UNDERSTANDING CHINA

By Earl Herbert Cressy

Christian Higher Education in China, 1929
Yellow Rivers: Adventures in a Chinese Parish, 1932
Daughter of Confucius (with Wong Su-ling), 1952
Daughters of Changing Japan, 1955

UNDERSTANDING CHINA

A HANDBOOK OF BACKGROUND INFORMATION
ON CHANGING CHINA

EARL HERBERT CRESSY

THOMAS NELSON & SONS
EDINBURGH NEW YORK TORONTO

Library of Congress Catalog Card No.: 57–11898

 Published in New York by Thomas Nelson & Sons and simultaneously in Toronto, Canada, by Thomas Nelson & Sons (Canada), Limited.

MANUFACTURED IN THE UNITED STATES OF AMERICA

This book is dedicated
to the
Average American Citizen
who carries the world on his shoulders
and
doesn't know what to do with it

Preface

The object of this handbook is to provide orientation for those who feel under the necessity of making up their minds concerning China. It will also serve the student as a rapid introduction to the main factors in a complicated situation.

It is a necessity today for America to make decisions on international policies. In a democracy like America the people make the final decision. The thoughtful citizen must evaluate each issue in the light of the findings of the experts and against the background of the past, and throw his influence and his vote on one side or the other.

One of the most vital issues concerns China, and the American people still have a deep feeling of outrage over the loss of China to communism. Thus far the American government has had too little of over-all policy and has dealt with one crisis after another as they have thrust themselves upon us.

The trouble with much of present policy-making is that it deals with the immediate practical aspects of a problem apart from its background. Thus, during World War II, American military strategists stressed the most direct method of gaining a military victory, and refused to attack through the Balkans as other allies urged. This blindness to past history and future political implications gave Russia its present control in that part of Europe.

Two kinds of facts are available as a basis for making decisions concerning China—the spot news of the daily press and the expert analysis of the specialist. Both have their limitations.

The spot news may be completely objective and merely report an event, or it may also include some spot interpretation as to whether it is merely an isolated occurrence or is related to other events, and whether these make a pattern.

The analysis of the specialist is generally from the standpoint of his own single discipline—anthropology, sociology, economics, political science—and even within the single discipline there are widely differing points of view. But the categories of the single discipline may apply to only a part of the total situation. Thus government is dealt with from the point of view of political science, whereas much that actually functioned in the field of government in China can be understood only in terms of the categories of anthropology, sociology, or even religion.

This information becomes available in fragmentary fashion. Both spot news and expert analysis have to be pieced together like some gigantic jig-saw puzzle with dimensions in both time and space.

The spot news trickles in, day by day or at long intervals, from this place or that, sometimes showing one aspect, sometimes another.

The expert analysis is also piecemeal in its own way, from the angle of this or that discipline, this or that point of view, always dealing with only a fraction, a single specialized aspect of the situation as a whole.

All of this, if it is to come to have unity and meaning, must be seen against the background of Chinese history and civilization.

But Chinese history is long, complex, bewildering. Many of the books available are written by specialists for specialists, and generally follow an ancient Chinese historiography. They present a weath of detail in which the reader gets lost. The result is a blurred background.

Such a background, to be significant, must portray the structure of Chinese society, the sweep of Chinese history that has made it what it is, and the development of Chinese thought.

That is what this handbook seeks to do—to provide a background and frame of reference for understanding China today.

What is needed right now is not more knowledge about China in general, but an understanding of the factors that bear on the present situation.

This handbook grows out of a graduate course given during my five years as Professor of Chinese Studies in the Hartford Seminary Foundation, after spending 38 years in China. This course was for persons actually about to go to China, some of whom had already been there, and aimed, not to produce sinologues, but to develop persons who could enter into Chinese culture, understand the Chinese people, and cooperate with them in practical ways.

Such an aim requires that this handbook concentrate on bare essentials, omit a mass of details interesting in themselves but not necessary for understanding, and further that it disentangle the various strands of Chinese history and thought so that each may be analyzed and its significance indicated. The first determines its streamlined character. The second determines its plan.

The first three parts deal with pre-communist China—structure of society, movement of history, development of thought. Part Four portrays the years of break-up and attempts at a modern synthesis. Part Five deals with the communist regime.

No solutions are presented. Merely the factors necessary for understanding future developments are explained. Chinese history covers some forty centuries. The communist regime has now lasted eight years. It is a little early to come to any final conclusions.

The bibliography is intended chiefly as a guide for those who will wish to go more deeply into the matter. It also serves to indicate the works consulted and the scholars to whom I am most deeply indebted.

EARL HERBERT CRESSY

Claremont, California
May 20, 1957

Table of Contents

Part V The Peoples Republic of China

PART I

The Structure of Chinese Society

The structure of Chinese society preserves patterns that go back to the New Stone Age.

These ancient patterns affect all aspects of Chinese life, except in modern cities, and condition much of present-day economics and government.

These patterns do not appear on the surface, are easily overlooked, and do not function through the institutional forms to which the West is accustomed. They have religious aspects, but of the nature of institutional ceremonial and magic, not of personal religion.

In preserving these ancient patterns, in spite of many changes, Chinese society has developed a unity, cohesion, and durability unmatched by any other people. China was modernizing only slowly, and in its own fashion.

Will these patterns be able to maintain their basic structure or be broken up by the impact of communism?

1

Anthropological Structure of Chinese Society

The key fact in understanding China is the continuance into our modern day of a very ancient clan structure of society, sanctified by Confucianism, largely invisible in its functioning, but still powerful.

Chinese society exists on three culture levels: the hill tribes of the southwest (5 per cent) go back to the Old Stone Age; the rural population (80 per cent) live in peasant villages of the type developed during the New Stone Age between five and eight thousand years ago; the walled-town and city dwellers (15 per cent) may perhaps best be classed as medieval, except for those in the new modern-type cities like Shanghai which are in large part foreign.

Persistence of Primitive Culture Levels

In an analysis of American society the anthropological structure can be ignored. It is deep buried in the past under countless strata of history, and has long since been forgotten, except for isolated tribes of Indians, and clan psychology among certain immigrant groups in a few cities.

But not so in China. For the continued existence of these ancient culture levels, especially as they function through the clan structure, although modified to some extent by the movement of Chinese history, gives Chinese society a characteristic structure which is complicated and not easy for the West to understand.

The three culture levels, with their different economic bases, social structure and psychology, are often side by side. Going from city to village may take less than an hour, but it covers 5,000 years of cultural development. The tribes, in the more remote mountain regions of the south and west, are usually within walking distance of the nearest villages.

The Tribes

The hill tribes are more isolated and vestigial, and are of less significance for an understanding of China, although there are some 20,000,000 of them. (The communists say there are 50,000,000.) They have advanced little beyond the stage of early hunting men and practice hoe culture or other elementary forms of agriculture. Some depend on barter and use no money. They preserve a number of customs of which there are traces in the folk songs of one of the earliest Chinese classics. But they have not yet become Chinese.

The Peasant Village

The peasant village was the supreme achievement of the New Stone Age, which constituted the first great period of human progress. It developed when food production was added to the precarious food supply provided by the hunting activities and the gathering of roots, nuts and berries which characterized the Old Stone Age. In some regions the first step was hoe cultivation, and in others the domestication of animals. These gave a more certain food supply. When agriculture and domestication of animals were brought together in certain favorable border-line localities, along with handicrafts, the peasant village was born, and for the first time in human history, achieved not only a stable food supply but a surplus. On the steppes this was paralleled by the development of nomadic pastoral tribes. In some parts of the world this New Stone Age type of organization continued, except for cities, until modern times, and was brought to an end only by the industrial revolution. China is one of those places, and most of rural China has been scarcely touched by the industrial revolution, which indeed is only in its beginnings.

The Walled Town

Most of the food surplus was taken over by entrepreneurs in irrigation and other lines, or by those who were especially skillful, or by the strong, and stored in a central granary. This called for clerks to make a tally of the amount stored by various individuals, and thus writing began. It called for guards, and government began. A wall of defense was constructed about granary, barracks and resi-

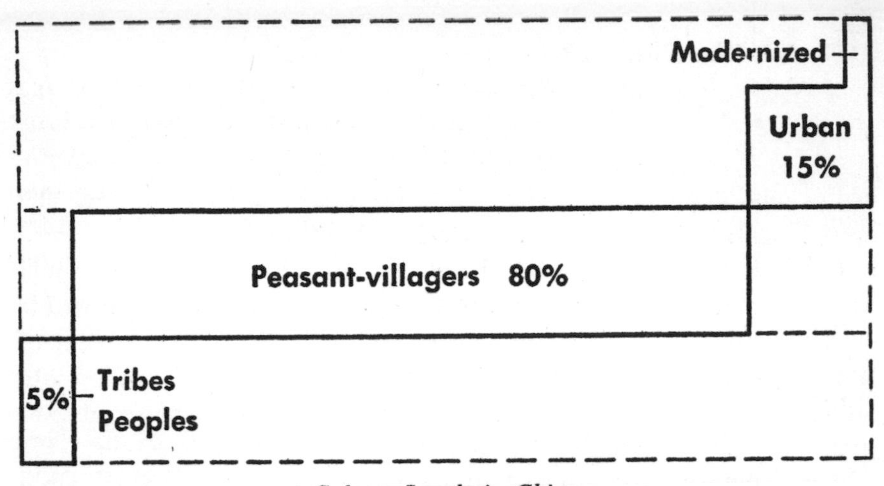

Culture Levels in China

Tribes level	Old Stone Age type	5%
Peasant-village level	New Stone Age type	80%
Urban level	Handicraft type	15%
Modernized urban level	Industrialized type	—

dences, and towns came into being. Here Chinese civilization arose. It was in such culture centers that it developed from its beginnings until the present. It may be noted in passing that if rural cooperatives had been invented in that ancient day, they would merely have distributed this surplus among the peasants who produced it. The result would have been an increase of the peasant population, but no civilization.

We thus come to what one writer has called the style of Chinese history. The Chinese landscape is dominated by the walled city surrounded by a large number of villages tributary to it. The radius of the tributary area is approximately one-half of a day's journey, or fifteen miles at most, so that the peasant can set out before daylight carrying his load of grain, take it to the central granary, and return home before dark.

Such walled cities to the number of about seventeen hundred have constituted the county seats for the counties into which the eighteen provinces of China have been traditionally divided. The great modern cities like Shanghai, Hongkong and Tientsin are recent developments and were not there a hundred and fifty years ago.

Who Are the Chinese?

A basic question is, who are the Chinese? History records the names of many peoples, both outside what is now China to the north and northwest, and within. There were also primitive hill tribes who lived in the marshes and mountains in the interior. The south was peopled with various kinds of barbarians.

Chinese history begins in what is now northwest China, in river valleys tributary to the upper Yellow River, but it is not possible to designate any one people as Chinese. The history is not that of a conquering tribe, or city like Rome, bringing other peoples into subjection, but rather that of an expanding culture that was able to assimilate all the peoples it touched and bring them together.

The Chinese then are not some particular race or tribe, but a group or confederation of related stock, possessing a culture that proved able to expand and integrate a quarter of the human race, so that they all came to be Chinese.

There were limits. To the north, the Mongols and various others remain outside the Chinese orbit. But the basic difference is cultural, for their steppe environment compels them to remain nomads. In the south and far southwest are the hill tribes of the Lolo, Miao, and others, who have not yet been reached by Chinese culture.

Out of this situation have grown two of the most significant movements of Chinese history. The first is the southward movement of Chinese culture and power, which still continues and can be seen in action today in Indo-China and Malaya. The second is the invasions of China by peoples from the north and northwest, of which the present Russian incursion might perhaps be taken as the latest instance.

Chinese Expansion Southward

In his expansion southward, the pioneering Chinese always found lands suited to his form of settled agriculture, and inhabited by peoples practicing agriculture of the same basic pattern, even if less advanced technically and socially. These various peoples were gradually sinicized and absorbed as the frontier of Chinese culture moved slowly southward during the centuries. Many have kept their own dialects, although adopting the Chinese written characters, and becoming Chinese in practically all other regards.

The Communists are taking measures to complete this process in their own fashion, and count some twenty-five tribes peoples in the south and southwest.

Nomad Invaders of China

In the north the process was reversed, with peoples from without penetrating into Chinese territory, but those who stayed were absorbed just the same.

This region to the north and west was one that the Chinese pioneer, depending on settled agriculture, could not penetrate. It belonged to the nomad. There were two quite separate ways of life, and the Great Wall drew a line between them. The Communists distinguish some twenty-one tribes in this region who have remained resistant to Chinese culture, and adopted alphabetic scripts from India or the Near East, along with culture patterns. Much of this they have passed on to China.

A considerable part of the history of China has been concerned with the give and take between these two worlds, and the invaders from outside ruled portions of China for over a third of the duration of the Empire. This interaction was a cultural stimulus, and provided part of the basis for the repeated syntheses that are the most important aspects of Chinese history.

Chou Invaders

Among the earliest invaders from the outside were the Chou, who established the Chou "dynasty," 1027–221 B.C. The leader belonged to the Chi clan, which was one of a group of militarily organized tribes of non-Chinese peoples. This leader, later the "king," and the leaders of the other tribes, constituted a new nobility, and developed a feudal system. This set up an ethnic superstratification upon the dominion of the earlier Shang "dynasty." But the number of the Shang cities and the size of the area in which their food supply was organized is not known.

The chiefs of the tribes of Chou invaders were assigned territory on a decentralized feudal basis, for communications were too difficult and slow for central control. Each one moved into his feudal domain with his own tribe and military force, and built a fortress city as an island among the natives of the conquered territory. This was the probable origin of the typical Chinese rectangular walled city.

The Chou were merely one of the first of a long series of outside peoples who have migrated into China, warred with China, at times ruled over portions of North China and twice over China as a whole. The rule of the last one, the Manchus, came to an end in 1911.

This anthropological structure of Chinese society underlies and deeply influences the sociological and political structure.

2

THE SOCIOLOGICAL STRUCTURE OF CHINESE SOCIETY

A sociological analysis of Chinese society reveals the kinship structure as its basis, and the clan as the primary unit.

Kinship Structure

The male members of the clan are descended from a common ancestor, have the same name, and usually live in the same village.

Large clans may have three thousand or more members and are often divided into a number of branches. Some branches may be in adjoining villages or cities. Often four generations live together in one big family which may number fifty or more persons. This has been for millenniums the Chinese ideal. Such a big family usually constitutes one of the branches of the clan.

The kinship structure of the clan is elaborately worked out. There are over two hundred technical terms in common use denoting the various degrees of relationship. All of this is carefully recorded and many clans have genealogies which go back for several centuries. These are brought up-to-date each year at the new year's season by entering births, marriages, and deaths.

The Chinese individual has a strong sense of social responsibility. But only to the members of his own clan. Other clans are expected to look out for their own. This provides a basis for social security and in China the clan takes the place of the government agencies of the welfare state. The *New York Times* commented editorially on the fact that during the depression no Chinese in New York received public relief, all being taken care of by their own people.

From the angle of government, clan loyalty is stronger than the obligations of citizenship, and very much stronger than national feeling. One result is that an official feels it his first obligation to amass a fortune for his clan even if this conflicts with his public duty as a government servant. His responsibility to his own relatives comes before his responsibility to the public.

The Chinese family is ordinarily described as democratic. It is not. All these relationships are between superiors and inferiors, as between father and son, husband and wife, and older and younger brother or sister. The obedience of the younger is balanced by the responsibility of the elder, but otherwise the whole set-up is aristocratic and paternalistic.

The Village

The typical situation is where a single clan inhabits a single village, although many larger villages include two or more. Smaller villages with a single clan often go by the clan name, such as Wong Family Village.

The one I know best has 1170 inhabitants, all related, all having the same name of Nyi, and all getting their living from their surrounding rice fields, 170 acres, of which 80 per cent is held individually and the rest by the clan as a whole.

Such a village has a six-fold unity. It has geographical unity in that it is closely built, with narrow streets and a maze of passages and courtyards, and its rice fields round about it. It has a biological unity in that all are related and bear the same name. It has a historical unity in that the men of this same family have continued in this same village for from one to five or ten centuries. All of the men in the clan have been born in the village, together with their male ancestors. It has an economic unity in that it lives off its own rice fields, is almost entirely self-sustaining, and needs to import from the outside only a few items such as salt, iron and cloth. It has a psychological unity in that the individuals are always conscious of themselves as part of a larger whole, and live their lives within the framework of the regulations and taboos prescribed by the ancients, and the social psychology of the clan overshadows the psychology of the individual. It has a religious unity in that the clan worships its own ancestors and the local gods of its own soil.

There is a central ancestral temple for the clan as a whole, each branch has its own branch temple, and each household has its own altar for the worship for its own immediate ancestors. In these temples the tablets of the ancestors stand in long rows and their souls are believed to dwell in the tablets so that the spirits of the ancestors continue to be present in the midst of clan and village, even as when they were alive. They actually function in the life of the living through the customs which they have helped to hand down and to which they give a religious sanction.

All of these unities mutually reinforce each other. The result is that the Chinese clan and village is a closely knit organization which is highly resistant to change. It has endured for forty centuries.

Clans govern themselves. If there is more than one clan in the village the elders of the several clans attend jointly to any business that is outside of the individual clan and concerns the village as a whole. This has been frequently described as democracy. It is not. It has been more accurately described by a Chinese writer as family-ocracy. Circumstances that in a western village would be governmental or legal matters, are in the Chinese village dealt with as family affairs. This includes cases of life and death. It may even involve the infliction of capital punishment. It is a primitive and patriarchal set-up carried into our modern day.

A Two-Class Society

China has been for millenniums a two-class society.

The typical Chinese is not one person but two. One is the land-lord-scholar-official who constitutes the ruling class. This class is the carrier of Chinese culture and has made China what it is. The other is the peasant in his peasant village who labors in the field, and whose main function is to provide food for the class above him.

The peasant leads a hard enough life, and to western observers and writers it has seemed that he has an impossibly low standard of living. But he has been on this basis for centuries and knows nothing else, and so long as he can get enough to eat and satisfy his simple needs, considers that he has a good life.

In a very real way the two classes complement each other. The peasant provides the food. The gentry control the irrigation system which the individual village would be powerless to deal with in isolation; they maintain order and adjudicate clan fights; and, what is more important, they have developed the culture and education which are the glory of Chinese civilization.

This two-class society has been taken for granted for centuries and it did not occur to anyone to question it. This was in part because there were actual advantages, and in part because it had always been that way. In fact, it is hard to imagine any other way in which civilization could have started.

In theory it has always been possible for the peasant to rise and become one of the ruling class. In practice, however, it has been difficult for any but the most exceptional students to accomplish this because of the long years of study which required money and leisure. Few peasant boys could compete with the sons of the aristocracy. The clans thus contained both literate and illiterate members. Universal education had never been even thought of. To become a scholar was a great privilege.

Clans were anxious to have a scholar who could give advice, deal on equal terms with officials, and provide liaison with the county government, and perhaps even become an official himself, thus adding prestige and wealth to the clan along with the further possibility that other members too might rise through his help and influence, which he was in duty bound to extend to his own clan members first. They were proud of him and looked up to him. This was true also to a considerable extent of those who acquired wealth.

Chinese civilization was largely the possession of the small landlord-scholar-official class. But a certain amount of this has been popularized, and a veneer of culture has been spread over a considerable part of the population.

A Gentry Society

There was at first a feudal nobility depending on birth or divine origin. This was largely destroyed with the rise of the Han dynasty, and was replaced by a gentry class based on education and socio-economic position, the landlord-scholar-official class. Centuries later, under the Sung, a class of small gentry grew up, and gained some share of power. During the last century a middle class developed and came to hold an important place in modern China.

The long history of China and its repeated nullification of foreign rule are due in large part to the extreme stability of the Chinese gentry society.

The reason for this stability was the two-fold base of the individual gentry clan, in the city and in the country. The country home was the economic base. Here lived the bulk of the clan in the midst of their land. The more enterprising members moved to the city and established the urban branches of the clan. This was the city base.

The clan which I described in *Daughter of Confucius* had eight branches in the neighboring city of about twenty thousand. The urban branches of fourteen such clans dominated the city, intermarrying generation after generation, and maintaining a monopoly of scholarship, prestige and official position. Those not in office lived a life of scholarly leisure. Some became merchants.

In times of revolution or conquest, the city branches could retire to their country base and live quietly and in safety. If the country base was attacked by bandits, they could take refuge with their clan in the city. Always the city branches could assist the country base in legal and financial matters. Always one could help the other. Seldom were both bases of a great gentry clan destroyed. One or the other nearly always managed to survive.

In Chinese society, the landlords, the scholars, the officials not merely belonged to the same class. They were closely related by blood or marriage. Furthermore, they intermarried only with other big gentry families, so that large groups of gentry clans were related by marriage, and formed cliques that presented a united front.

In *Daughter of Confucius*, a middleman brought an offer of marriage for a daughter of the gentry clan from the family of a country pastor of peasant origin whose son had recently graduated from the university and was beginning a successful career. Her grandmother would have none of it, saying that he was doubtless an able and estimable young man, but that they married their slave girls into families like that, not their daughters.

However, this young woman's brothers fell in love in college with girls from other than gentry families, and married them on the basis of their value as individuals, and not of their status as members of another gentry clan. This individualism affected their own clan very little, but tended to put an end to their close cooperation with the clans with which they had intermarried and made common cause for centuries.

The Masses

During a large part of Chinese history the common man simply does not count. At least not in a way comparable to the citizen in a democracy.

The clan is not on a level. Individuals and branches differ in thrift, ability and enterprise. Some attained wealth and high official position. A large part of the wealth, scholarship, and official positions of a clan tended to be in its city branches. Some lost their land and became tenants or hired hands—often on land owned by more prosperous members of the same clan. But they all belonged and economic differences were tempered to some degree by a feeling of mutual responsibility.

The gentry at the upper end of the social scale tended to stability. At the bottom, poverty and the narrow margin of food supply tended to instability and produced a floating population which included men out of work, beggars, magicians, bandits. There were always bad elements and local gangsters. Some were aristocratic adventurers who had come down in the world.

Gradual Differentiation

Thus a gradual differentiation has been under way for a long time, resulting in three sizes of units and three levels of clan psychology.

In the country village, expansion of the clan can be taken care of by adding rooms or courtyards, and the branches remain close together and maintain the clan psychology. In cities where the surrounding land is already built up, often by other big families, this is impossible, and the result is that the different branches are usually separated and tend to become more individualistic.

In more recent years small families, made up of husband, wife, and the children of this pair, have gone in considerable numbers to the more industrialized cities. This has resulted in a still further degree of isolation from the clan as a whole and the development of a small family psychology.

The communists are now trying to carry this a degree further, and relate the individual to the state instead of the clan, the large-family branch, or even the small family.

3

Economic Structure

The basic fact in the understanding of China's economy is that it takes eighty per cent of the population to provide the food supply.

This compares with a farm population in the United States of thirteen per cent.

This imposes an absolute limitation on everything that China attempts to do. It means that only twenty out of each hundred workers are available for industry, communications, the professions and government. It inescapably curtails the production of consumer goods, limiting the necessities and excluding the luxuries. It condemns China to a low standard of living. This is the chief problem faced by the communists today.

High Labor Cost of Rice

This situation grows to a large extent out of the enormous labor cost of raising rice, which is the staple food crop of all except the northern one-fourth of China, which depends on millet and wheat.

Hand labor is used almost exclusively. The land must be terraced in small level fields, so that the water used for irrigation can flow from one to the other next below it. This involves a retaining wall which, in a level valley or delta, may be merely a mud embankment a few inches above the level of the field and wide enough for a narrow footpath, or on a hillside may be a stone wall two or three feet high.

The soil is broken up by using a sort of forked hoe, or a water-buffalo wallows through a flooded field dragging a primitive plow. The young plants are started in small plots and when about six inches high are transplanted by hand into the soft mud of flooded fields. The rice grows rapidly in the water under the hot sun. Soon the fields must be fertilized. Then weeded. This last is sometimes done with hoes, standing up, but often on hands and knees. I have seen rows of men and boys, down on all fours in the mud and water, processing the rows of growing rice plants with their bare hands.

Traveling an hour southwest from Shanghai across the Yangtze delta, the first hill is reached. From the summit one can see six or seven miles in all directions—an unbroken expanse of rice fields, save for villages and intersecting canals and rivers. It is awesome to consider that of the billions upon billions of rice plants in the hundred or so square miles visible, every last one has been transplanted and cultivated by human hands. But that is not the end. When the grain ripens, the water is drained off, and the rice is harvested by hand with a sickle, threshed by hand in the field by whacking it against the sides of a box, and later winnowed by hand at a threshing floor and lugged away by hand to be stored for the winter.

Even with all of this prodigious expenditure of labor, the Chinese food supply is precarious. Famines are frequent and cause appalling loss of life. Even in normal times a considerable amount of food has to be imported.

Basis of Dense Population

Although rice culture requires much more man-power than wheat it gives a 48.8% larger average yield per acre. Thus the Food and Agriculture Organization of the United Nations stated in its year book that world production of wheat in 1954 was 151.5 million metric tons from a total area of 135 million hectares, while rice was planted on only 97.4 million hectares but the yield was 162.2 million tons of paddy (unhusked rice).

This provides the basis for the dense populations of China and Southeast Asia.

Possibility of Mechanization

The question arises today whether rice culture can be mechanized and thus cut down the amount of hand labor and free a larger portion of the population for work in factories and urban centers. Thus in the United States in 1940 there were 6,100,000 farms with

1,500,000 tractors, and in 1950 below 5,000,000 farms with 3,500,000 tractors. This is the basis of American productivity.

In China there is the immediate difficulty that the people are too poor to buy machinery and the rice fields too small and too soft for its use.

These difficulties might be overcome to some extent but there still remain two insurmountable technical problems. Thus the great rice-producing region in the delta of the Yangtze in the region of Shanghai is intersected by hundreds of canals, often a quarter or half mile apart. These constitute the highways. The few bridges over them are of the camel-back variety. It would, therefore, be impossible to move mechanized equipment from one field to another except with the greatest difficulty. See map.

Most of the remaining rice area is in river valleys. Here the fields

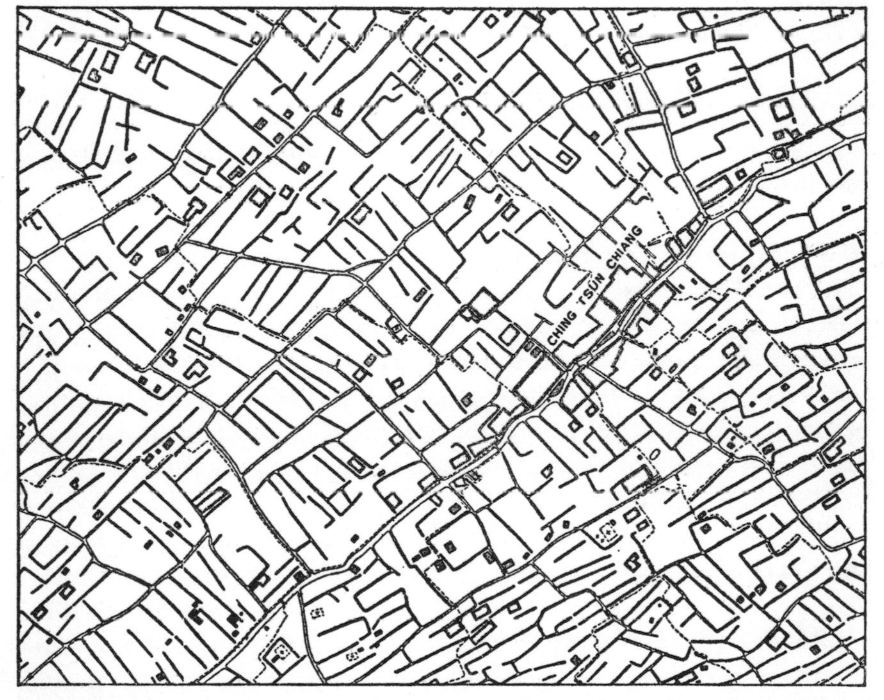

Area in Fenghsien County in the Yangtze delta, about 20 miles south of Shanghai. The scale is 1 inch to 2000 feet. The average spacing between canals is 380 feet. After G. B. Cressey in the *Geographical Review* based on Whangpoo Conservancy Board survey.

are terraced, the difference in level varying from a few inches to several feet according to the slope of the land. This makes the use of machinery impossible.

In the regions above the irrigation level where dry rice is cultivated, and in the north where the crops consist of wheat or millet, mechanization is possible. But these constitute only a fraction of the total.

Geographic Foundation

Geography is more important in China than in the West, for the process of mechanization has only begun. Rivers and canals still carry far more freight than railways and motor roads. Travel in the interior is thirty miles a day. Produce is still borne miles to market on the shoulders of men. Geography still holds a veto over many enterprises and the limitations it imposes on many others are severe.

Mountains, Rivers and Regions

China is a mountainous country, much more so than is generally realized.

In other lands mountains are a source of wealth, but in China only to a very limited degree. All accessible mountain areas have long ago been denuded of trees and even shrubs for fuel. Forest products will not be available in any quantity until reforestation takes place, which will require several decades. Mining is still sporadic. Superstition, particularly fear of demons, has limited or prevented developments like grazing and dairying. With a few outstanding exceptions, mountain roads are non-existent or very bad.

The mountain ranges have served chiefly to wall off a predominantly agricultural country into three main regions and five lesser ones. These regions are basic for the development of the Chinese economy and the movement of Chinese history. See map, p. 102.

China is a land of rivers. Three major river systems and five minor ones occupy the corresponding regions for which they provide irrigation, fertilization, and transportation.

The rivers were prone to disastrous floods, but probably compensate for their destructiveness by enriching the soil. Thus the peasants of the Han dynasty had a song when the Po Canal in 95 B.C. brought the silt-laden waters of the Ching River to a large agricultural area in what is modern Shensi.

> Ching water carries mud.
> It flows and fertilizes all.
> It makes the five grains bud,
> And feeds the court and capital.

These main river valleys formed "key economic areas" that for centuries were highly self-sustaining and independent of each other and had the localism and exclusiveness of an agricultural economy.

Chinese culture developed along these rivers. As population increased, the cultivated fields squeezed further up the valley of every stream, and hillsides were terraced. They invaded the territory of the hill tribes, and gradually these were absorbed.

Chinese culture did not penetrate northward into the steppe region as that was not suitable for the settled agriculture on which Chinese culture was based. To the south they always found agricultural land, hence the southward movement of the frontier of sinification.

Chinese civilization began in the valleys of tributaries of the upper Yellow River.

Indeed the economic history of China, on which the political history is based, is precisely the conquest and successive incorporation of food-producing areas, beginning in the north and moving to the south and southwest.

China is in the monsoon rice area of East Asia, and shares the characteristics of this region. The monsoon is a periodic wind. One of the characteristics of monsoon climate is a variation from year to year, particularly in rainfall. This served as a stimulus to the early Chinese and led them to develop irrigation. This called for constant labor, resulted in the fixed Chinese habit of industry, and had a definite effect on the formation of Chinese character.

Likewise floods and other disasters called for courage and endurance. In 1912 I investigated a famine district for the Famine Relief

Committee, going through half a dozen villages in a howling snowstorm with flashlight and notebook. In each house I took the lid off the cooking pot to see what they were eating. It was ground bark and sweet potato leaves, flavored with straw and an occasional bit of hoarded grain. This diet was poisonous, and their stomachs slowly swelled until death ensued. The mess was nauseating and almost made me sick. But every time, without fail, someone would make a joke about the fearsome stuff.

Irrigation and Water Control

The economy of China is based on irrigation as industrial capitalism is based on iron and coal, and China has from the beginning made great progress in water conservancy.

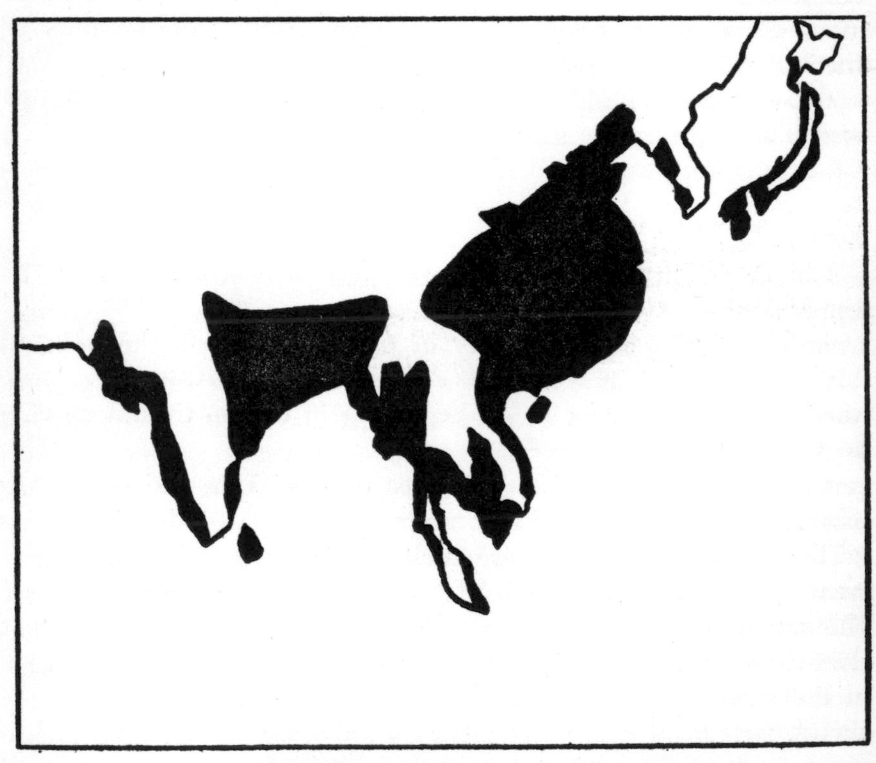

The Monsoon Rice Area in Asia

Water control was necessarily a public function, as the individual clan could not control the entire flow of a stream but had to share it with many others. The largest unit of cooperation in Chinese society was the village. Any enterprise beyond the capacity of one or two villages required that the government step in. Witness the edict of the great Han emperor, Wu Ti, in 111 B.C.

> Agriculture is the basic [occupation] of the world. Springs and rivers make possible the cultivation of the five grains . . .
>
> There are numerous mountains and rivers in the domain, with whose use the ordinary people are not acquainted. Hence [the government] must cut canals and ditches, drain the rivers and build dikes and water tanks to prevent drought.

This edict states the basic problem of agricultural production in China, namely, the proper use and regulation of water, and acknowledged the major economic function of the state, in regard to production, to be construction and maintenance of water-control public works. A proper understanding of these two problems has always been a prerequisite of constructive statesmanship in China.

Key Economic Areas

Such an agricultural economy fitted into the regions that were at first independent of each other. Communication between them was limited and state centralization was impossible.

A centralization of state power came about only when an able ruler secured control of an economic area, developed irrigation so as to provide a food surplus, dug canals for transporting the accumulation of grain to strategic points, and used it as a basis for the conquest of a neighboring area.

Thus the government bureaucracy developed three main departments: military affairs, irrigation, and transport of surplus grain. The stored surplus of grain was the basis of military power. The chief duty of local officials was to remit the grain tribute for storage in the granaries at the capital and other strategic points. Until almost the end of the nineteenth century the main function of the government of China continued along these same lines.

Movement of Chinese History

The chief movement of Chinese history has been territorial expansion and the gradual inclusion of other key economic areas.

This has taken place practically without change in the character of society or its political superstructure or its economic forms.

This lack of change has usually been interpreted as stagnation. It is really an evidence of the sturdiness and vitality of Chinese civilization, which in an expansion of four thousand years and including eventually a quarter of the human race, has maintained conformity to its original ethos and structure, instead of suffering fragmentation, as in Europe.

This began to change only during the last 150 years when the development of foreign commerce led to the growth of key economic areas of a different sort—port cities and manufacturing centers like Shanghai, and manufacturing and trans-shipping points in the interior. But the historic key economic areas which provide the food supply still maintain their basic importance.

Transportation

China has some 24,000 miles of railway against 240,000 in the United States. Motor roads have increased greatly in recent years, but are still inadequate.

The main reliance is on river and canal transport. Steam is used on the lower reaches of rivers and on canals. Sailboats, with trackers when the wind opposes or gives out, go further up, and when the shallow head-waters are reached, bamboo rafts are laboriously towed by man-power. On land, caravans, two-wheeled carts, and wheelbarrows are used in the north. In the south much is still transported by human carrying coolies.

Travel in a large part of the interior is thirty miles a day. I have myself, since 1940, traveled at that rate, by sedan-chair, by ricksha by the day, and by bamboo cargo raft, drifting slowly down level reaches, and shooting wild, foaming rapids, the raft undulating over the waves like a long serpent, the bamboo withies, with which it was tied together, snapping like firecrackers, so that the raft threatened to come apart, and after each rapid had to be retied.

Such transportation is slow, expensive, and uncertain. It constitutes another serious handicap. Millions have died of famine, with abundance in other provinces, but without means of transport.

Industrial Revolution

The countries of Europe were once where China is now. They were snapped out of it by the industrial revolution. It is usually assumed that China will do likewise. But the modern age was an indigenous development in the West, but only a sudden, and not always welcome, importation in China, where the industrial revolution has not yet taken place.

China does not have extensive deposits of coal and iron, and thus lacks a basis for heavy industry, except in Manchuria. This limits the possibility for industrial development on a modern scale, and makes it likely that China will continue to be predominantly an agricultural country and a producer of raw materials.

Population

The population of China is usually taken as four hundred fifty million. (The present People's Government claims 600,000,000). No one knows exactly. The one certain fact is that it is increasing.

This population pressure is due to several factors: the clan structure of Chinese society, the Confucian emphasis upon having many sons as the first requisite of filial piety, and the religious sanction of ancestor worship.

One of the very few intensive and scientific studies of the population dealt with a small district halfway between Shanghai and Nanking, for the four-year period 1932–35. It was found that there were 1573 persons per square mile. However, a portion of the district was not under cultivation so that the number of persons per square mile of cultivated land was 2673.

The amount of cultivated land per capita was .24 acres. Thus the average family of 4.7 persons had to live off 1.128 acres of land. The problem of population is therefore acute. Nevertheless, the average population increase per year for the four years of the study was found to be .64%.

The Narrow Margin

In this study the population was classified as rich, well-to-do and poor, defined as follows: those families with sufficient food and clothes were classed as rich; those with a doubtful sufficiency of food and clothes as well-to-do; and those with very insufficient food and clothing as poor. In terms of American dollars at the time of this survey the rich families had an annual income of about $135 and up, the well-to-do from $35 to $135, and the poor $35 or less. The rich constituted 4.2% of the population, the well-to-do 27.1%, and the poor 68.6%. The average size of family varied as follows: for the rich 6.8, well-to-do, 5.7, poor 4.1 persons.

This is in one of the most prosperous regions in China.

It is possible for an average family of 4.7 persons to live off 1.128 acres. I know personally a number of families in a similar district who make a living off the same amount of land and get on fairly well.

Millions do. But only so long as everything continues to go right. They are too close to the edge. Any disaster pushes them across into want, often into famine.

Possibility of Improvement

The question arises as to the possibility of improvement. Various solutions have been proposed. The one most emphasized has been in the field of better farming such as seed selection, better fertilizers, and animal husbandry. Another line has been rural cooperatives.

In view of the age-long Chinese emphasis upon large families, it does not seem likely that these would solve the problem. The conclusion of the expert who directed this study is as follows:

> I cannot conceive of any significant improvement in village life which will not be accompanied by a decline in the death rate, nor of one which will have any marked effect upon the birth rate in the near future.
>
> Therefore, I cannot but feel that a large part of any increases in productiveness will be needed to support their increased numbers rather than be available for the improvement of standards of living.
>
> This is the tragic dilemma in which those who would improve village life in China will certainly find themselves.

The figures above as to size of family bear this out, that of the "rich" family being 6.8 as compared with 4.1 for the poor family or 66% larger. Why? The number of children born is much the same. It is simply that there is not food enough and the weaker ones die. Provide the food and the number of survivors increases. The population goes up. The standard of living remains where it was.

4

The Political Structure of Chinese Society

The political structure of Chinese society presents an incongruous assembling of elements that do not articulate. On the local level are the clans, and on the national level was the imperial government. The two did not meet, for the national government stopped at the county, and the governmental gap in between constituted a vacuum which left the way open for gangs, secret societies, and bandits.

The clans can be fully understood only in terms of the categories of anthropology, and the imperial national government only in terms of political science. The two are not merely different in operation. They are different in kind.

A Conglomerate Political Structure

The persistence of a primitive anthropological structure, the kinship structure of society as embodied in the clans, and the intrusion of the clans into the field of government, is something outside Western experience or imagination. It is one of the chief obstacles to an understanding of China by the West, and contributes to the failure of the West to develop a China policy that will work.

Difficulty in understanding this is the greater because the kinship structure is invisible. It is there behind the facade of modern political organization, behind the modern social and economic structure, but not apparent to the average Western observer. This calls for some explaining.

These were incommensurable types: the imperial national system of government superimposed on a new stone age type of local government—which was not government at all in the modern sense, but merely a patriarchal handling of clan affairs. The two did not fit. However, it served as a workable makeshift for over two thousand years.

The national government, functioning through the province and the county, did not arise from among the people, but was handed down from above. The clan was introvert, concerned with its own affairs, and wanted only to be left alone to handle its own affairs in its own way.

The difference was the greater in that nation, province, and county are based on territory, as in the West, whereas the clan, although in part at least localized in the village, is based on blood relationship.

The Provinces of China as of 1946

So there was a gap between them, a sort of no-man's-land where custom ruled with the stable elements of the population, and among the unstable elements various extra-legal or semi-legal groups functioned in their own fashion in default of a regularly constituted government apparatus.

The Three Areas of Government

There are thus three areas of government to be considered: the clans, which handled most of the local functions of government; the national government; and the governmental gap between the two.

The first must be analyzed in terms of anthropology, the second in terms of political science, and the third in terms of sociology. All have religious aspects. Together they make up the picture of the actual government situation, a picture that is never one hundred per cent complete or accurate.

The Clan as a Political Unit

The clan, with the peasant village in which it is typically embodied, has been described in the previous chapters. It now remains to indicate its functions in the field of government.

It will help to begin by comparing a local unit of government in America, say a village of a thousand persons, with one of the same size in China. In both, matters within the household are treated as family affairs with which government has nothing to do as long as they do not break the law.

The difference is that in America these thousand persons would be divided into some two hundred separate households, only a few of which would be related to each other, whereas the thousand in the Chinese village would all belong to one clan, having the same name, being blood relatives, and under control of the elders of the clan.

In America, village affairs are quite extraneous to the affairs of the two hundred individual small families. In China clan and village are identical. Many local government affairs in America become merely family matters to be settled within the clan in China.

This clan control might be in terms of formal judgment and direct action, but was more often by indirect pressure. Thus when one of the slave girls in the big household of fifty-one persons portrayed in *Daughter of Confucius* was found with child by one of the husbands, she came before the grandmother who dominated the household, confessed, and stated she was ready to endure any punishment, even death. No one in the family ever had the slightest doubt that if the grandmother had ordered her to commit suicide, the girl would have done so without hesitation.

Of course, all were subject to government control, particularly as to taxes, and, especially in cities and the larger towns, they were subject to police action. But in general the policy of the government from time immemorial has been to allow the clans to govern themselves so long as no major disturbance breaks out.

But this setup had serious defects.

The Disunited Clans of China

A Chinese writer has made the striking statement that where we have the United States of America, they have the united clans of Asia.

Only they are not united.

The number of clans in China, possibly of the order of half a million, is unknown. Each one is a tightly organized and isolated social unit. There is little carry-over from one to another except as certain clans intermarry with certain others. There is little that is cumulative. The clans have to be dealt with one by one. They are like unicellular organisms that do not combine into any organic structure. (Recent Communist figures indicate a total of over one million.)

Thus the national government is like a small ship of state sailing a vast ocean of which the individual waves are the individual clans.

Such an aggregate of small, disunited clans could offer no resistance to armed invasion, except as the central government was strong enough and near enough to take effective action in time. Thus Japanese pirates, or the early European mauraders, could make a landing on the coast and find the clans defenseless. It was equally easy for any internal armed force—such as the Communists.

Most of Southeast Asia is in the same situation today.

The National Imperial Government

The Chinese Empire was established by force of arms in 221 B.C., but its first dynasty lasted only fourteen years, because the First Emperor had not yet learned how to organize his vast territory effectively, although he laid down the pattern that was perfected under the Han, and continued for 2132 years until 1911.

The imperial government consisted of three levels. At the top was the emperor in the metropolitan capital, along with the court (imperial clan), the army, the granaries, and the central government ministries. The second was the provincial (or vice-regal) level, with imperial representatives at strategic points, with adequate garrisons and granaries. The third level was that of the county magistrate, who collected taxes, kept records, administered justice, maintained order, and performed a minimum of government functions.

The imperial government did not penetrate below the level of the county magistrate. It stopped short of the village.

Attention has been centered on the civilian bureaucracy of the Chinese centralized empire and the examination system by which it was recruited, and this has tended to obscure the fact that all dynasties were established by force and as the outcome of fighting, and that a dynasty continued only so long as it retained its ability to crush any revolt. This resulted in a concentration of military strength at the capital.

The civilian bureaucracy was merely the agent of the imperial power.

This has been largely overlooked, particularly in the early years of the Republic. As a result, the national government under the Republic represented merely a vacuum of power, and war lords arose in various areas.

All this seems quite understandable from the Western point of view, but it is by no means the whole story.

The East Asian Idea of the State

It is a mistake to apply western ideas of the state to East Asia. In fact, the word "state" should properly not be used at all, for most Asian peoples think of something quite different from the western state with exact boundaries, organized government, and geographical and political subdivisions.

In many East Asian lands the concept—with various modifications—is something like the following. At the center is a hill or pyramid, on the summit of which a divine ruler—a son of heaven—comes into contact with the overarching and overruling divinity of the heaven. The Altar of Heaven in Peking may be considered a stylized parallel to this. About the hill or pyramid lie the imperial court, the camp of the imperial armed forces, the granaries to feed army and court and the imperial treasure houses. This was usually the only large city, which dominated the country in a way that is not possible in western lands.

Here was the center of a mystical entity, a divine potency, implemented by the victorious imperial army. That is so long as it continued to be victorious.

From this center the power of the government faded off into the vague distance to an undefined boundary that varied with the strength and ability of this emperor or that. Government was the business of the emperor and the court and no concern of the common man. What he wanted was to be left alone.

China shared in this concept, which was probably, in a vague way, the point of view of the average uneducated villager in the interior.

The Governmental Gap

The gap between the local clan government in the village and the national imperial government was bridged to a limited extent by the gentry who mediated the government directives to their own clans. This was not part of the machinery of government, but was merely de facto, a matter of custom.

From the gentry, the county magistrate, representing the imperial government, generally received cooperation. They were persons of substance and represented the good elements of society.

But dealing with the bad elements of society was another matter. This called for finesse on the part of the official, for the use of force was generally considered evidence of a lack of administrative ability.

Local Hoodlums

The increasing over-population led to the wide prevalence of a considerable proportion of floating population. This was the unstable element in rural China. Locally they were petty gangsters, who might or might not have land or jobs, and who perpetrated minor depredations, largely along lines of intimidation, which ordinarily did not come to the ears of the officials, or could be ignored.

This floating population, with its gangs of local hoodlums, later played the most important part in the communist seizure of power, under Mao Tse-tung.

Banditry

Banditry in China rises almost to the dignity of a profession.

In many cases banditry is rationalized on a basis of unemployment, or of inequality and injustice suffered by the poor at the hands of landlords and officials. The bandit often appears as the champion of the poor—a sort of Chinese Robin Hood. Indeed a common term for them is Greenwood Hero.

In three cases bandits have become emperors. In many other cases they have achieved high official position. The line between the two has not always been clearly drawn.

Secret Societies

From the point of view of political science, the numerous secret societies formed a method of transcending the particularism and isolation of the individual clans so as to make possible, on a wider scale, united action arising from among the people.

Secret societies were thus a Chinese halfway substitute for democracy.

This wider relationship, transcending the biological boundary of the clans, appears in the famous oath in the Peach Garden, often referred to in later secret society rituals:

> We three, though of different families, swear brotherhood, and promise mutual aid to each other.

Having sworn this oath, they called themselves the "three brothers."

Such societies generally had a religious aspect, either Taoist or, later, Buddhist, which introduced a mystical atmosphere, and a magical potency which gave them assurance of success. This was enhanced by ritual. This always embodied the idea of a blood-brotherhood wider than the clan into which the initiates entered when they pricked their fingers, dripped their blood into a cup, drank it, and swore the oath of blood-brotherhood.

Extra-Legal Tendency

Seeing that they arose from among the people and unrelated to the government handed down from above, they tended to be opposed to it. They had an extra-legal character. This made them easily become instruments of rebellion.

The lotus is a Buddhist symbol. Its roots are in the mire, but it rises to purity and beauty, and thus the individual may rise out of the mire of this mundane world to a better realm. It also may have the revolutionary implication that a new and better government may rise above the old one.

The lotus also symbolized the composition of the secret society itself. At the top are to be found scholars and leading gentry. These are designated "pure water" members. At the bottom may be beggars, magicians, robbers. These are designated "dirty water" members. Here again the secret society shows its extra-legal aspect, and combines the forces of order and disorder. It cuts across class lines and serves to allay the insecurity of the more unstable group while serving upper class ends.

A local secret society might appear as a benevolent organization and build bridges or perform other public services. In fact, this was a usual aspect. Its more nefarious members might pull off robberies, from which both high and low might benefit, and no questions asked. They had secret signs which might prove useful on meeting robbers who might be members of a brother society, and in all sorts of emergencies.

A description of such a society in San Francisco in 1892, based on translations of secret documents seized in a police raid, stated:

> Its members are drawn from all ranks of life—rich and poor, learned and illiterate, honest men and swindlers, bandits of the mountains, pirates of the seas, and tramps of the public streets . . . a resort for all who are in distress or in debt or discontented.

In Singapore, Chinese secret societies were given official status in 1882, for it seemed to the government that they included the most substantial leaders in the Chinese community. Later police records make it clear that they were also involved in most Chinese criminal activity.

Such secret societies went by many names in various regions, but were essentially the same. But they lacked a strong organization linking them together.

The first secret society recorded in Chinese history as revolting against the government was the "Carnation Eyebrows" toward the close of the Former Han dynasty which ended 9 A.D., who painted their eyebrows red to terrify their enemies. At this time there were also the "Copper Horses" and the "Iron Shins."

These secret societies were related to the Taoist religion and the Taoist mountain monasteries served as refuges when they were defeated. The "Yellow Turbans" revolted in 184 A.D. after a leader had gone from monastery to monastery uniting them and the Taoist priests had gone from village to village bringing the lowly and oppressed into a secret army. They had wide success at first but were eventually defeated.

The most widespread was the Lotus Society, founded by a famous Buddhist scholar (died 416 A.D.) which became a leading religious sect, but probably did not become political until about 1277 when it served as an underground basis for organizing a revolt against the alien Mongol dynasty, which was overthrown soon afterward. The leader was a Buddhist monk who established the Ming dynasty and became the first Ming Emperor. This Chinese dynasty continued from 1368 to 1644 when it was overthrown by the alien Manchu dynasty, and the secret societies again became political.

This close relationship between Taoist and Buddhist sects and revolutionary activities made the Chinese government suspicious of all religious organizations. This came to include Christianity which provided a considerable part of the religious aspects of the Taiping revolt.

Limitations of Secret Societies

Secret societies could stir up revolt, at times on a large scale. But generally it ended with negative action. They had little widespread organization. They were uninstructed in methods of organization of power, even when it was in their hands.

Their religious ideas provided an ideology which a revolting peasantry could oppose to the Confucianism of the government. But such ideologies remained magical and anarchistic, and failed to develop any constructive political theory that could replace the existing government order.

Effects of Governmental Maladjustment

The attempts in recent years to combine modern government with this ancient governmental structure have not worked. Democracy failed to be effective against forty centuries of a two-class society run by aristocrats where the common man simply did not count. The mystical idea of a vague region ruled by the magic of a semi-divine king forms little basis for citizenship and the duties and responsibilities of modern government.

There of course had been some modification of all this as individuals had moved to the growing and partially industrialized cities. But this was still a small part of the picture, too small to be effective.

This failure to carry government down to the level of the masses, and to implement government organization at the local level, left the Chinese without experience in the organization of government.

This is the explanation of much of the failure of powerful revolts, like the T'ai-p'ing Rebellion, and of the Republic as established in 1912, or of the Nationalist Canton government in 1923. It was this that gave the Russians their great opportunity to come in and take control.

This lack of experience in local government was illustrated by the wartime city election in Chengtu. This was the first time any member of the faculties of the several universities there had ever voted. They were at a loss to know how to set up a campaign until some remembered that a recent American movie had portrayed an election, and this was taken as a model for such guidance as it provided, much to the amusement of all concerned. But it was all they had to draw upon.

Such an amorphous national government set-up meant that a dynastic weakening permitted fragmentation of the government machine at the provincial level, resulting in war lords. Secret societies, bandits, and war lords might struggle or coalesce, and local leaders might rise to power. This was always an invitation to adventurers watching for opportunities and plotting for power. The most popular novels, like the *Three Kingdoms* and the *Sui Hu Chuang* (*All Men Are Brothers*), glamorized the stratagems and victories of such men of derring-do. The communists are in this succession.

5

Religious Aspects of Society and State

Every social Chinese institution had its religious aspect. This was not personal religion, but household, clan, and official ceremonial. It grew out of the necessity for adjustment to the environment, which they did not understand, but on which they were dependent—the seasons, the fertility of crops. This called for the right magic.

The West thinks largely in terms of personal religion, but this concept does not apply to China before the coming of Buddhism. The aim was the prosperity of the clan or state of which the individual was a fractional part, and in which he shared. Any personal religious feeling was incidental and subsidiary. Even the king or the clan head who performed the ceremonial did so in a corporate capacity.

Popular Religion

The general popular religion was shamanism. The *wu* or shamans were medicine-men, mediums, and specialists in the occult, who did many strange things. They were often women, and are found in most country villages to this day.

This religion of the masses was largely incorporated into the Taoist religion after its development in the third century. It has continued with very little change up to the present, and still has a strong hold over the great majority.

Clan Religion

The religious aspect of the clan was ancestor worship. The dead were reverently encoffined and venerated with the correct ritual, so that the deceased ancestor would continue to watch over the welfare of the clan, bring good fortune, and prevent ill fortune.

Thus the orifices of the body were closed with jade stoppers of magic potency which would prevent any spirit from entering the corpse and using it as a vampire for its own malign purposes.

Filial piety—the chief Confucian virtue—is an anticipation of ancestor worship, and provides a religious sanction for the clan relationships, which constitute the Confucian ethic.

Religious Aspects of the State

The state was basically a magical entity, as indicated above, with indefinite boundaries determined by the outreach of the magical power of the ruler. Supplemented and implemented by force of arms.

In the *Analects* is a saying of Confucius concerning Shun, the legendary model king.

> The Master said, among those that ruled by inactivity surely Shun may be counted. For what action did he take?
>
> He merely placed himself gravely and reverently with his face due south; that was all.

Waley comments that he is said to have ruled by non-activity, through the mere fact of sitting in a majestic attitude with his face turned to the south. This is the conception of the royal magic power that regulates everything in the land. It is one which is common to all early Chinese thought.

The ruler was one who was en rapport with heaven, one who could induce rain in season, guarantee the food supply, and overcome the malign spirits that could prevent prosperity. The state ritual was his business just as the clan ritual was the function of the head of the clan. It was his business to know the seasons. There were no calendars and it was necessary to tell the people when to sow. He was of divine descent and worshiped Shang Ti, the Supreme Ancestor. Only he could worship heaven. He worshipped mountains and rivers in person or by deputy to invoke clouds for rain and water for irrigation.

In other matters he obtained the guidance of the Supreme Ancestor by divination, and the earliest written records are the "oracle bones" recording the royal divinations of the Shang period.

It is almost impossible for Western men, habituated to the use of a calendar for several millennia, to imagine a state of things when the seasons were not accurately known, and a basic function of the ruler was to tell his people the exact time to plant, so that they might reap in due season. This had in it something of divinity, as the people of that day saw it. He was the Son of Heaven in China. He held the Mandate of Heaven. And in Japan he was the descendent of the Sun Goddess, and a Manifest Deity.

A later development along this line was that of the influential Buddhist sutra entitled "Benevolent Kings Protecting Their Countries," where an elaborate ceremonial, on a large scale, featuring the chanting of this sutra, was believed to have great magic power in inhibiting the malign activities of the countless spirits that would otherwise imperil the well-being and stability of the nation. This was elaborated in T'ang dynasty China, and was extensively used in Japan, where it had great influence commending the adoption of Buddhism to the imperial court.

Ideas of this sort have continued to our own time. When Sun Yat-sen began to advocate a republic rather than a restoration of the Ming dynasty, as was the aim of the other revolutionaries, he summed it up in a key slogan: "The mandate of heaven is not forever."

In Japan, a messianism based on the divinity of the emperor provided a religious certainty of world conquest and the mystique that underlay Japanese fanaticism.

It is necessary for the man from the West to get inside this enchanted world if he is to understand China and indeed most of Asia. The geography of this world is not the precise maps of the West, with the orderly play of natural forces, but the fantastic geography of primitive folk lore, or of a Buddhist tale of a journey to some Western paradise.

Religious Aspects of Secret Societies

This factor of magical power is why revolutionary movements in China nearly always took the form of secret societies that had a distinctly religious character, usually Taoist or Buddhist. The government was always Confucian. This religious factor brought a magical assurance of success and the emotional drive that only religion can give.

Thus, in the Northern Sung dynasty, the revolt which was the basis of the famous novel *Sui Hu Chuan*, did not spread to anything like the same extent as another revolt led by one Fang La in Chekiang about the same time.

A significant and perhaps decisive factor was the element of local superstition and debased religion of which Fang La made capital. The adoption of certain heretical Taoist doctrines which also flourished in the vicinity contributed greatly to the morale of his followers. Fang preached rebellion to masses filled with indignation, fanned the flame with this heresy, and became, at least for a time, invincible.

As has been indicated above, the religious aspect of the secret societies provided them with an ideology which they could oppose to the official Confucianism. This was in a number of cases provided by foreign religions, such as Buddhism.

Rise of Personal Religion

Religion continued for centuries to be almost completely institutional until with the coming of Buddhism at the end of the Han dynasty came the beginnings of personal religion. This was supplemented by the highly individualistic Taoist philosophical development which followed, as will appear later. However, personal religion developed slowly, and has occupied a subordinate place in China up to the present.

Cultural Function of Monotheism

What is perhaps the most profound difference between East and West grows out of religion.

The first commandment is basic in this connection: "Thou shalt have no other gods before me." And the Old Testament emphasizes that God is a "jealous" God, and will not tolerate the worship of any other. The result was that the other gods had to be liquidated. And with them went their cults, and that portion of the culture that was closely associated with them. This was both a theological and a cultural purge.

It resulted in a unified culture.

This was a culture with a horizontal stratification, in which the earlier culture levels—with their old religions and their old cultures—

were buried beneath the strata of the more recent culture levels. Or else they were amalgamated to the newer culture level and became a part of it.

China, lacking this unifying principle, has three religions—Confucianism, Taoism, Buddhism—not counting the more primitive religion of the masses. Here the strata are vertical. The earlier ones are not buried beneath the later ones, but appear side by side with them on the surface.

This gives China some of the characteristics of a pluralistic society. Of course, not to the extent of a society like Malaya, where the population is split into three large groupings of Malays, Chinese and Indians, with differences of national origin, culture, and language. The Chinese pluralism, much less in degree, is not linguistic or national but internal within China's own culture itself.

Indeed, the same person may belong to all three religions. But that does not imply a synthesis. It has been said that the Chinese is a Confucianist in office and a Taoist when he loses his job. He makes use of Buddhism when he is concerned with death. He thus displays a multiple personality in this aspect of his culture.

But it goes still deeper. The religious situation is a symptom and an outcome of China's pluralistic structure, or from another angle, of the failure to achieve a complete cultural integration. This shows in the persistence of the three anthropological culture levels, in the pluralistic sociological structure with little on the local level but isolated and unrelated clans, and finally in the conglomerate political structure.

Of course, this is one aspect only of China's culture—although a very important one—and must be set over against China's tremendous achievements, such as the uniting a quarter of the human race, as compared with Europe's fragmentation into twenty-five warring nationalities.

PART II

THE MOVEMENT OF CHINESE HISTORY

The movement of Chinese history may perhaps best be understood as a series of expanding circles, whole new areas of geography, social conditions, techniques, philosophy, and religion being synthesized into a larger unity, modified by including these new factors.

There have been four main periods of synthesis, each preceded by what has been usually considered an age of confusion but has really been a formative period. This has not been merely the repetition of a cycle. Each synthesis has established a wider equilibrium and fixed a revised pattern, but has retained its characteristic Chinese quality. The fifth synthesis has not yet been fully worked out.

In addition there have been certain long-term trends, many of which still continue.

Military conquest and political developments have played their part, but China is best understood as a cultural entity, and the most significant aspect of the movement of Chinese history is the Chinese cultural expansion.

China embraces half of East Asia and a quarter of the human race. The peoples of this vast territory were no more homogeneous than those of Europe, and China, like Europe, was subject to repeated invasions from without. But where Europe remains Balkanized, China is one, with a tradition of unity reaching back to the establishment of the empire in 221 B.C.

THE FOUR SYNTHESES OF CHINESE HISTORY

I. The Confucian Synthesis

Formative Period	1273 years	1994?–722 B. C.
Period of Synthesis	244 years	722 –478 B. C.

Political Synthesis: None. Followed by period of the Warring States
Cultural Synthesis: Defined the pattern of Chinese society

II. The Han Synthesis

Formative Period	257 years	478–221 B.C.
Period of Synthesis	441 years	221 B.C.–220 A.D.

Political Synthesis: Establishment of the empire
Cultural Synthesis: Standardization of written characters, examination system, university, Confucian dominance

III. The T'ang Synthesis

Formative Period	369 years	220–589 A.D.
Nomad invaders of North China		
Period of disunity		
Indianization, coming of Buddhism		
Period of Synthesis	317 years	589–906 A.D.

Political Synthesis: Re-establishment of the empire
Cultural Synthesis: Flowering of Chinese culture, poetry, art; conflict between Confucianism and Buddhism; invention of printing

IV. The Sung Synthesis

Formative Period	54 years	906–960 A.D.
Period of Synthesis	320 years	960–1280 A.D.

Political Synthesis: Minimum. Pacifistic, limited frontiers, divisions. Tartars rule the north, Chinese the south
Cultural Synthesis: Neo-Confucianism

V. Formative Period Leading toward a Fifth Synthesis

Formative period	494 years	1280–1774
Mongol dynasty	88 years	1280–1368
Ming dynasty	276 years	1368–1644
Manchu dynasty	267 years	1644–1911
Break up and attempts at a modern synthesis		
Under Manchu dynasty	137 years	1774–1911
Early Republic	15 years	1912–1927
Nationalists	22 years	1927–1949
Peoples' Republic	8 years	1949–

1

The Confucian Synthesis

The Confucian synthesis was the first of the four main syntheses that mark the movement of Chinese history.

It may be conveniently dated at the death of Confucius, 478 B.C. The formative period leading up to this synthesis includes all previous Chinese history—the Hsia, Shang, and Chou "dynasties." The period of synthesis may be taken to include the period covered by the Annals, 722–481 B.C.

Chinese Historiography

The first great history of China, the first of the series of twenty-five dynastic histories, was written during the Han dynasty, when China had been unified and the empire established. It tended to read into the past the imperial and dynastic pattern. This was followed by all later historians.

This resulted in an artificial pattern being superimposed. The Hsia, Shang, and Chou "dynasties" were not dynasties in the later imperial sense of the word. It also resulted, as will appear later, in numerous brief kingdoms of limited territory being designated as dynasties, especially during the period of disunion 220–589 A.D., that followed the Han dynasty.

This historical pattern, as developed by Chinese historians, has been followed by most western books on Chinese history, with the result that the course of history is cluttered with an immense amount of detail, and the main trends are lost amid a flood of irrelevant events.

This handbook departs from this ancient pattern and goes behind the dynastic facade to present the broad outline of Chinese history in its four main synthesis so as to uncover and focus attention upon its main movement.

Character of the Confucian Synthesis

Confucius said of himself that he was a transmitter, not an originator. This was the characteristic of the Confucian synthesis. It defined and fixed the pattern of Chinese society. It was a cultural, not a political synthesis.

Beginnings

Chinese history traditionally begins with the Hsia and Shang dynasties. Modern scholarship considered both to be legendary until in 1928 excavations uncovered the Shang capital of Anyang and brought to light some hundred thousand oracle bones with inscriptions. Indeed, archeology has revealed two still earlier cultures, known as Yang Shao and Lung Shan—perhaps paralleling the Hsia—and has established the continuity of these two with the Shang which followed them. Seventy sites of the Lung Shan or Black Pottery culture have been found, where there were communities of circular pit dwellings, which had domesticated the pig, made pottery, and begun simple agriculture with stone-bladed hoes.

Hsia and Shang

The oracle bones contain the names of twenty-three of the thirty-one Shang kings on the traditional list. This verification of Shang history makes the Hsia tradition probable. But in any case, neither one was a dynasty—that was a reading back of the later organization of the empire. What is known is little more than the list of names of kings, embellished with a few anecdotes. The dates are approximately as follows:

Hsia	1994–1523 B.C.
Shang	1523–1027 B.C.

There was probably a special priesthood that wrote on flat bone or tortoise shell the questions of the prince and interpreted the replies of the deity from the cracks in the bone when heat was applied. There are indications of human sacrifice. Sea shells show that Anyang was in touch with the coast. There was a high level of material culture, and highly artistic ceremonial vessels of bronze.

Chou Invaders

The Chou invaders were bronze age chariot fighters from the northwest, probably of pastoral origin, and were more virile and crude than the more highly civilized Chinese of the Shang "dynasty" in the middle Yellow River valley. They settled to the west, and rapidly adopted the culture of the people they had conquered.

Duke Wen, who later became the ideal ruler of Confucius, consolidated the Chou rule. To placate and win over the more highly civilized Shangs, the conquerors put forth the theory of the mandate of heaven: that when a ruler failed in good government, the mandate was withdrawn and conferred on someone more worthy. This was merely Chou propaganda, but that did not prevent it from being accepted and becoming very influential in its later Confucian form.

The Chou invasion was in 1027 B.C. The first certain date is 841 B.C., verified by an eclipse. Here actual history begins. By this time the Chou control had relaxed, and the country gradually disintegrated into an increasing number of large and small states.

In 770 B.C. a nomad people from the steppes sacked the Chou capital, and the Chou moved it to Loyang, further east in the Yellow River valley. This ended the hegemony of the Chou, and left them only the priestly function of the Son of Heaven, and the nominal headship of the feudal system. The real power was now in the hands of the feudal states.

Extent of the Chou Realm

The China of that day included the Yellow River valley, and one or two states to the south. The total number of states is estimated at 1440. Many were very small. Some were enclaves within larger ones. See Map.

The Age of the Annals

The classic Spring and Autumn Annals, not written by Confucius as traditionally held, provide a picture of the period 722–481 from the viewpoint of the small state of Lu, in modern Shantung, where Confucius was born.

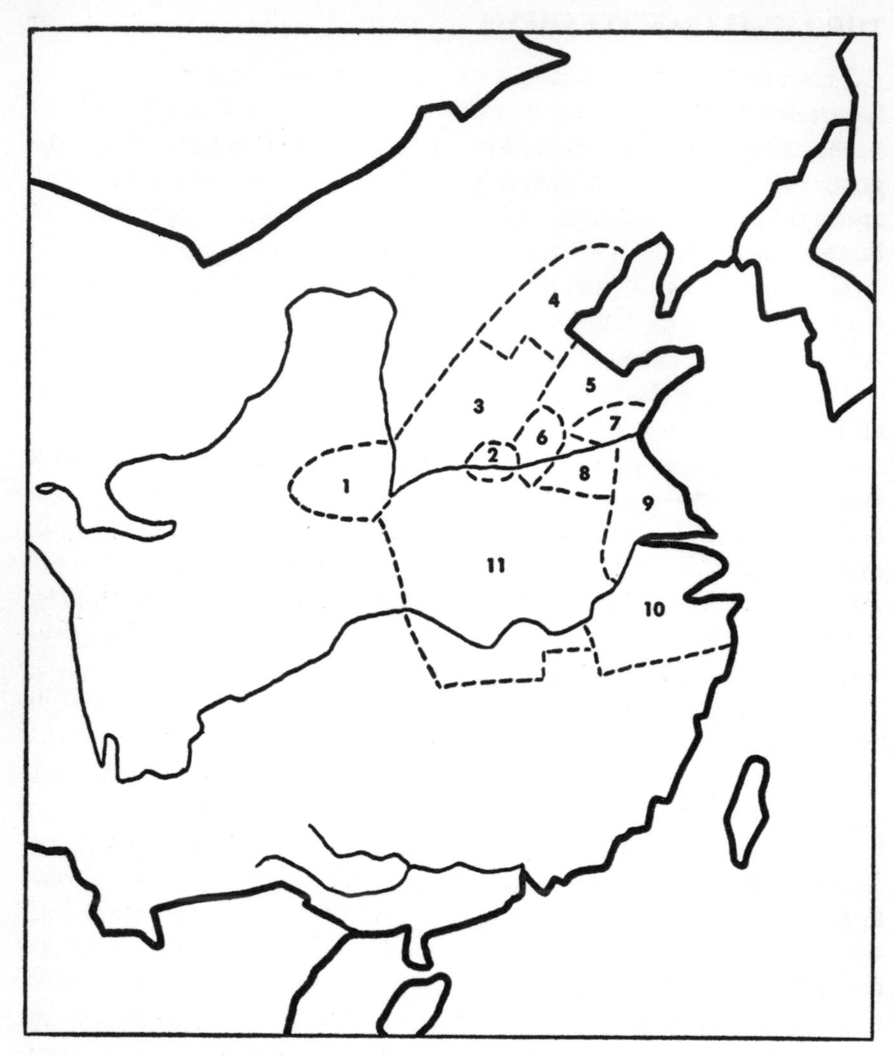

China about the Time of Confucius

The 11 main states are indicated on the map as follows:

1. Ch'in (which later conquered the rest and established the empire)
2. Chou
3. Tsin
4. Yen
5. Ch'i
6. Wei
7. Lu (the state of Confucius)
8. Sung
9. Wu (this and the two following were frontier regions at this time)
10. Yueh
11. Ch'u

The various states did not occupy the whole area but were separated by uninhabited marshland, and in the mountains were barbarian tribes. The Chou invaders probably took over cities and good lands and drove the earlier peoples to new settlements or marginal regions. Thus the Shang rulers continued as the rulers of Sung, a territory to the east.

The nobility were members of a clan system, sharply separated from the masses. Some twenty-two clans are mentioned in the Annals of the small state of Lu. All political power was in the hands of these noble clans, who were also the great landlords. They held all the government offices.

The common people did not count. They tilled the soil for their landlords in peace, and fought for them in war.

The elaborate ancestor worship was the privilege of the land-owning clans. The higher rites of sacrifice to the gods of the soil and the crops were reserved to the prince. The formula for recording the fall of a state was that "the sacrifices were discontinued." This was official sacrificial magic rather than religion.

The nobles were known as lords and the aristocrats in general as "sons of lords," *chun-tzu*. This became the standard Confucian term, which later came to mean merely the princely or superior man.

Chivalry

The basic characteristic of these nobles was that they were fighters, knights. They were also polished aristocrats. They had tutors and education was honored. They followed an elaborate ceremonial which governed all social relationships. This was related to religion and was the expression of a moral order approved by heaven. Good form was virtue, and with the Chinese people rises to the dignity of a religion.

In these early days etiquette was observed even in warfare, which was conducted according to a code of chivalry. But by the time of Confucius, population had increased and states had expanded and come into contact with each other. This developed into conflict as the pressure increased, and at last came to be a life and death struggle for the supreme power.

What Confucius tried to do was to bring back the courtly chivalry of the good old days. But times had changed. He failed. But he refused to give up his ideal. And throughout Chinese history, Confucianism has retained an academic and impractical position in contradistinction to the political realities.

Wandering Adventurers

This period, and the one which followed, was characterized by numerous vagabond adventurers, and modern research indicates that they had an increasingly significant influence in Chinese society.

The increasing anarchy stimulated intellectual activity. Old loyalties were destroyed. Established institutions were overthrown. Men groped for a new pattern of relationships, for a new morality. Some began to question about a world order.

The swallowing up of many states left their previous nobility stranded. They were cut off from their old income, from their old relationships, their old loyalties. Many became footloose adventurers.

Some were wandering scholars, of whom Confucius was one of the first. He was a descendant of the royal house of Shang which had now transferred to Sung, and his junior branch of his princely clan had gone still further east to the state of Lu. Some of these scholars, like Confucius, became professional teachers. Others took up the search for knowledge itself and became dialecticians.

Some became "legalists." These were wandering scholars who were displaced aristocrats owing no loyalty to anyone, least of all to the new authorities who had usurped their old prerogatives and thrust them out into the world to seek their fortunes. They tended to become attached to some princely or aristocratic household, and the general name for these was "house guests." This gave men like Confucius a special interest in government.

Such legalist adventurers from the more advanced central states received a warm welcome in the more barbarous states on the border, and many rose to high positions. These states had been little touched by the old code of ceremonial and chivalry, and were far more ruthless and unscrupulous. The wandering scholars readily fell in with this and proposed stratagems for conquest and the gaining of the supreme power. No state was more ready to disregard the old code than was Ch'in, the one farthest to the west. Here, much later, came several of the most realistic and most able of the wandering legalists who were an important factor in aiding Ch'in to conquer all the rest and establish the empire.

The practicality of the legalists was in sharp contrast to the academic idealism of the Confucianists. This has continued as a basic and interesting contradiction throughout the course of Chinese history.

Two other main types of adventurers emerged in addition to scholars—men-at-arms, and practitioners of the occult who were adepts in magic, exorcism and fortune-telling, and were the precursors of the later Taoist priests.

These three tended to form a team. A ruler—or a bandit chief or a captain of a group of marauders—might have a legalist as adviser, employ men-at-arms in his fighting forces, and have a magician who could by divination foretell the best course of action and, by magic, render the fighting forces invulnerable.

This also has been a continuing factor in Chinese society. A prominent war lord in West China, only a few years ago, had such a team, complete with magician.

At first these wandering adventurers were chiefly displaced aristocrats, but as time went on they included an increasing number of commons of ability, who were more often fighting men. The importance of this type is attested by the fact that one of them, a commoner, became the founder and first emperor of the great Han dynasty.

The Curriculum of Confucius

Writing was known nearly a thousand years before Confucius, as the oracle bones prove. The diviners who wrote them were probably the first intellectuals.

Other documents began to appear. Court annals recorded administrative decisions. Archives included edicts and rituals.

Confucius collected everything available out of the past and made it the curriculum of his teaching. The result was a conspectus of the civilization of his time, an epitome of Chinese culture. This fixed the pattern of the Chinese way of life and ethical ideal, and of Chinese scholarship. These books became the Chinese classics. There were five: Annals, Book of Historical Documents, Book of

Rites and Ceremonies, Book of Changes, a handbook of divination, and Book of Poetry, containing ritual chants and primitive folk songs. Some other documents have survived, but were relegated to the place of commentaries on the classics.

Confucius the Man

Confucius exemplified his own teaching, and was the typical Chinese whom succeeding generations have taken as a model. This representative character has been the basis of the strength of Confucianism.

There had been court tutors, but he was the first to make teaching his profession and accept as pupils any who could pay his modest tuition.

Confucius loved the learning of the past. He was precise about all ceremonial details of dress, food, personal relations, and court etiquette, which he considered essential for the orderly conduct of life and the welfare of clan and society.

He had a passion for propriety. It is recorded of him that he would not sit on his mat unless it was straight.

Confucius and Government

The chief interest of Confucius was government. The teaching he gave his pupils was in preparation for official position. This was natural for a descendant of a royal house, now a displaced aristocrat.

He felt he could best accomplish his own mission by becoming minister to a prince and inspiring his policies. He had absolute confidence in his vocation, and felt that if he found a prince "capable of making use of him, at the end of a cycle of twelve months some result, and at the end of three years, perfection, would be achieved." And he was likewise confident of his own wisdom. "When one has fully achieved wisdom," he once said, "if one remains without employment, the shame is on the head of the nobles."

Confucianism has been described by Professor Fung Yu-lan as a "code of honor for the feudal lords." It was implemented by ceremonial. Force was used only to control the serfs, the common men who did not count.

His reliance was on nobility of character and on moral suasion.

Below was the properly educated aristocrat, above was the prince, whose virtue would have a compelling influence on the nobles in his government. This "virtue" was in part moral character in the Confucian fashion, but even more it was magical power, something like "the divinity that doth hedge a king."

It was easy for Confucius to think in such terms, for his state of Lu was small. Even in that day of slow travel he could probably cross from one border to the other in a few days. Indeed all but a few of the states of that day were small, because there were so many of them.

But no prince made him a minister after he left Lu, and he continued to wander from state to state, teaching his hopeful followers, some of whom did get positions. So he came to his end.

Rationalizing the Clan Structure

Basically, however, Confucianism is a rationalization of the kinship structure of Chinese society. It put the structure of the clan into words. The first three of the five relations, which were the essence of Confucianism, were those between father and son, older brother and younger brother, husband and wife, which constitute an analysis of the relations within the clan, setting forth the duties of the inferior and the responsibilities of the superior. Confucianism is not democratic. One is above the other. The other two, prince and minister, and friend and friend, envisage the noble clan at court, with its members holding office as the various ministers of the prince, or on polite terms with the members of the other noble clans at the court.

Confucius thus saw the government as an enlargement of the clan. The rules that enabled the clan to live together harmoniously and prosperously would suffice for the government of the state.

This was partly true—at the New Stone Age peasant village level. But it was not true at the level of national government to which it was later applied. This was the basis of the academic and impractical character of later Confucianism.

The Confucian synthesis was cultural and educational only. Its significance was that it summed up the history of Chou and the two preceding "dynasties" back to the beginnings, and gave definitive form to the Chinese civilization of its day. It was historically minded. In the words of Confucius:

> Chou had the advantage of surveying the two preceding dynasties. How replete was its culture. I follow Chou.

The significance of this synthesis appeared more in retrospect than at the time.

2

The Han Synthesis

The second of the four main syntheses that mark the movement of Chinese history was the Han synthesis. This was both political and cultural.

The formative period of the break-up of the Chou "dynasty" and the warring states covered the 257 years from the death of Confucius to the establishment of the empire. It was a time of confusion and anarchy, but also it was the chief creative period of Chinese history.

This was followed by the brief Ch'in Dynasty which established the Chinese Empire in 221 B.C., which was to last for 2132 years until 1911. This began with the conquest of the other states, and was characterized by gigantic works of reconstruction based on forced labor.

The Han Dynasty, which continued for 400 years, consolidated the nationwide unity of the centralized empire, synthesized the Confucian and legalist positions by putting the Confucian scholars in control of the government through the examination system, and replaced the feudal nobility by a landed gentry class, whose status was based on scholarship.

The main periods are as follows:

Warring States	403–221 B.C.
Ch'in Dynasty	221–207 B.C.
Han Dynasty	206 B.C.–220 A.D.

Warring States

In the brief year-by-year records that have come down to us, there is scarcely a year which is not marked by fighting, in spite of frequent councils to make peace or set up coalitions. The central

Chou authority was weak. There was urgent need for some system of protocol to keep the turbulent feudal nobility in order and maintain peace.

From the point of view of later historians, writing under the centralized empire, who read the imperial organization back into the Hsia, Shang and Chou "dynasties," the period of the warring states was one of breakdown. Actually it was a formative period.

Age of Philosophers

This was the period of the Hundred Schools. The political diversity made for intellectual freedom. The breakdown of the old ways and loyalties stimulated a search for new criteria. There were many varieties of theory. But three main lines emerged that were to dominate Chinese history.

Confucius began with man and rationalized the social order. The Taoists began with nature—legends, cosmology, divination. The actual solution was worked out along the third line by force of arms, and rationalized, analyzed, and organized by the legalists.

These and others of the Hundred Schools will be dealt with in Part III as systems of thought. Here it will suffice merely to indicate the part they played in the movement of history. Confucianism has already been described.

Taoism was not for everybody. It was a method for the ruler, who should practice a masterly inactivity, sit facing the south, and delegate everything to his ministers. It was an escape from responsibility for the aristocrats, also, who could take to the mountain fastnesses with a plentiful supply of wine and beauteous maidens to serve it. It was a mysticism just the opposite of the Confucian fussiness about everything. It was as paradoxical and fantastic as Confucianism was practical and matter of fact. As Confucianism became more rationalistic and less superstitious, more humanistic and less religious, Taoism took over the superstitions that Confucianism discarded, and eventually developed along two lines and became a rather crass religion on the one hand and a philosophy on the other.

Basis of Ch'in Supremacy

The state of Ch'in conquered the others and set up the empire as a result of a combination of circumstances. It was the one farthest west and the world currents of cultural diffusion brought iron weapons to them first. They were barbarians who had more recently entered China and were less civilized, particularly in warfare, where their aim was not merely to conquer the enemy but to liquidate his fighting forces. They attracted legalist scholars and organizers from the more culturally advanced states further east who did not think in Confucian terms of moral suasion, but in terms of law, applied equally to all and rigidly enforced without exception, and in terms of organization that would implement the central authority. They built the first large-scale irrigation canal. Lastly, there was the organizing genius and vast administrative ability and energy of the First Emperor himself.

The state of Ch'in became the country of legislators and economists. The Prince of Shang, an outstanding refugee from an eastern state, took the lead in this. In 359 B.C. he caused the laws to be codified, reformed punishments, encouraged tillage. Feudal dues were replaced by taxes. Chivalry was discarded. War ceased to be an implementation of the judgment of Heaven, or a mere punishment of the guilty, and aimed at the destruction of the enemy.

The Ch'in territory was a great natural fortress, with mountains and the Yellow River forming formidable barriers. Within it was the valley of the Wei, whose fertility had been greatly increased by the construction of canals about this time. To the east was the narrow corridor of the Yellow River valley, which opened out into the lower valley and coastal region, where there was a group of more developed states. In this narrow corridor were strategic cities, and the immense granary at Ao, on a mountain near the Yellow River. This later provided food for three years for an army of over a hundred thousand.

The rest of the present China had not yet become important. See Map.

Establishment of the Empire

The Chinese Empire, established in 221 B.C., was the only revolution in Chinese history until 1911, and was its most profound and far reaching social upheaval.

The First Emperor had developed the most effective government in China. It was of the power and punishment school as opposed to the Confucian moral suasion method. It had a realistic philosophy of government. But he was first of all a great destroyer in the utterly ruthless and wholesale fashion of the Huns and other bar-

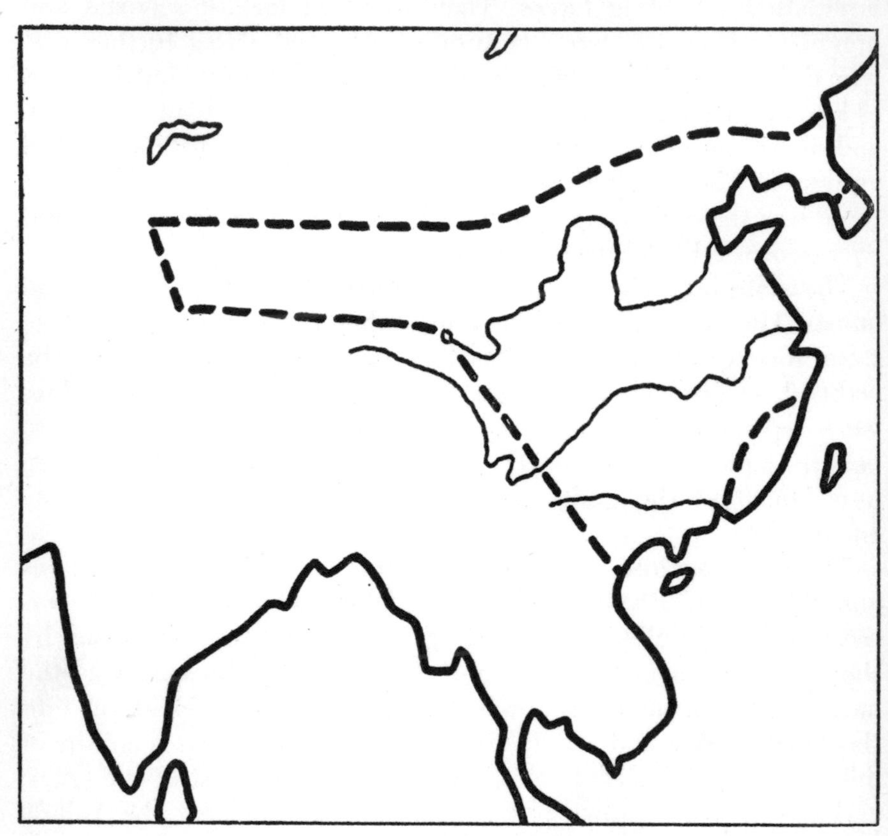

The Han Empire about 100 A.D.

barian hordes that devastated Europe and Asia over the centuries, and from whom his own population was probably derived.

He ruled for thirty-seven years, the last eleven as emperor of all China.

He first established rigid control. He massacred defeated armies. To further ensure security all weapons were collected and melted down. The Great Wall was completed, and the report persisted for centuries that it cost a million lives.

Thought Control

His was not merely a superficial unity of conquest. He and Li Ssu, his minister, set up a structure of centralized government that has endured almost to our day with little basic change.

He smashed feudalism and transported 120,000 families of the aristocrats from all over China to his own kingdom, thus destroying their landed power.

Education and learning were in the hands of these same aristocrats, now bitterly opposed to the new regime. So he ordered the burning of their books, except technical works on medicine, divination, agriculture, arboriculture. His edict states the case:

> Formerly the princes were continually at war. They esteemed the wandering scholars and sought their advice. Now the empire has been pacified. Laws and commands emanate from a single authority. The common people are engaged in industry and agriculture, the superior classes study law and methods of administration.
>
> Nevertheless the scholar nobles do not conduct themselves in the new way, but study the past in order to defame the present. They cause doubt and trouble. . . . They oppose the new laws and commands. . . . At court they conceal their resentment, but elsewhere debate these matters in the public streets and encourage the common people to believe calumnies.
>
> Those who praise ancient institutions to decry the present regime shall be exterminated with the members of their families.

Some 460 scholars were put to death for concealing the proscribed books. The burning of the books and proscription of the teaching of ancient history, on top of the transportation of the scholar nobles and the abolition of their fiefs, broke their power.

Also it partly destroyed the memory of the ancient institutions. When under the Han Dynasty the ancient literature was painfully pieced together, it had ceased to be the expression of a living political and social system.

Economic Unification

The unification went still deeper. The Ch'in law code was put into force everywhere. Ch'in weights and measures superseded the varying standards that had hindered commerce and complicated the collection of taxes. A system of trunk roads was built and several important canals. The length of axles was fixed so that cart wheels would fit the ruts in the roads everywhere and thus avoid reloading goods or changing axles at boundaries. This removed a great obstacle to commerce and to the transport of tax grain and army supplies.

Language Standardization

Perhaps the innovation that had the most far-reaching results was the standardization of the Chinese written characters which had differed from kingdom to kingdom. This made the written language intelligible all over China. And more than that. For the Chinese ideograph was the symbol of an idea, not of a sound, and its pronunciation might therefore vary with differing dialects and even languages. It thus cut across all language differences and gave all China a semantic and intellectual unity.

This is perhaps the most important factor in the unity of China that has endured for over twenty-one centuries.

The First Emperor was a great administrator who each day handled a hundred and twenty pounds of state papers—written on slips of wood or bamboo, sometimes on silk. His conquests had extended the borders of China almost to its present size. He was the founder of China's national unity. But the ruthlessness of his measures led to universal revolt, and his vast program of palaces, trunk roads, canals, fortifications like the Great Wall, and other public works, impoverished the country. The scholar nobles could not forgive their loss of power and the burning of the books. Later historians held him up to execration:

> A man with a very prominent nose, with large eyes, with the chest of a bird of prey, with the voice of a jackal, without beneficence, and with the heart of a tiger or a wolf . . . to devour men.

That such was the only portrait that has come down is an indication of how far the point of view of the writers was divorced from the realities of the situation, and of the academic character of Confucian scholarship.

The Han Dynasty (206 B.C.–220 A.D.)

On the death of the First Emperor there was a struggle for power that began as palace intrigue but soon spread into nationwide civil war.

But there was a difference. Previously the nobles had had a code of punctilio. Now it was a fight to the finish. All the more so as many leaders were commons who had a simple-minded regard for the realities.

Each seized power as and where he could. The aristocrats had the prestige and frequently became the rulers. The feudal system was momentarily restored. But the aristocrats proved inferior to the shrewd and hard-bitten commons, and it was Liu Chi, a man of humble birth, who came out on top as the first emperor of the Han dynasty.

The four hundred years of the Han Dynasty was the first great period of the Chinese Empire. The Chinese people have ever since looked back upon it with pride. They ordinarily call themselves Han men.

The Han Dynasty established an undying tradition of unity, which Europe still lacks and the four centuries of actual unity under the Han Dynasty gave to this a reality which has made it a basic conviction of the Chinese people ever since. The Han Dynasty also established a conviction of success and solidarity. It made the Chinese people deeply conscious of their strength and greatness. It gave them a national self-consciousness and assurance.

Conquest

It was a time of conquest and political expansion. The country had already been unified by the First Emperor, whose armies had taken over a large part of what is now China. The Han emperors and their brilliant generals extended the boundaries still further. To the northwest they conquered all of Turkistan and Chinese armies met the Roman legions in battle close to the Caspian Sea. To the south they carried Chinese sovereignty into what is now Indo-China and Siam and to the southwest penetrated to the Burma border. This determined the boundaries of China for the next 2000 years.

China entered upon an international period. The conquests of the Chinese armies brought the empire into touch with new and strange lands and civilizations. Embassies were exchanged and trade routes developed, the most famous being the silk route which opened trade with the Roman Empire.

The trade winds seem to have been discovered about this time, with the result that there was a great development in sea-borne commerce from the southern ports of China extending as far to the west as India and Arabia. It was during this dynasty that Buddhism entered China, coming first along the silk route from Central Asia but also along what is now the Burma Road into the Yangtze Valley, and by sea into Canton and other southern city centers. All of this added new factors that would call for a new and wider synthesis some centuries later.

End of Feudalism

Liu Chi actually restored the centralized organization and autocracy of the First Emperor, but at first he kept a facade of feudalism. But only members of his own family might be kings, and his generals who were rewarded with territory were almost all liquidated sooner or later. At the time of his death nine of his family were kings.

This was a further blow to the feudal system, and later under another emperor a decree (144 B.C.) divided the inheritance of a noble among all his sons, so that as the number of fiefs increased, they became smaller, and ceased to be important after the time of the Han emperor Wu (141–87 B.C.)

Social Revolution

The establishment of the Han Dynasty marked not only a political revolution but a social revolution as well.

The ruin of the feudal aristocracy left a gap which was often filled by undesirable elements. A new conception of society gradually evolved in which education and culture rather than divine or noble descent were the qualifications of the ruling class. The 1400 states large and small of Confucius' time had been swallowed up and the princes and nobility who had ruled them had come down in the world.

Liu Chi had been first a petty military official, then a bandit. He had come to the supreme power as a result of his own ability and that of the comrades in arms whom he had very shrewdly chosen and whom he was able to trust. These three changes, the destruction of feudalism, the impoverishment of the nobility, and the rise of a commoner to become emperor, brought about a new spirit and a new initiative.

The scholars and officials of the centralized empire who became the inheritors of the Confucian ideal of the superior man were no longer a hereditary nobility, but a class, including many of the old aristocratic families, marked off from the masses by education, and by education only.

Rise of the Gentry

The gentry were the landlord-scholar-official class which had filled the gap left by the abolition of the feudal nobility.

When feudalism collapsed landed property became salable and was bought by wealthy merchants, and successful farmers who also acquired more land by inheritance, marriage, or by bringing new land under cultivation. Such lands were worked by tenant farmers and the landlords moved to the towns and lived off the rents. Slavery did not develop. Foreign slaves were few. Chinese could not be forced into slavery because of the clan system. A slave's clan could back and avenge him.

The gentry had standing and power. They naturally handled the collection of taxes. They had the leisure for education. They formed the best material for officials and came to have a monopoly of government positions.

The new Han Dynasty began with a mixed administration. Part of the empire was governed by the new princes created by the new dynasty, and part was organized into provinces and prefectures administered by the central government through its appointed officers, who were from the gentry. A struggle went on between these two for about a hundred years and the gentry officials won out.

Thus began the gentry-state that has lasted to the present.

As the gentry moved into the towns their standard of living rose and they became more and more a class apart from the general population. They began to identify themselves with the nobles of feudal times and to adopt the ceremonials and ideals of the Confucian books. Thus Confucian ideals penetrated the official class and then the government. What the government examinations tested was not special training or efficiency, but knowledge of the gentry ideals and the Confucian literature on which they were based. These were considered sufficient qualifications for government office.

In theory, education and official position were open to all except those in dishonorable callings, such as dancers, soldiers, slaves and the like, but in practice no peasant stood a chance. Even if he had money for fees, no tutor who valued his standing with people of influence would jeopardize his position by accepting the son of a peasant as a pupil.

This whole system had its limitations, but also its good side. Eberhart says of it:

> The Confucian moral system gave a Chinese official . . . a spiritual attitude and an outward bearing which . . . always commanded respect, and integrity that has always preserved its possessors, and in consequence, Chinese society as a whole, from moral collapse . . . and has thus contributed to the preservation of Chinese cultural values in spite of all foreign conquerors.

Rise of Confucianism

Confucianism had not flourished greatly up to this time. Both Mencius and Hsun-tzu, his chief disciples, had felt isolated. The period of the warring states was not a good time to revive the order and chivalry of a past that was out of date, and by the end of the period Confucianism was merely the teaching of a few pedants in semi-retirement.

But by the end of the Former Han Dynasty, Confucianism had become the official philosophy of the government and had to be adopted by anyone who hoped to enter public life; it was now on the way to becoming beyond question the dominant influence in Chinese culture.

In this, the examination system was the most important factor, but there were two others: the ceremonials that Confucius so much emphasized and the fact that scholarship and Confucianism were almost synonymous.

Examination System

One of the characteristics of Liu Chi which contributed largely to his success was his shrewd judgment of men and his genius for attracting and using men of ability.

This at first applied in military matters, and when the conquest of the empire was complete he still continued along military lines. A scholar pointed out to him the need of a civilian administration.

"I won the empire on horseback," he replied.

"But can you govern it on horseback?" asked the scholar.

Hence he began to seek capable men. His edict of 196 B.C. stated:

> Verily, We have heard that no king was greater than Wen of Chou, and no Lord Protector was greater than Huan of Ch'i—both needed capable men in order to make a name for themselves. At present in the world there are capable men who are wise and able . . . The trouble is that the ruler of men does not meet them . . . Now I, by the spiritual power of Heaven, and by my capable gentlemen and high officials have subjugated and possess the empire and have made it one family. I wish it to be enduring, that generation after generation should worship at my ancestral temple without cessation. Capable persons have already shared with me in its pacification. Should it be that capable persons are not to share together with me in its comforts and its benefits? If there are any capable gentlemen who are willing to follow and be friends with me, I can make them honorable and illustrious.
>
> Let the foregoing be published to the world . . . the Palace Secretary shall transmit it to the Commandary Administrators. If any have an excellent reputation and manifest virtue, the officials must personally urge them to come. . . .

Capable men were accordingly sent, received in an eastern hall in the palace, and interviewed. This was the earliest stage of the Chinese examination system. Under a later emperor in 165 B.C., when men were sent up, the emperor questioned them in person, and for the first time set literary exercises for prospective officials.

Confucian Ceremonial

Confucius had sought to tame the turbulent nobles by ceremonial, protocol, and rites that carried a religious sanction. Of the thirteen classics finally developed, three dealt with this.

Liu Chi began with a violent prejudice against Confucianism. On one occasion when a group of scholars came to him, he snatched off the ceremonial scholar's bonnet of one of them and urinated in it. Later, as emperor, he no longer liked the rough free ways of the army camp, particularly when his old comrades in arms had been drinking, and realized that such boisterous manners must be stopped and replaced with more of respect and formality. So when a Confucian scholar proposed to construct a court ceremonial along Confucian lines, he accepted.

"Make it easy," he admonished.

But after the ceremony he was greatly impressed.

"Now," he said, "I have today known what is the greatness of being an emperor."

Confucianism Epitomized Chinese Culture

A third factor was that the Confucianists were the ones who conserved the past. They made themselves the scholarly authorities and teachers of the ancient lore and came to have a proprietary interest in the great books of the past which formed their curriculum and were finally considered to be Confucian books. The Confucian school was not the protagonist of some new-fangled theory but the embodiment of the accumulated wisdom of the ages.

When things settled down scholars began to seek out and piece together the ancient books, some of which were extant only in the memory of very old men. This necessitated textual criticism, and was the beginning of a careful critical method that was to be characteristic of the Ming and Manchu dynasties. This interest in the past also led to the writing of the first history by Szu-ma Ch'ien, the Shih Chi, or Historical Records. This furnished the precedent and pattern for the series of twenty-five dynastic histories, really historic encyclopedias, which provide China with the most extensive historic documentation of any country.

The Three Ways of Thought

The three main trends that had appeared during the period of the Warring States and were to dominate the entire course of Chinese history, now became clear-cut. These were represented by the Confucians, the Taoists, and the Legalists.

At the beginning of the Han Dynasty many Taoists held high positions. Thus the chancellor or prime minister of the second Han emperor was a Taoist. He followed the policies of his predecessor in office, but (as described by Prof. Dubs) gave himself to drinking day and night. When anyone would come to talk with him, he would give them a drink before they could get started, and give them more drink whenever they showed any signs of reopening the subject, so that they went away drunk without having had a chance to speak. His subordinates likewise fell to drinking and singing and shouting daily so there was no business done in his office.

The youthful emperor reproved him. He replied that since their predecessors had subjugated the world and laws and ordinances had all been made plain, the emperor should sit with unruffled garments and folded hands, while he guarded the empire. The emperor agreed.

He thus followed the Taoist doctrine that the best government was the one that governs least. Also he sought to give the people relief from the harsh government of the First Emperor, and rest after the wars at the establishment of the Han dynasty. In addition, the real power was then in the hands of the empress dowager who already had several murders to her discredit, so it was politic to lie low.

The Legalists were really the ones who had provided the firm basis for the organization and administration of the empire, which had actually been established by military force. In comparison, the Confucian theory of government was academic and utopian. This was recognized by able men of the time. Thus the History of the Former Han Dynasty records the Emperor Hsuan as admonishing the heir-apparent that the institutions and laws of the Han Dynasty had been taken from both Confucian and non-Confucian sources, and that the Confucian principle of using only moral suasion to bring about conformity to right principles was utterly impractical.

Confucians Gain Control

Thus, at first, scholars of many of the Hundred Schools held positions at court and the Confucians were only one of the most influential groups.

But persons interested in literature or scholarship naturally gravitated to the Confucians, and they inevitably became the tutors of the crown princes.

The slow process of the ascendency of the Confucians came to a climax in the long reign of the Emperor Wu, 141–87 B.C. The great Confucian scholar of the period, Tung Chung-shu, in a famous memorial proposed that there should be an intellectual unification of the country by destroying all non-Confucian philosophies. The Confucians who had never forgiven the First Emperor for burning the books were now ready to institute their own type of thought control. Confucianism soon became the political philosophy of the government, the Confucian party gained control, and Confucianism dominated the last half century of the Former Han Dynasty and the whole of the Later Han period.

This introduced a fatal contradiction. The empire had actually been established and organized on a harsh basis of reality, of law and its drastic enforcement. The Confucian training of candidates for office and the Confucian theory of government was based ethically on moral suasion and sociologically on a rationalization of clan relationships, especially filial piety.

The nobles opposed this, so the Confucians revived an old law that the nobles should reside at their estates. This the nobles did not want to do and, as many of them had married imperial princesses, they appealed to their relative, the Grand Empress Dowager, grandmother of the emperor, who was an ardent Taoist. The Confucian party countered this by proposing a law that government affairs should not be brought to the attention of an empress dowager. At this the old lady became really irked, and so exerted herself that two leaders of the Confucian party had to commit suicide and two others were dismissed, all great officers of state. The Confucians could not withstand the emperor's grandmother. Family and clan were too much for them.

After the old lady died they tried again with better results, although many Taoists and others continued to hold important positions.

In 124 B.C. the Imperial University was established on Confucian initiative and along Confucian lines. Here students spent a year before taking the examinations and could earn the title of Literary Scholar or Authority on Ancient Matters. The curriculum and teachers were Confucianist. Confucians graded the examination papers. So the historian Szu-ma Ch'ien wrote, "From this time on, most of the minor officials in the offices of the ministers and officials at the capital were Literary Scholars," that is, Confucians.

The princely or "superior man" of the time of Confucius had now become the gentleman bureaucrat, and this he remained.

Government vs. Filial Piety

The fighting that went on among the nobles under the feudal system continued under the empire in the form of a series of palace revolutions that undermined and eventually led to the fall of both the Former and the Later Han dynasties.

This was due primarily to the status of the empress as determined by the kinship structure of society and by the Confucian principle of filial piety.

Chinese society had a strict rule of exogamy. It was forbidden to marry within the clan and when names came into use this was applied to anyone with the same name. The feudal nobles had been able to marry into other noble families and thus form alliances that added to their strength. The emperor could not marry into a collateral branch of the imperial house for they were relatives and bore the same name. So the emperors had to marry their subjects.

The consort of a feudal prince had come from a foreign state and could have little influence on government policy, and she had no family to back her in her new country. But the family of an empress was right there, in line for favors and high position, and grasping for power at every opportunity. The empress naturally favored her own kin and put their interests first.

The empress usually outlived the emperor. If the heir was a child, as he frequently was, she became regent and the imperial authority passed into the hands of her family and her uncles and brothers held the highest positions and filled the government with their relations.

If the heir was of age, the empress dowager and her family continued to wield great power, for here Confucianism came in with its exaltation of filial piety as the supreme virtue, and the emperor had to be subservient to his mother so long as she lived. Thus the welfare of the state was subordinated to the whim of some old woman who happened to be the widow of an emperor.

On the death of the first Han emperor, his wife barely succeeded in enthroning her son against the rival son of another powerful favorite, who had almost succeeded in displacing her as empress. At the first opportunity she murdered both the mother and son. The emperor wept himself into a nervous breakdown and kept his bed for a year. But in the face of the Confucian doctrine of filial piety he could do nothing to his own mother, even for murder. However, she proved a good ruler. She knew her position was not strong enough to weather the unpopularity of misrule and was too intelligent to indulge in it.

Such an empress might be merely a pretty concubine or dancing girl who had caught the emperor's fancy, and her family might be the merest upstarts with no idea of government beyond grasping wealth and power for themselves. But such power had a precarious basis in harem intrigue and was easy to lose, so the fatal logic of the situation led most of such consort-families to attempt to seize the throne itself. All failed except the last, Wang Mang, who usurped the throne and brought the Former Han Dynasty to its end. The Emperor Wu had realized this situation and considered it such a menace that when he decided on his successor he had the mother of the future emperor put to death in order to rid him of the pressure of her clan when he became emperor. No other took such harsh measures.

Confucianism is given the blame for this situation by Prof. Dubs, an authority on this period, seeing that it added a moral sanction for this administrative weakness in the central government.

> Confucianism encouraged nepotism and removed the bulwarks afforded by common sense against the abuse of imperial relationships. The inevitable result was the eventual downfall of the dynasty. Confucian idealism was thus the most important contributory factor in the downfall of the Former Han dynasty as well as that of the Later Han dynasty.

Confucian Pedantry

In other ways the Confucians were not much more practical.

The Han emperors engaged in almost constant warfare with the nomad tribes on the northwest border, particularly the ones later known to Europe as the Huns. The Great Wall, completed by the First Emperor, helped, but had to be garrisoned. The great difficulty was not military strategy, for the Chinese won most of the battles, but logistics because of the great difficulty of transporting grain to the garrisons. The rivers ran in the wrong direction, and other transport was extremely difficult.

This drain, together with the ambitious conquests of the Emperor Wu, caused a financial crisis. The old forms of taxation, chiefly on agriculture, were insufficient, and the government had not yet learned to tax the new forms of wealth that had arisen among merchants and manufacturers. Gradually this was done, together with a method of providing the border defense budget from a government monopoly on salt and iron, two new forms of business productive of great wealth. This worked satisfactorily, but was opposed by a group of Confucian scholars who argued that this made salt too expensive for the people to purchase, and furthermore that there was no precedent for this sort of thing.

The minister asked how they proposed to defend the border if the monopolies that supported the army were abolished. They replied with standard Confucian arguments.

> Confucius observed that the ruler of a kingdom . . . is not concerned about his people being few, but about lack of equitable treatment, nor is he concerned over poverty, but over the presence of discontent. . . .
>
> They should cultivate benevolence and righteousness, to set an example to the people, and extend wide their virtuous conduct to gain the people's confidence.
>
> Then will nearby folk flock lovingly to them and distant people submit joyfully to their authority. Therefore, the master conqueror does not fight; the expert warrior needs no soldiers. . . .

The minister had to deal with a real situation, which he put up to them thus:

> The Hsiung Nu, savage and wily, boldly push through the barriers, and harass the Middle Kingdom, massacring the provincial population and killing the keepers of the Norther Marches.

To this the scholars replied:

> Your majesty has but to manifest your virtue toward them and extend your favors to cover them, and the northern barbarians will undoubtedly come of their own accord to pay you tribute at the Wall.

The minister went to the root of the Confucian failure to understand the situation in his reply.

> Your learned men . . . compare the conduct of the affairs of some village with the great business of the nation. . . .

The monopolies were not repealed, for the barbarians were not to be tamed by moral precepts. The crisis was solved, not by the Confucian bureaucrats, but by a member of the new merchant class who previously had not been considered fit to hold office.

Thus the brilliant and imperial synthesis of the Han Dynasty carried with it the seeds of its own break-up, which was already evident by 180, forty years before the official end of the dynasty in 220 A.D. The prestige of Confucianism, together with its conservatism, had perpetuated its rationalization of the primitive clan structure of society, and had tried to apply it to the government of a vast empire.

3

THE T'ANG SYNTHESIS

The third of the four main syntheses of Chinese history took place in the T'ang dynasty which the Chinese consider the most brilliant period of their history.

It was preceded by four centuries of disunion, followed by a brief dynasty that reunited the country, after which the actual synthesis took place during the three centuries of the T'ang dynasty. It thus had the same three phases as did the Han synthesis, but under different circumstances and with greatly differing content. The first phase began at the end of the Han dynasty. The whole period covered seven centuries.

Period of disunion	221–589 A.D.
Unification by Sui dynasty	589–618 A.D.
T'ang dynasty	618–906 A.D.

Wider Circle of the T'ang Synthesis

An influx of nomadic peoples from the northwest broke north China into a shifting series of small kingdoms with new blood and differing cultures. Indian and Persian influences penetrated China, especially Buddhism.

The center of the widening circle of Chinese culture shifted south, and the Yangtze valley displaced the Yellow River valley as the chief basis of food supply.

Period of Disunity 220–589 A.D.

The 369-year period of from the end of the Han dynasty to the reuniting of the empire under the Sui is generally looked on as a sort of Chinese dark ages, a period of confusion and chaos. But this was due in considerable part to the disgruntled point of view of the Confucian historians.

Actually it was much more than that.

There was economic expansion. The Han empire broke into the famous Three Kingdoms based upon the rise of two new key economic areas, in Szechwan in the west and the lower Yangtze valley in the east, that had come to rival the original one in the Yellow River valley. And a temporary unification came when the original area forged ahead again. But the other two continued to grow. One method used in the Yangtze valley was that of military colonies. Then the country fell apart in a welter of small states.

It was another intellectually free period. The political unification of the Han dynasty had hardened free philosophizing into classical scholasticism, culminating in Confucian orthodoxy and control of learning, education and government. Its reverence for the past and academic impracticability brought down the dynasty and the Confucians together. This opened the way for Taoism.

Dominance of Taoism

The Taoists now found themselves in the position of leadership. They formed two schools.

The Rationalists developed the "dark learning," called neo-Taoism in the west. They also made a reinterpretation of Confucius, whom they considered greater than Lao Tzu or Chuang Tzu.

The dark learning held that things are spontaneously what they are. It denied the existence of a personal creator by substituting an impersonal Tao. When there is a change in social circumstances, new institutions and morals spontaneously produce themselves. Non-action is therefore to follow the natural.

The Sentimentalists had a spirit transcending the "distinctions of things" and lived according to themselves, not according to others. This quality is *feng liu*—wind and stream—a quality of elegance and freedom.

The Han style had been characterized by dignity and grandeur, the Confucian style was pedantic. This was romantic and elegant. The way of life that went with it was living by impulse, living according to oneself. This was exemplified by the famous Seven Worthies of the Bamboo Grove.

Merely following what was natural, or living by impulse, was not helpful in preventing the fragmentation of China.

Political Chaos

The political situation was one of confusion. In little over a century, from 304 to 431, some seventeen dynasties ruled larger or smaller parts of north China, and only two of them were Chinese, the rest being of barbarian and nomad stock. Many of them adopted Chinese culture and were eventually absorbed, but that was a slow process, and largely took place after they had ceased to rule.

In the meantime refugees from north China fled to the south in such large numbers that the population increased an estimated five-fold. So the south, particularly the Yangtze valley, advanced culturally as well as economically.

In 439 the Wei dynasty of the Toba Tartars unified the north, and for the rest of the period to 589, the country was divided into two parts, ruled by Chinese in the south and Tartars in the north. But the tradition of unity, established by the First Emperor and maintained by the Han dynasty for four hundred years, still remained strong. Every prince and adventurer strove to restore the empire.

International Influences

It was an international period and Chinese culture was Indianized and enriched by other foreign influences. Much of this was in the field of philosophy, religion, and culture, and appears in Part III. But Buddhism was also one of the international influences that interacted with Chinese society and government in many ways.

In 399 Fa Hsien, one of the first of a long succession of Chinese pilgrims made the long, arduous journey to India to visit the holy places, and bring back Buddhist scriptures. He was gone fourteen years.

Until the coming of Buddhism China had been regarded by the Chinese as the only civilized country, all others being considered barbarians.

The first step was the realization that there were other civilized lands. The second was the beginning of the Indianization of China. The third was the rule of non-Chinese dynasties in north China which brought this home to them in pragmatic fashion. The idea that the Chinese emperor was the son of heaven enthroned at the center of the world lost some of its reality.

Buddhism

It was largely under the non-Chinese rulers in the north that Buddhism, which had entered from the northwest and in the form it had assumed in Central Asia, reached a dominant position. Various factors contributed.

Toward the end of the period of disunity political confusion was augmented by social unrest, largely due to problems of land and taxation. Many land owners were forced by the difficulties of the times to sell at a loss. Buddhism provided a refuge. A historian of the time, Wei Shou, wrote in 554:

> The empire suffered much anxiety, and the services demanded of the people became increasingly oppressive. Thereupon they everywhere entered religion, pretending a love for the sramanas, but in reality avoiding assignment for military service . . . Calculated in round numbers, the monks and nuns were estimated at a total of two million, and their monasteries thirty thousand odd.

This was a large number for that day and meant a considerable loss to the government, for these properties were not taxed.

Monks Replace Gentry

In the non-Chinese dynasties in the north, foreigners, particularly Buddhist monks, played a greater part than the Confucian gentry, and replaced them as government officials.

According to Chinese historians, who were Confucianists, nothing of importance happened in north China during this period. That is, no one came into prominence as a celebrated Confucian. The gentry had maintained Confucianism since the Han period. Taoism had also been dependent on the gentry. Until the fourth century, these two maintained themselves as the dominant philosophies.

Now the gentry had been largely destroyed, and those who remained were shut out from political leadership.

Who could take their place? The alien ruling class could not write

Chinese, but had to have officials who could do so in order to govern their Chinese subjects.

Educated Chinese were seldom available, for the gentry retired to their estates, which they protected as well as they could from their alien rulers, and so long as they had no prospect of regaining control of political life, they were not prepared to provide a class of officials and scholars for the anti-Confucian foreigners.

Thus educated persons were needed at the courts of the alien rulers, and Buddhists were engaged. These foreign Buddhists had the important scriptures translated into Chinese, and so made use of their influence at court for Buddhist propaganda.

Buddhism and Business

Many traders from Turkistan set up branches in China. In the capital were whole quarters inhabited only by aliens from Turkistan and India. With the traders came Buddhist monks; trade and Buddhism seemed to be closely associated everywhere. In the trading centers monasteries were installed in the form of blocks of houses within strong walls that successfully resisted many an attack. Consequently the Buddhists were able to serve as bankers for the merchants, who deposited their money in the monasteries, which made a charge for its custody.

Religious Appeal of Buddhism

Buddhism as a religion made a strong appeal and much of the literature and philosophy of this period are Buddhist. How did Buddhism gain such influence?

Buddhism came to China overland and by sea during the first century A.D. It had interested only a few cultured people, and not for its religious or philosophical content but for the scientific knowledge that accompanied it, except in Taoist circles. It had much in common with philosophical Taoism, and at first the Taoists thought they were the same, and Buddhist monks were called *Tao Shih,* Taoist priests.

But generally the missionary monks that came from abroad with the foreign merchants found little approval among the Chinese gentry. They were regarded as second-rate persons, belonging to an inferior social class. Thus the monks had to turn to the middle and lower classes. Among these they found widespread acceptance, not of their philosophic ideas, but of their doctrine of the after life. But this was not the original Buddhism, and was perhaps due to Persian influence.

Buddhism had undergone extensive modification on its way from India to China. Its original Hinayana form is a purely individualistic religion without God. Mahayana Buddhism, on the other hand, developed a religion of salvation. It did not interfere with the indigenous deities, did not discountenance life in human society; it did not recommend Nirvana at once, but placed it after a future life in a paradise.

Social Implications of Paradise Sect

This doctrine was in a sense revolutionary: it declared that all high officials and superiors who treated the people so unjustly, and who exploited them, would in their next incarnation be born in poor circumstances or inferior rank, and would have to suffer punishment for their ill deeds. The poor who had to suffer undeserved evils would be born in their next life to high rank and have a good time. This doctrine brought a ray of light to the country people who had suffered so much since the later Han period, and the Chinese country population became Buddhist.

The merchants who made use of the Buddhist monasteries as banks and warehouses, were also well inclined toward Buddhism and gave money and land for its temples. In those times a temple was a more reliable landlord than an individual alien, and the poorer peasants readily became temple tenants, which augmented their inclination toward Buddhism.

Buddhism as Official Religion

The Toba dynasty needed an official religion. They were attracted by Buddhism, especially by its shamanistic element, for some Buddhist monks had a knowledge of shamanistic practices. The Buddhist monks at the Toba court regarded the emperor as a reincarnation of Buddha. Thus the emperor became the protector of Buddhism, and Buddhism became a sort of official religion. The emperor conveyed large gifts to the Buddhist establishment.

The alien rulers showed great interest both in Buddhist and in Chinese shamans. Not infrequently competitions were arranged. Thus the private religion of the aliens consorted perfectly with shamanist Buddhism and with the shamanistic popular Taoism.

Like other Turkish peoples, the Toba possessed a myth that their ancestors came into the world from a sacred grotto. So with money from the emperor the great Buddhist cave temples at Yun Kang, with their famous sculptures, were constructed.

Rise of the Taoist Religion

This period of confusion and new developments saw the rise of the Taoist religion.

It was greatly influenced by the example of Buddhism, and may be understood in part as an indigenous parallel and reaction to the foreign religion. But there were Chinese factors and probably other foreign causes of its emergence.

As Confucianism became more rationalistic it excluded more and more superstition, and much of this was taken up by Taoism, and the ancient shamans came to be called Taoists.

During the second century Chang Ling appeared in Szechwan and preached strange doctrines which Professor Dubs considers were "actually the Persian Zoroastrianism of that day," for numbers of Buddhist missionaries and others were coming from or through Persia. Ahura Mazda was called creator, Dadhvah, which Chang Ling translated as Tao. This gave rise to the Five Pecks of Rice Sect, so called from the annual contribution made by each devotee. Chang Ling's grandson spread the religion, and moved with the court to Nanking and this became the dominant religion of the Yangtze delta. In 399 a rebellion led by a priest of this cult almost overthrew a dynasty. Later a Taoist practitioner in the capital, Loyang, amalgamated the two sects, in 415, as both used the word Tao.

It imitated Buddhism in developing a pantheon, scriptures, and cultus. Its supreme deity, the Jade Emperor, first mentioned in the ninth century, "was almost certainly Ahura Mazda."

It became a popular religion at the lowest level of superstition and the occult, and must be distinguished sharply from the Taoist philosophy.

Confucian Infiltration of Government

The Toba were glad to employ more Chinese, and Chinese pressed more and more into the administration. In this the differing social organization of Toba and Chinese played an important part. The Chinese had a patriarchal system of wide clan relations. The Toba also had a patriarchal family system, but as nomads with no fixed abode, they were unable to form large family groups. Among them the individual was much more independent. So when a Chinese obtained an official post he was followed by countless relations. When a Toba had a position he remained alone. So the sinification of the Toba empire went on incessantly. With this growing influence of the Chinese gentry, Confucianism gained ground again, until with the transfer of the capital to Loyang in 494, it gained a complete victory, becoming the official religion.

Second Foundation of the Centralized Empire

The unification of China in 589 by the short-lived Sui dynasty and its consolidation by the T'ang dynasty marked the second foundation of the centralized empire, which had been in abeyance for 369 years.

This needs emphasis, for every ruler of even a small state assumed the title of emperor, and set up as a dynasty. Chinese historians have tended to consider the ruler who governed the largest area as emperor of all China. This has given a misleading impression of a succession of national dynasties.

Sui Dynasty Unification of All China

As the Ch'in had briefly preceded the Han, so the Sui preceded the T'ang and did the work of pulling things together, putting through the necessary harsh measures, building canals and other requisites of economic unification, and all on an imperial and grandiose scale, bordering on megalomania, and leading to widespread revolt that brought the brief dynasty to its end. A later Chinese administrator wrote of the Sui emperor:

> He shortened the life of his dynasty by a number of years, but benefited posterity for ten thousand generations. He ruled without benevolence, but his rule is to be credited with enduring accomplishments.

The two Sui emperors not only unified China but also pursued a career of conquest, and greatly extended its borders.

The T'ang Dynasty

This was carried forward and broadened by the T'ang dynasty and for a century the T'ang empire was the greatest in the world

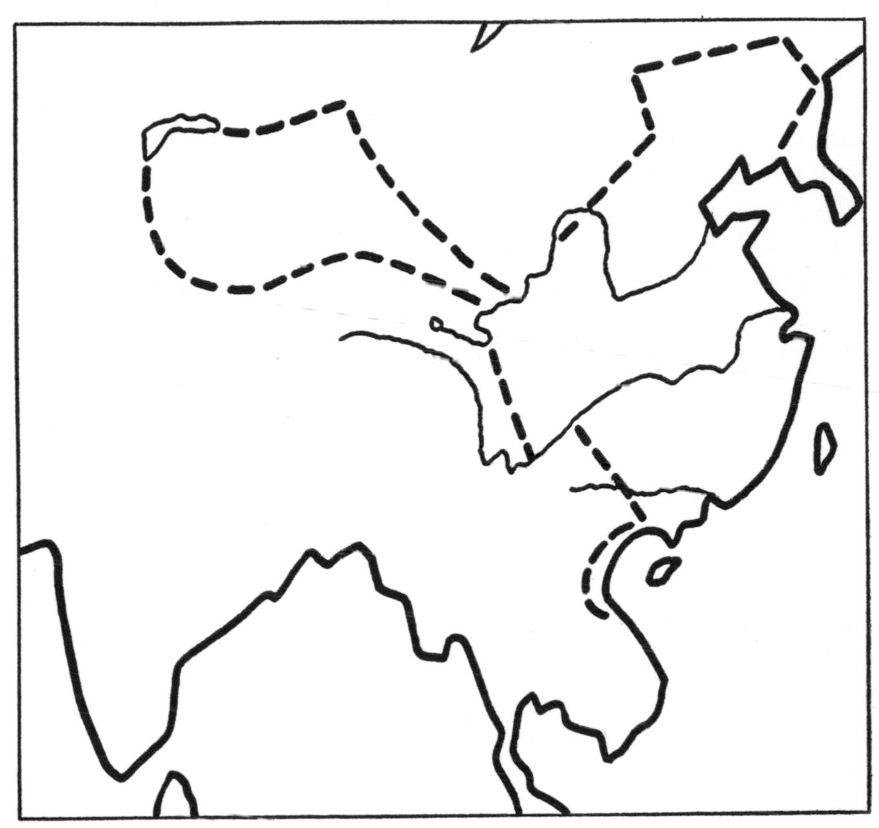

The T'ang Empire about 750 A.D.

and the most civilized, and its capital at Ch'ang-an was a great cosmopolitan city and center of religion, scholarship, and culture.

It was founded in 618 by Li Shih-min, the greatest of Chinese emperors, and lasted 300 years. See Map.

His reign was the beginning of a hundred and thirty-two years of internal peace including the long reigns of two great successors, the empress Wu, and the emperor Ming Huang, known in history as Hsuan Tsung, whose reign came to a tragic end in 755 with the revolt of the Tartar general and court favorite An Lu-shan. The emperor fled and abdicated, and it took eleven years before peace was restored. This destroyed the regular army which An Lu-shan had commanded and led into revolt, and thus crippled the imperial government which now had to contend with attacks from Tibetans on the west and generals in the various provinces who were constantly setting themselves up as war lords.

Four years earlier in 751, and in far off Central Asia, the Chinese armies had been defeated by the Arabs in a great and decisive battle near the Talas River. Turkistan was lost to China. The Buddhist monasteries in Central Asia that had developed their special type of Buddhism compounded with Persian influences, and had provided the missionaries to carry it to China, were soon displaced by Islam, and Buddhism in China was largely cut off from its sources in Central Asia and India.

Here the Arab empire that reached all the way to Spain and Morocco was face to face with T'ang China. Here was fixed a boundary line between the east and the west.

Even more serious was the damage to the prestige of the dynasty from An Lu-shan's rebellion. However, from its end in 766, the T'ang provided 102 years of peace and prosperity until the second great rebellion in 868, when the T'ang empire entered a period of intense strife, the prelude to its end in 906.

The first rebellion, however, had hardly touched the south, which enjoyed almost uninterrupted peace for 250 years since the founding of the dynasty. There have been few periods in the history of the world when so large and so civilized an area has had no war for two centuries.

However, in the north the Tibetans attacked repeatedly, but were resisted and eventually driven back. But the long drain on the weakening T'ang government contributed to its decline.

Confucianism Returns to Power

With peace and stable government and the reorganization of the civil service, Confucianism again returned to power.

In this education was the decisive factor. The Taoist emphasis on spontaneity and "living according to one's self" made education impossible for them.

The examination system was revived. Confucian temples were established. Staffs of scholars worked on dynastic histories. The university grew to 8,000 students. Printing was developed, and the oldest known printed book is from this period. A historian originated the epitaph, one of the useful inventions with which China is credited. He wrote his own:

> Fu I loved the green hills and the white clouds.
> Alas! He died of drink.

It was the golden age of poetry. The great anthology contained 48,900 poems by 2,200 poets. This was the flowering of Chinese culture.

Confucianism won out over Taoism, and Taoist books were excluded when the classics, fixed by imperial decree, were cut on stone slabs and set up in the university in 836.

Taoism remained influential, however, and furnished inspiration for poets and painters.

Buddhism

Confucians attacked Buddhism at a great debate at the court of the first T'ang emperor, but toleration continued. Tolerance was particularly due to the Empress Wu favoring Buddhism, since Confucianism did not allow a woman to occupy the throne.

Other pilgrims continued to go to India, the most famous of whom was Hsuan Tsang, the foremost figure in Chinese Buddhism, who brought back and translated—far more accurately than previously—a large number of Buddhist scriptures, and founded one of the most important Chinese Buddhist sects. On his return in 645 he was met by the emperor himself.

Two other main Chinese Buddhist sects, Hwa Yen and T'ien T'ai, had been founded toward the close of the period of disunion. These were formulations of Buddhist philosophy in Chinese terms. Buddhism now became Chinese.

Indian astronomy, mathematics and medicine were influential. A Chinese Buddhist monk developed a reformed calendar which was adopted by the state in 721.

Other foreign cults entered China. Zoroastrianism is the first mentioned in Chinese texts. It too came over the Central Asian trade routes soon after 500. It received imperial patronage and several rulers in two states participated in its cult and ritual dancing, partly to gain the favor of the people of the west, probably Persia. Nestorian Christianity was widespread in China during the T'ang dynasty.

Thus new documents, new learning, new cults, new arts entered China and were studied and assimilated. Chinese culture came to flower. It was a time of stimulating influences and creative vigor.

But the intellectual synthesis of all this mass of diverse material had to wait to the Sung dynasty.

Persecution of Buddhism

There had been a number of attacks on Buddhism by Confucian officials and scholars.

Things came to a climax when a Buddhist relic, a supposed bone of the Buddha himself, was brought to the capital in a state procession, and received by the emperor. A famous Confucian scholar, outraged by such superstition, wrote a stern protest that was one of the factors in bringing about the persecution of 845 that broke the power of Buddhism in China.

This was also aimed at taking over the wealth of the Buddhist monasteries to strengthen government finances. Also the Buddhist orders had become a state within a state. By this the secular state remained supreme. The imperial edict reads as follows:

> We therefore ordain the destruction of 4600 temples, the secularization of 260,500 monks and nuns who henceforth shall pay the biennial tax, the destruction of some 40,000 shrines, the confiscation of millions of acres of arable land, the manumission of 150,000 slaves, both male and female, who shall henceforth pay the biennial tax. The monks and nuns shall be under the control of the bureau for foreign affairs. Those who are obviously propagators of foreign religions, as the Nestorian and the Zoroastrian, shall be compelled to return to secular life lest they contaminate any longer the customs of China.

Buddhism never recovered from this, although there was a considerable amount of rebuilding. But China ceased to be a center of Buddhist influence for East Asia as it had been before.

Beginning of Neo-Confucianism

Confucianism was once more the official teaching of the state. But nearly a thousand years had passed since Confucius, and Confucianism had by this time lost the vitality it had once manifested in Mencius, Hsun Tzu, and Tung Chung-shu. The original texts were still available with the commentaries and sub-commentaries, but they failed to meet the spiritual needs of the new age.

There was now an interest in metaphysical problems, due to the revival of Taoism and the dominance of Buddhism.

This called for a new interpretation. But it was still lacking in spite of the efforts of the emperor's scholars. But, in the latter half of the T'ang dynasty, the Confucian scholars Han Yu and Li Ao developed the philosophy called Tao Hsueh, the Study of the Tao or Truth, known later in the West as Neo-Confucianism.

This was the beginning of the fourth synthesis which took place in the Sung dynasty.

4

The Sung Synthesis

The fourth main synthesis of Chinese history took place under the Sung dynasty and covered a period of nearly four centuries.

It included—at first—another unification after a period of break-up, but this political phase was mild compared with the harsh military measures of the brief Ch'in and Sui dynasties that paved the way for the Han and T'ang.

Indeed, it was rather a synthesis in the fields of philosophy and education, and in this resembled the Confucian synthesis more than the Han and T'ang. The Sung synthesis was completed while the country was again divided, and non-Chinese dynasties held north China.

It also had three phases, but of a different pattern.

Five dynasties	906– 960 A.D.
Northern Sung	960–1127 A.D.
Southern Sung	1127–1280 A.D.

T'ang Collapse and Five Dynasties

The break-up of the T'ang empire began with the first successful peasant revolt in 860, some forty-six years before the end of the dynasty. A second rising was led by an unsuccessful scholar who joined the hungry peasants and became emperor of the state of Ch'i.

The end of the T'ang in 906 was followed by the period of the Five Dynasties. These were in the north. There were ten in the south.

This was also a formative period. There was a development of trade. Some idea of the scale of such relationship is given by an Arab source that states 120,000 foreigners in Canton lost their lives when the city was captured and burned. There were government monopolies in trade in salt and tea. Porcelain was widely exported. Books were printed in quantity, which opened the way for the Sung renaissance. See Map.

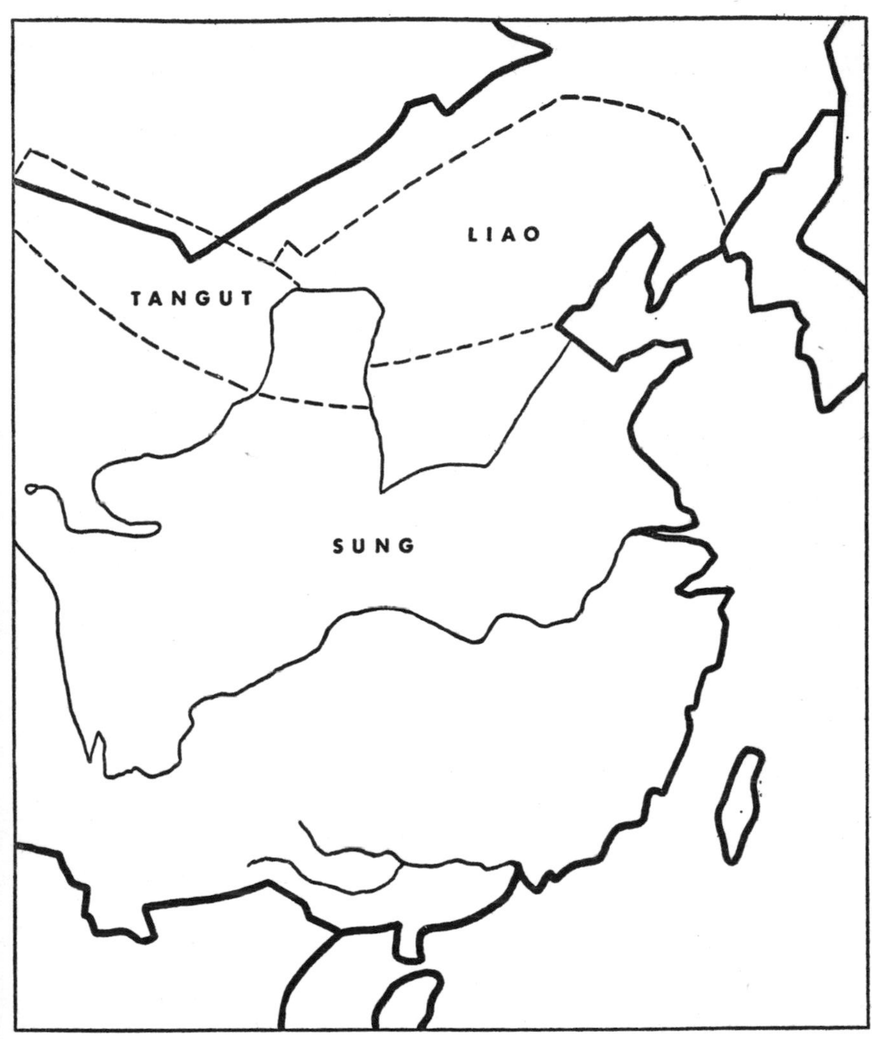

The Sung, Liao, and Tangut Empires about 1100 A.D.

Northern Sung Dynasty

The Sung dynasty was the third centralized empire. But it was different in many ways from the Han and the T'ang, for the reunion of the empire was not through fighting, but through wise policy. This was due in large part to the character of the first Sung emperor and the confidence and respect in which he was held. Fitzgerald relates the following.

The emperor of one of the five dynasties died in 959 and made the mistake of leaving his throne to a child with an empress as regent.

The army, which had been sent north to repel an invasion, were discontented for they felt that with an infant on the throne their services would go unrewarded. The chief officers led a mutiny and entering the tent of the general in the dawn, with drawn swords, robed him in a yellow gown and presented him to the army as the new emperor, a situation unique in Chinese history.

He refused to accept unless they took an oath to obey him, which they did. He then ordered that no harm should be done to the imperial family or to the city. The capital was occupied without disorder, the dominant civilian element in the government was restored, and within the year he got rid of the army that had made him emperor.

In the course of time all the independent states submitted and the nation was again a unity.

Unlike the Han and T'ang emperors, the Sung emperors did not go in for conquest. This changed temper of the imperial government under the Sung had led to treaties and tribute, first in relation to the Kitans of the Liao dynasty, later with the Tartars. But the situation was different. These were now powerful states, not merely tribal confederations as in Han and T'ang times. China had lost the defense line of the Great Wall and was at a disadvantage. The Sung empire never extended over the whole of China, and under the Southern Sung included only the part south of the Yellow River basin.

But the Liao dynasty and later the Tartars were virtually Chinese dynasties, although the rulers were nomad conquerors. They established their capitals in purely Chinese cities, assimilated Chinese culture. They took over the capital Kai Fung, the center of Chinese civilization. They were simple nomads with nothing to contribute but their fighting spirit, which they soon lost. Thus the loss of political control over north China by the Sung dynasty did not impair the cultural unity of the country. Confucius was as much honored by those Tartars as by the Sung.

Civil officials came into control of the Sung government, and military officers were relegated to the inferior status they held in China from that time on.

The peace with the Liao, 1004, continued for over a hundred years, and during this time Chinese civilization reached its apogee. There was an alliance of scholarship and politics that was typical of the Sung. The conservatives won control, resulting in a rigid orthodoxy, and relegated religion to the common people as superstition.

The Tartars, further to the north, conquered the Liao dynasty, and went on to take all of north China in 1127, bringing the Northern Sung dynasty to an end.

The Southern Sung Dynasty

The Sung capital was moved to Hangchow, south of the Yangtze, and peace was made with the invaders. This lasted 153 years until the conquest of China by the Mongols under Kublai Khan. During that period the Sung continued a brilliant philosophical, artistic and literary culture.

The Sung synthesis found its supreme expression in Neo-Confucianism, which was the final fixation of Chinese culture. Here China took what it wanted from Buddhism, and squeezed the juice out of the Chinese Buddhist philosophical sects which afterward counted for little. This will be dealt with in detail in Part Three.

The country was divided, so this was in no sense a political synthesis, and illustrates the fact that the basic history of China is the record of an expanding culture.

5

Formative Period Leading toward a Fifth Synthesis

Since the end of the Sung dynasty, 1280 A.D., the China that had resulted from the four earlier syntheses has continued to develop along much the same general lines, under the Mongol, Ming, and Manchu dynasties. No further synthesis of equal importance with the four earlier ones has taken place.

This period, up to the present, may be looked upon as a formative period leading to a fifth synthesis. The impact of the modern world has not yet reached the point of synthesis. The present communist phase may be interpreted as an attempt at a synthesis under an alien concept, but in view of the 4000 years of Chinese history with its ups and downs it would be premature to define the present Peoples Republic of China, established in 1949, as the fifth synthesis.

This formative period of 630 years may be dated as follows:

Political

China ruled by Mongols	1280–1368 A.D.
Ming dynasty (Chinese)	1368–1644 A.D.
Manchu dynasty	1644–1911 A.D.

Cultural

Development of critical scholarship, encyclopedias
Rise of middle class
Western influences and education

The period of break-up, which began in 1774, and the attempts at synthesis which began about 1880, will form the subject of Part IV.

The Mongols

The Mongols completed their conquest of Sung dynasty China and established their dynasty in 1280 A.D. See Map.

They were the most destructive of the long series of nomad invaders. Genghis Khan and his sons ruled over the most extensive land empire that has ever been formed, before or since. They not only were little affected by Chinese civilization, but set up new

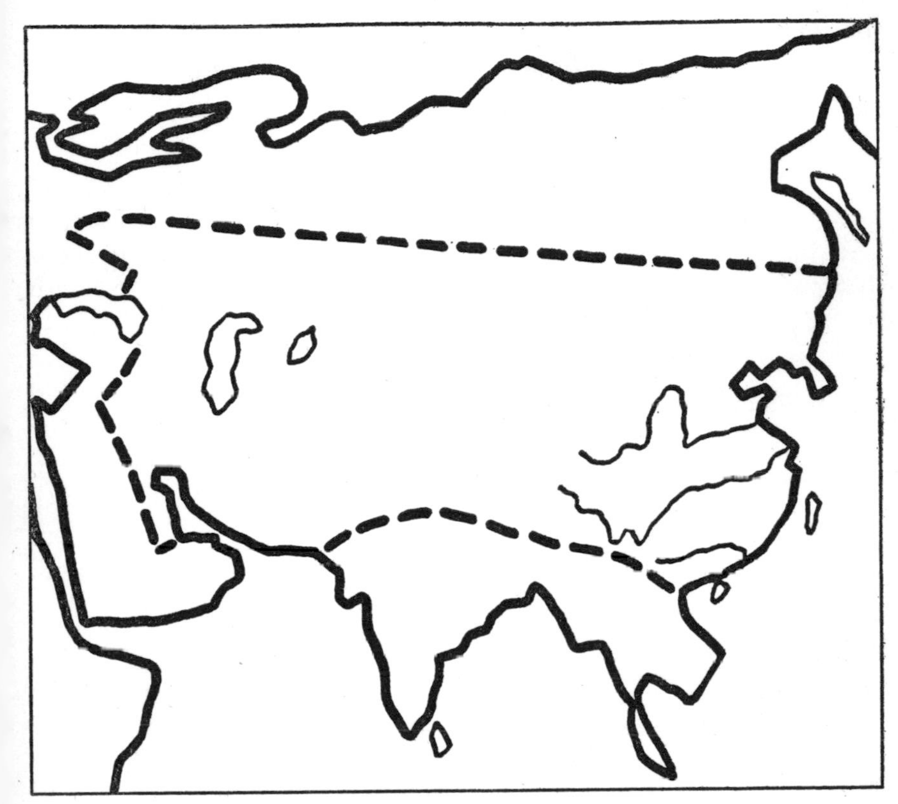

The Mongol Empire about 1300 A.D.

standards of ferocity. Genghis Khan laid down the rule, which his successors followed, that if a city made any defense whatever, its inhabitants should be exterminated to the last woman and child. He also stated their ideal:

> The greatest joy is to conquer one's enemies, to pursue them, to seize their property, to see their families in tears, to ride their horses, and to possess their wives and daughters.

They ruined the northwest of China which had been the center of Chinese civilization in Han and T'ang times, and had been cultured and wealthy. The diminished population could no longer keep up the irrigation systems. Many cities on the frontier were never reoccupied and were in time overwhelmed by the encroaching sands of the desert. The region became permanently a semi-desert, the poorest and most backward in the empire.

Then they began on the rest of China. Peking was taken, burned, the inhabitants slaughtered. The Mongols were disgusted to see the whole country under cultivation with no place to pasture their horses. One put it thus:

> Although we have conquered the Chinese, they are no use to us. It would be better to exterminate them entirely, and let the grass grow so that we can have grazing land for our horses.

Genghis was ready to put this into operation, but was dissuaded by a councillor who pointed out that he could get a vast revenue by taxing them instead. This was done, and this policy saved most of the rest of China from devastation and massacre.

In the Sung period the peasants had been exploited by the big gentry landlords. The Mongols deprived the gentry of political power but left them their estates, as they had at once gone over to their side.

The peasants had to support four groups: gentry, a million Mongols, Buddhist temples, merchants. The temples were given great estates. All this decreased the number of free peasants who were the ones who paid the taxes. The country was impoverished. There were general risings. The Mongol garrisons could not handle them. The dynasty fell.

One reason was the failure of the effort to rule the country without the assistance of the Chinese gentry who knew the sources of revenue.

The Ming Dynasty

With the Ming dynasty the alien Mongols were driven out and China was again ruled by a Chinese dynasty.

The new dynasty took the T'ang dynasty as its ideal, for the Sung dynasty had lost half the empire to the Tartars, and had finally been overwhelmed by the Mongols. So the Ming followed the T'ang policy of conquest, rather than the Sung pacificism, and extended the boundaries of China to a greater extent than ever before.

During the Mongol period the formation of a middle class began, and this was now carried further, for the establishment of the dynasty had grown out of revolts against bad economic conditions. The increased number of books made self-education possible. A class arose who were not landed gentry, but who could pass the examinations and thus get official position. They would begin in debt, and this led to corruption. They found that much of the power was in the hands of the eunuchs, so some of them voluntarily became eunuchs, and this educated type of eunuch soon came to the front, so that the rise of the middle class and the increasing power of the eunuchs went hand in hand.

The third Ming emperor, Yung Lo, had been in charge at Peking when he decided to oppose the new emperor, and after defeating him at Nanking, he moved the capital to Peking, where he was already living in the sumptuous palaces of the Mongol emperors.

This was a mistake, and had unfortunate consequences. Under the Southern Sung, the north and south had been separated, and still more so under the Mongols. This accentuated their differences. Furthermore, the key economic area had long since shifted to the Yangtze valley, and the problem of the transportation of food was difficult. The wealthiest gentry, and the new middle class, on whom the government depended in many ways, were largely in the south. The north had been devastated and had lost most of its powerful families and much of its importance.

For the nomads who had ruled China, Peking was ideal, putting them in touch both with their original steppe domain and with their new agricultural conquered regions. But the Ming capital at Peking was exposed to constant raids, and the government had to spend much time and strength in defending itself. This deepened the rift between north and south.

This showed up in connection with the civil service examinations. The gentry of the south attended in large numbers, and were in control to such an extent that few candidates from the north were able to pass. When this was made an issue, it was decreed that a third of the successful candidates must be from the north.

The dynasty was unfortunate in having a number of boy emperors who had been brought up in the harem and under the influence of the eunuchs. One of these eunuchs led a campaign into Manchuria, taking the emperor along. Neither knew anything about warfare; they were defeated and the emperor captured. This defeat in 1449 brought to an end the Chinese military supremacy and thereafter the empire was on the defensive.

During the reign of Yung Lo a great navy was built that made a number of trips as far as the East Indies, Arabia, and Africa. It was later discontinued, possibly because it was more profitable to leave trade in the hands of foreign merchants, possibly because the canals had been repaired and grain could move in the interior.

The government situation gradually got worse, and more into the hands of eunuchs and palace cliques. The eunuchs were largely from the north and that increased the difficulties between north and south. The coast cities suffered from Japanese pirates. There were peasant uprisings. The dynasty was brought to an end by internal conflicts.

During this dynasty Chinese civilization for the first time began to lag behind Europe.

The Manchu Dynasty

The Manchus were brought in by one of the warring factions and stayed to establish their own dynasty.

Two able emperors—K'ang Hsi and Ch'ien Lung—had long reigns of sixty years each. They were patrons of Chinese culture and kept a great staff of scholars busy on a great encyclopedia of Chinese learning, and won their cooperation to a considerable degree.

However, secret societies multiplied with the object of restoring the Chinese Ming dynasty and ousting the alien Manchus.

During the latter half of the eighteenth century overpopulation became acute for the first time, and individual land holdings decreased in size. The petty gentry and poor scholars who had become prevalent during the Ming dynasty now increased in numbers, and many became impoverished. This led to a floating population which came into prominence in a new way.

In 1774 came the first large-scale peasant revolt, which was the beginning of the break-up of the Manchu dynasty, which came to an end with the revolution in 1911.

This break-up and the abortive attempts at a fifth synthesis will be taken up in Part IV. But it is necessary first to summarize the long-term trends of Chinese history so as to bring out certain characteristic aspects.

6

Long-Term Trends of Chinese History

The four periods, each culminating in a synthesis as elaborated above, form a schematism for the understanding of Chinese history. But it is necessary also to take into account certain long-term trends which constitute the dynamic patterns of its forward movement. For it has neither been static nor a case of arrested development, as used to be believed.

Misleading Dynastic Pattern

Before tracing these long-term trends it is necessary to re-emphasize the artificial character of a considerable part of the dynastic pattern.

Later historians read back into the past the dynastic pattern of the centralized empire with which they were familiar, and in periods of disunity tended to portray the ruler of the most powerful state as emperor.

This was natural for the great series of twenty-four official dynastic histories. The practice was for a new dynasty to turn over the archives of the previous one to an editorial board, entrusted with the compilation of the history. All such official thinking was inevitably in terms of dynasties. Wittfogel comments:

> The establishment of a new type of state with a centralized imperial bureaucracy paved the way for a new type of systematic, institutional and cultural historiography. It was this situation that in the Earlier Han dynasty led to the writing of the first dynastic history.

The Shang was a dynasty in only a loose sense of the word. The Chou people were a conquering group that dominated the rest on a feudal basis, but this headship was largely nominal after the barbarians sacked the Chou capital in 770. To speak of the Chou dynasty after that, particularly during the period of the warring states, obscures the actual situation. This is true of the period of disunion, 220–589, also of the Five Dynasties, 906–960.

China's Place in World History

Certain long-term factors in China's history become more clear when seen as a part of the movement of world history.

The optimum temperature for human efficiency is put at about seventy degrees. It was under such conditions that civilization was most likely to flourish. The isotherm of this temperature cuts across four river valleys—Nile, Tigris-Euphrates, Indus, and Yellow River. It was at these points that the earliest civilizations developed about 3000 B.C. or earlier. Here cities grew up, based on the peasant village food surplus, and developed writing, handicrafts, and the arts of civilization. Here the most powerful city conquered the others and the first empires arose. China was probably the latest of these four to develop.

The Direction of History

Anthropologists believe that some 15,000 years ago the American continent was settled by people from Asia who crossed a land bridge where Behring Strait now is, and made their way southward. This establishes a direction of history, a movement fanning out from a probable area of human origin in Central Asia.

In line with this are movements of population from Central Asia into China, and cultural influences from the west. This was the case also with Korea and Japan. In historic times waves of peoples infiltrated northwest China or came as conquerors, forming an important factor in the dynamic movement of Chinese history.

The movement of cultural diffusion was in the same direction. The infiltration from the west brought not only people but cultural innovations. China received from the west the chicken and the water-buffalo, two important factors in the Chinese agricultural economy, also the use of iron and other techniques, and Buddhism, which was a carrier for a whole new world of ideas and practices.

The states in the northwest of China usually received these first, and profited by them to achieve a position of leadership and supremacy. There was thus a time lag, and these innovations penetrated only slowly to the east and south, and the states in the northwest at first had a monopoly of the new techniques.

This time lag appears most clearly on the various charts on which the cultural levels in China, Korea, and Japan are arranged in chronological sequence in parallel columns. Most developments appear later in Korea and still later in Japan.

This was modified to some degree in later centuries when south China ports developed sea-borne commerce with the west. This, however, was chiefly commercial, limited in scope, and subsidiary to the main movement from the northwest to the east and south.

Thus the political history of China was modified by the incursions of non-Chinese peoples from the north and northwest, its cultural history by borrowings from the west, and the development of Chinese thought by Buddhism and the Indian and Iranian influences that came with it from Central Asia.

Chinese culture was never overwhelmed, but on the contrary absorbed its conquerors, and was only modified, never changed. Its political unity, repeatedly interrupted by conquerors from outside, was never completely disrupted, and was always restored. The Chinese state did not perish along with the others of antiquity, but has maintained its existence for 4000 years. China has no dead language.

This long life and extreme stability are due primarily to the structure—both anthropological and sociological—of Chinese society, of which Chinese culture is the expression, and in which it is firmly embedded.

Barbarian Invasions, and Non-Chinese Dynasties

From the earliest times to the last imperial dynasty, the Manchu, which ended in 1911, China has been subject to barbarian incursions, infiltrations, and invasions from the north and northwest. Indeed, the present communist regime might almost be included in the same category.

No one people can be characterized as Chinese at the beginning. There was merely a group of peoples of somewhat similar stock who developed a common culture.

The history of China is the record of the expansion of that culture. Many peoples have had a part in this. Sooner or later all of them have become Chinese.

The first was the Chou "dynasty" which conquered the earlier Shang, but became so basically "Chinese" that Confucius took Chou as his ideal.

The history of the Chinese Empire falls into ten main divisions. In half of these the power was in the hands of non-Chinese dynasties. This is exhibited in the following table (after Wittfogel):

Chinese Dynasties	Dynasties of Conquest
1. Ch'in and Han (221 B.C.–A.D. 220)	
2. Chinese dynasties during the Period of Disunion (220–581)	
	3. Wei (386–556) and other northern barbarian dynasties directly before and after
4. Sui and T'ang (581–906)	
5. Sung (960–1279)	
	6. Liao (907–1125)
	7. Chin (1115–1234)
	8. Mongol (1280–1368)
9. Ming (1368–1644)	
	10. Manchu (1644–1911)

During the period of disunion, the so-called dynasties in south China were all Chinese. In north China there were seventeen "dynasties" of which all but two were non-Chinese.

However, all except the last two—Mongol and Manchu—conquered and ruled over only a part of China, always in the north, and generally only a part of that.

Conquest of an amount of territory was relatively easy. But for the conquerors, organized on a tribal and nomadic basis, to administer a China that was agricultural and by this time highly organized, was complicated and presented problems that most of the invaders were unable to solve, so most of their dynasties were short-lived.

It involved the bringing together in one organization two highly specialized but quite different cultures. A loose tribal organization had to be changed into a centralized military one, then into a centralized governmental machine. The invaders lacked the knowledge and experience. They were a small minority. They had to get the cooperation of Chinese officials, who in many cases looked down on them as barbarians.

Several such dynasties appointed to the bureaucracy various skilled foreigners, from Central Asia, India, Persia and even Europe. Marco Polo was one of these. In this way Manicheism and Nestorian Christianity were introduced, and this was an important factor in the propagation of Buddhism.

The invaders were faced by a cultural dilemma. Their shamanistic religion was regarded by educated Chinese as on the same level as the superstitions of the Chinese masses. Superstition could not be the religion of a ruling group. But if they adopted Confucianism, they merely adopted the culture and way of life of the Chinese gentry. One solution was to seek to disguise their shamanism as Taoism. But the most common solution was to adopt Buddhism or even to make it the state religion in place of Confucianism.

The barbarian invasions were always by a minority who were on a lower culture level.

China survived them.

The bureaucratic machine was too much for them, they could not make it work. They either failed, or by the time they had learned, they too became Chinese.

Key Economic Areas

Chinese civilization began in northwest China in what is now the province of Shensi, in the valleys of the Wei and Ching, two small western tributaries of the Yellow River. The expansion of China was based on the development of a succession of three major food-producing areas of increasing importance, and their successive conquest and incorporation. See map.

The earliest irrigation project began about 600 B.C. The previous method of water-control had been to provide a bride for the river god and each year drown a selected peasant maiden in the river.

There are a number of records of progressive administrators who opposed this and converted the peasants to the advantages of irrigation. But when they were mobilized to dig canals, they complained bitterly over the forced labor. The old way was easier. Irrigation was an innovation, and they were skeptical about getting any real benefit.

The First Key Economic Area

The first major irrigation project, the Chengkuo canal, opened in 246 B.C., so increased the food surplus of the state of Ch'in that its ruler was able to feed a much larger army and thus conquer the other warring states and establish the Chinese Empire in 221 B.C., twenty-five years later.

This canal thus marked—and made possible—the main turning point in Chinese history, the transition from the feudalism of the Chou and the warring states to the centralized empire. And public works for water-control had a great influence on all subsequent political development.

This canal, fifty miles long, and named after the engineer who built it, irrigated some 1,100 square miles of alkali land with the silt-laden waters of the Ching River. This region thus became the key economic area of the China of that day, and the economic base of the power of the new imperial central government.

This canal system involved the mobilization of tens and hundreds of thousands of peasant laborers for its construction. It established a precedent for forced labor on a vast scale, which was used by the First Emperor to complete the Great Wall, inaugurate gigantic public works, build enormous palaces, and engage in foreign wars against the Tartars.

But these ambitious projects overstrained the national economy, led to widespread revolt after the death of the First Emperor, and brought the Ch'in dynasty to a swift end, to be followed by the Han dynasty in 206 B.C.

The Second Key Economic Area

The commoner, Liu Chi, who founded the Han dynasty, first gained control of this key area, which enabled him to defeat his rivals.

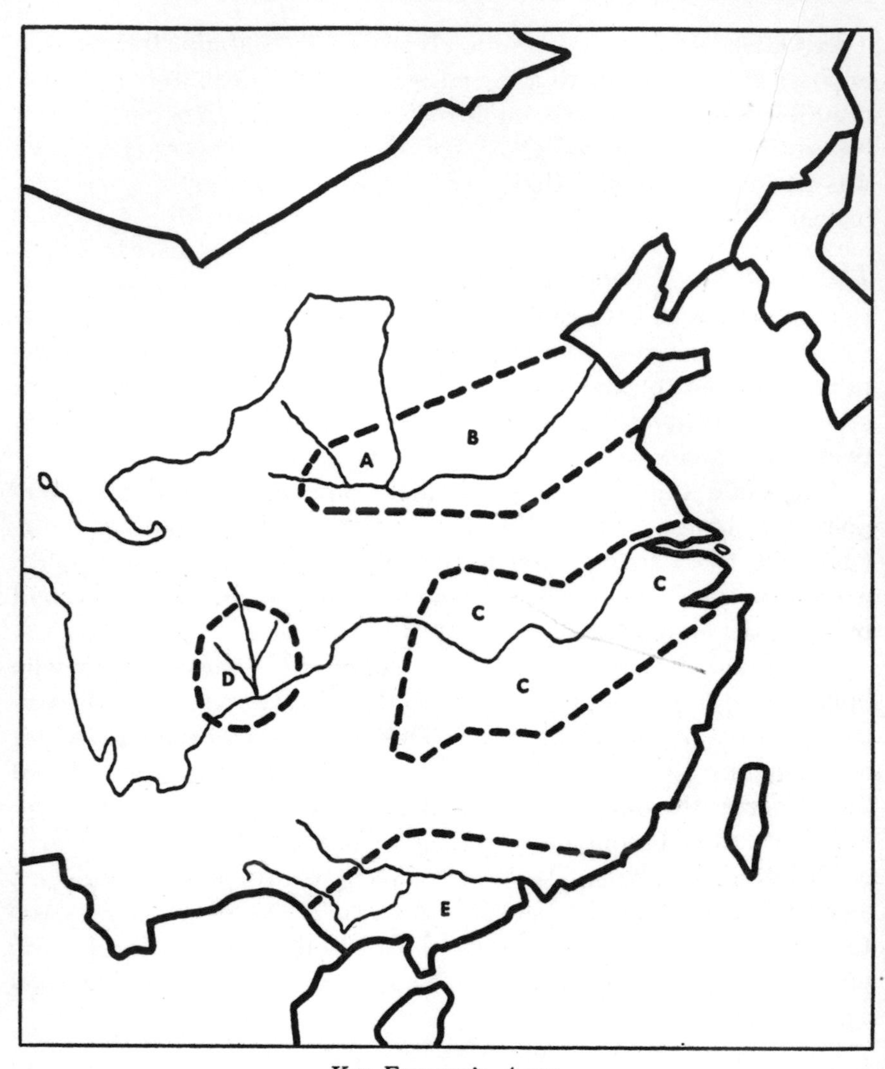

Key Economic Areas

A First Key Economic Area. Cradle of Chinese culture. Valley of tributaries of the Yellow River.

AB Second Key Economic Area. Yellow River Valley. Han Dynasty.

C Third Key Economic Area. Yangtze River Valley. T'ang and later dynasties.

D Chengtu Plain in Szechwan. Secondary Economic Area.

E Canton Area. Secondary Economic Area.

This area maintained its economic dominance for the first century of the Former (western) Han dynasty. The first dynastic history states that it had a third of the territory and three-tenths of the population, but six-tenths of the wealth of the Chinese Empire of that day.

By the time of the great Han emperor Wu Ti, a century later, a second economic area had developed in the lower Yellow River valley, including the modern south Shansi, north Honan and west Shantung, and the imperial grain tribute from this area had increased nearly ten-fold to the order of 400,000 tons per year. This created a new and difficult problem of the transportation of what was a vast amount for that time to the capital which was still in the far west.

Therefore, Wu Ti's first two public works in the field of water-control were to facilitate the transportation of the grain tribute. Later, the Po Canal, 95 B.C., was a reconstruction of the Chengkuo canal which had become silted up in its 160 years of use. This and six supplementary canals restored the productivity of this region.

But these and similar expenditures once more led to financial difficulties, and no major water-control public works were constructed during the remainder of the Han dynasty, with the result that the irrigation system was neglected and the original Shensi key economic area declined, and was soon replaced by the lower Yellow River valley as the main economic area.

Liu Hsin, founder of the Later Han dynasty, grasped the importance of the shift from the first key economic area in Shensi eastward to the second area in the lower Yellow River valley, and seized it at the critical stage of his campaign of conquest, entrusting it to his ablest general.

> This is the base from which I shall conquer the country. Guard it firmly, and transport a sufficient supply of grain to my army.

When the fighting was over he moved the capital to Loyang in the lower Yellow River valley. The two economic areas were thus consolidated, and constituted the basis of support and seat of power for the remainder of the Later Han dynasty which ended in 220 A.D.

The Three Kingdoms 221–65

Meanwhile new food production areas had begun to develop in the lower Yangtze valley and in Szechwan in the far west, where another extensive irrigation system had been developed.

Upon the break-up of the Later Han dynasty, these two appeared as rival kingdoms, strong enough and far enough away to enable them to challenge the authority of the overlord in the main economic area in the Yellow River valley. This produced a stalemate of power for the period of the Three Kingdoms, 221–65.

All three resorted to increased digging of irrigation systems and canals for transport as part of the logistics of military conquest. The Wei dynasty in the old Yellow River area won out, largely by use of military agricultural colonies, enlargement of their own irrigated supply base, and by starving out the opposing expeditionary forces rather than fighting them. This began the period of disunion, due in large part to barbarian invasions, but based to a considerable extent on the various economic areas.

The Third Key Economic Area

During the Former Han dynasty (206 B.C. to 9 A.D.) the lower Yangtze valley had a small and scattered population on a primitive basis. In addition to these "southern barbarians" there were a considerable number of settlers from the north, bringing with them the equipment of an advanced agricultural civilization to the incomparable natural fertility of the Yangtze valley.

During the Period of Disunion, 221–589, non-Chinese peoples from the north and northwest continued to enter, and this with the destructive wars drove the Chinese, both commons and aristocrats, to move into the Yangtze valley in larger numbers, so that by the end of the period this had developed into the third key economic area, which was to continue to the present as the most important one. Indeed by the middle of the T'ang dynasty dependence on the supply of rice from the south had increased so that the land tax from Kiangnan (the modern provinces of Kiangsu, Anhwei, Kiangsi, and Chekiang) was nine-tenths of the total land tax of the entire empire.

However, the capital and the political center of gravity remained in the north, largely because of the continued menace of nomadic invasion on the northern frontier, partly because of tradition and political inertia. This involved an increasingly difficult problem of transportation.

Secondary Economic Areas

Another economic area developed in the south in the region where Canton is now the center. This developed later, and while it became a chief secondary economic area, along with Szechwan, it never became a national key area as did the Yellow River and Yangtze River valleys. Other areas developed along the coast in Chekiang and Fukien.

The Rise and Dominance of the Gentry

The anthropological and sociological structure of Chinese society gave rise to a two-class society. The lower class simply does not count—at least until comparatively recently. The upper class, the gentry, have made China what it is.

A landowning nobility consisting of the leading clans of the Chou conquerors ruled the 1400 or so feudal divisions, large and small, of the early Chou period. There was constant fighting among them and before the time of Confucius many of the smaller units had been swallowed up and their nobility thrown out upon the world as adventurers.

With the establishment of the centralized empire, feudalism and the feudal nobility came to an end together.

Their place was taken by a landlord class which gradually gained in prestige and power. This was the beginning of the gentry class that has dominated China ever since.

The unification called for a bureaucracy to manage the far greater extent of the empire. This called for officials with training and experience, which led to the examination system. The members of the landlord class were the only ones with the leisure for the years of study, and naturally took over the bureaucracy, and added the prestige of scholarship and the power of official position to their wealth. Candidates for the examinations were often recommended by officials, who naturally included their own sons and relatives.

The gentry were thus the landlord-scholar-official class. Although in theory others could rise from among the lower classes if they could pass the examinations, in practice the great gentry clans had a monopoly.

This class was firmly established in power during the first century B.C. under the Former Han dynasty, and some of the great gentry clans of that time were among the most powerful clans in the government a thousand years later, with a continuous genealogical record to prove it.

There are records of about a hundred of these great gentry clans.

After the invention of printing and the popularization of education and knowledge in the early years of the Sung dynasty, members of other clans with less wealth were able to pass the examinations and become officials in the provinces, or minor officials in the capital. Thus arose a class of small gentry. They had scholarship, prestige, and some power, but little money. And they were thus more open to corruption.

The great clans could maintain a branch in the capital. The small gentry could do this with difficulty but usually as clients of one of the great clans. In the provincial capitals they could do better, but still in a subordinate role.

The government of an empire of the size and complexity of China could not be carried on without a bureaucracy made up of officials of training and experience. So that no matter what dynasty, Chinese or non-Chinese, came to the top in the fighting and gained control, they were dependent on the great gentry clans for the collection of taxes and the successful operation of the governmental machine.

The Dynastic Cycle

It has been noted that the main dynasties or groups of dynasties have a length of three to four hundred years. This has led to the theory of the dynastic cycle.

According to this theory, the Confucian system with its emphasis on filial piety and the maintenance of large families favors the scholar-landlord-official class, as the resulting overpopulation provides a surplus of workers and tends to hold wages down. When this situation reaches the breaking point, widespread distress ensues, resulting in banditry, civil war, and finally the overthrow of the dynasty. Such a period of disorder may last for fifty or a hundred years.

At length some strong man establishes a new dynasty. The surplus population has been killed off by war, banditry and famine, and the cycle is ready to start again.

This explains the economic situation from the basis of population and labor, as the economic area theory does from the basis of food supply.

Actually, there were frequent peasant rebellions but they had little success. Only three leaders of such revolts became emperors, the founders of the Han (206 B.C. to 220 A.D.), the Later Liang (907–923) and the Ming (1368–1644) dynasties. It was only a special combination of circumstances that made this possible. It is significant that the impact of the West in our modern day came toward the end of a dynastic cycle, as will appear in Part IV.

The Advancing Frontier

Chinese civilization was first consolidated to form a basis for empire in northwest China. This area was soon enlarged to include the entire Yellow River valley. See map.

Political conquest easily outran cultural integration. The First Emperor extended his rule over most of the China of today. This continued under the Han. However, political control usually involved little more than garrisons and government administrative centers at a few strategic points, and had only limited cultural impact. So the populations south of the Yellow River valley still lagged far behind, and the cultural frontier was on a line half way between the Yellow River and the Yangtze.

The fact that the Yangtze Valley was outside the frontier of Chinese civilization at that time, comes out clearly in the first dynastic history written during the Han Dynasty about 130 B.C.

> In the territory south of the Yangtze River the custom was to fertilize the land by burning the vegetable overgrowth and, as the seeds were planted, flood the fields with water. The land was low and wet.

> This was a large territory sparsely populated, where people eat rice and

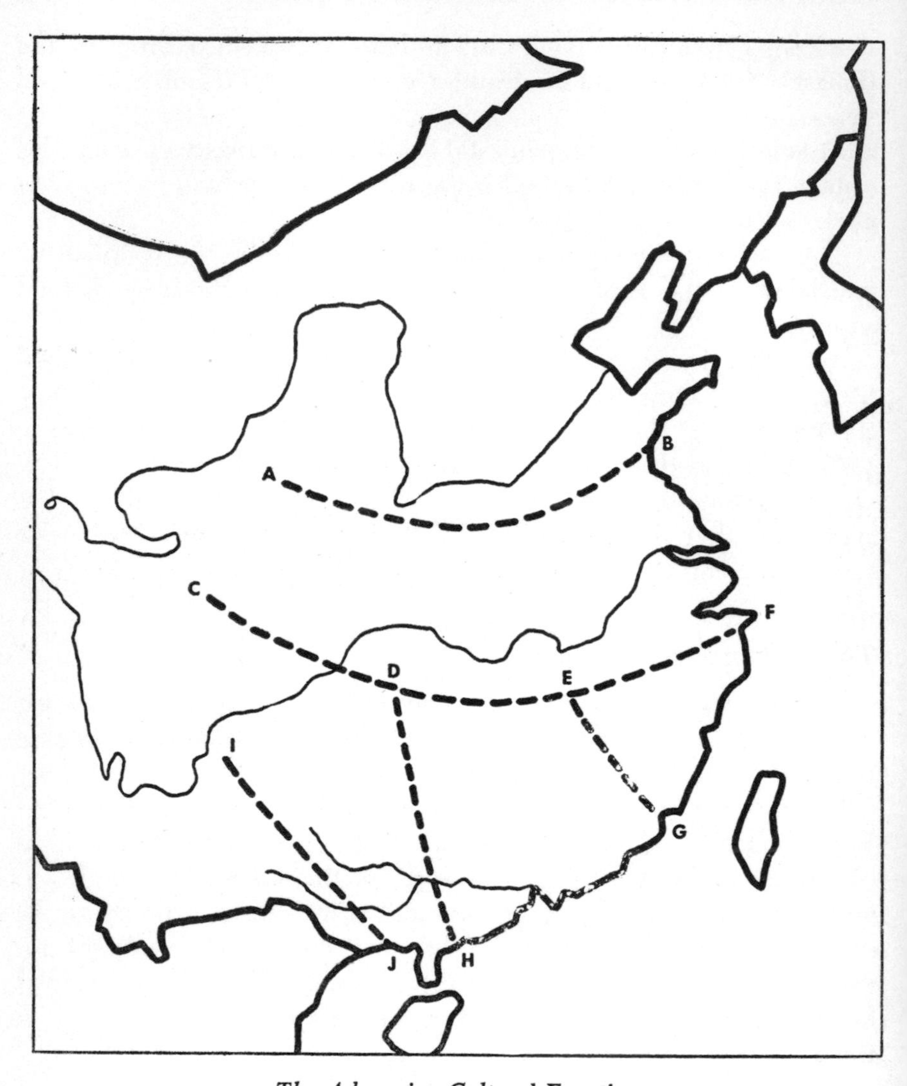

The Advancing Cultural Frontier

Cultural sinification lagged behind political conquest. The cultural frontier moved south and southwest as follows:

Han	AB
T'ang	CDEF
Sung	CDEG
Ming	CDH
Manchu	IJ

drink fish soup; where people collect fruits and shellfish for food and enjoy self-sufficiency without commerce.

The place is fertile and suffers no famine and hunger. Hence the people are lazy and poor and do not bother to accumulate wealth. There are neither hungry nor frozen people nor a family which owns a thousand gold.

Heavy migration from the Yellow River Valley during the Period of Disunion resulted in the establishment of clans and colonies in the south, who gradually amalgamated with the more primitive earlier inhabitants and integrated them into Chinese culture. This went on during the four hundred years of this period, and under the T'ang Dynasty (618–906) the Yangtze Valley caught up with the Yellow River Valley culturally.

Under the Sui and T'ang all of China was again unified, and the political boundary was pushed south and southwest to include practically all of present-day China. However, the cultural boundary moved southward very slowly. This comes out in the Sui dynastic history, referring to Kwangtung.

South of the mountain range, the central government gave official sanction to the authority of local chiefs over their subjects and in return exacted tribute from the chiefs, whose riches consisted of animals, kingfisher feathers, pearls, elephant tusks, and rhinoceros horns.

During the Sung dynasty the cultural boundary moved southward to include the present provinces of Kiangsi and Fukien, and during the Ming the present provinces of Kwangsi, Yunnan, and Kweichow were included in part.

It was only during the last dynasty, the Manchu Dynasty, that the rest of the southwestern provinces were sinized. Indeed, even at the present time there are some twenty million tribes peoples still largely untouched by Chinese civilization.

A large factor in all of this was the constant movement into frontier lands of adventurous and pioneering individuals and families.

The more recent emigration of some ten million Chinese to the South Seas is a continuation into modern times of these long-term migratory trends.

The foregoing chapter has summarized the sociological, economic, and political trends of Chinese history.

It has been repeatedly stressed that China is basically a cultural entity. In this the intellectual factor is of great significance, both as an expression of that culture, and as determining its direction.

This aspect calls for more detailed analysis of the development of Chinese thought, to which it is now necessary to turn in Part III.

PART III

The Development of Chinese Thought

China is fundamentally a cultural entity rather than a military state and its history can best be understood in terms of its cultural development.

This finds an important expression in the development of Chinese thought.

The three original ways of thought were Confucianism, which was a rationalization of the structure of Chinese society on the practical level where people lived; Taoism, which was a naturalistic revolt against the Confucian social order; and legalism which furnished the basis for the actual organization of the empire.

Later, during four centuries of break-up and disunity, Neo-Taoism developed a paradoxical philosophy of non-action and a romantic naturalism, and Buddhism entered from India. Under the reunited empire, Confucianism, again dominant, amalgamated elements of Neo-Taoism, Buddhism, and the Taoist religion into Neo-Confucianism.

China developed a massive scholarship which had probably produced more books by the beginning of the modern age than all the rest of the world put together. It developed a body of scholar-officials who governed the empire, but served the dynasty in power rather than taking over political control.

This scholarship turned back upon itself and became classical. It looked back to the original creative period, and later changes were integrated into the classical pattern.

1

The Pre-literate Intellectual Tradition

The invention of writing led to the division of the population into two classes, literate and illiterate.

The illiterate majority continued the mentality of their pre-literate ancestors. The literate minority entered into a new world of ideas, and were able to use their written records of the past as stepping stones to progress.

These two levels have been called the high intellectual tradition and the low intellectual tradition. The high intellectual tradition was carried by an elite urban minority, the low intellectual tradition by the peasant masses.

The content of the earliest writings was the existing pre-literate, low intellectual tradition which was thus preserved. It was all that was then available.

This is summed up by Prof. Fung as including divine beings, divination and magic, heaven and God, and the beginnings of rationalism growing out of this tradition.

Most of these early ideas have been preserved to the present by the conservatism of the peasant villagers, and are today the living beliefs of the great majority. But their incorporation in books gave a distinctive character to the Chinese high intellectual tradition.

Belief in Spirits

The Chinese held the universal primitive belief in spirits. One of the earliest books (Kuo Yü) contains the following, dated about the time of Confucius:

> In ancient times people and divine beings did not intermingle. Among the people were those who were refined . . . sincere and upright . . . Their perspicacity could illumine everything.

When there were people of this sort the illustrious spirits would descend in them. If men, such people were called sorcerers (*hsi*), if women they were called witches (*wu*).

Such witches are found today in a considerable proportion of country villages. The record of fairly recent contacts with a number of them appear in *Daughter of Confucius*, which I wrote with Wong Su-ling. I have myself seen a sorcerer casting out demons from a haunted house.

Divination and Magic

The catalog of the Imperial Han dynasty library enumerated six classes of divination: astrology, almanacs, those connected with the Five Elements, the method of the tortoise shell and the stalks of the divination plant, miscellaneous diviners who keep records of phenomena, especially dreams, and the system of forms, including fortunetelling based on physiognomy.

Heaven and God

The most ancient doctrines contain numerous references to a deity high above the spirits. Two terms were in common use. Heaven, Tien, personalized, was the concept of the Chou nomads, and does not appear earlier. Shang Ti, the Supreme Ancestor, was the concept of the agricultural peasant-villagers.

High Intellectual Tradition

Among the literate holders of the high intellectual tradition, rationalism early arose.

Confucius would not discuss prodigies—or supernatural beings. He counseled to respect the spirits but keep them at a distance.

But much of the content of the pre-literate intellectual tradition was already embodied in the books that came to be the classics, and was thus permanently influential.

The high intellectual tradition developed education, philosophy and literature, but it remained close to the low intellectual tradition.

Closeness of the Two Levels

The most distinctive characteristic of Confucianism was that it was a rationalization of the Chinese social order, and that it never lost that character.

Prof. Ralph Turner states that Confucius

> gave classic form to the Chinese high intellectual tradition . . . ensured that its carriers in subsequent ages would not abandon the peasant-village mentality of which the first written materials were an expression. This resulted in the fixation of Chinese culture on a basis which was, even more completely than in the Western world, the mentality of the peasant-village masses.

> Confucius did not make the mistake of the exclusive projection of knowledge in an ideal individual existence possible only in subjective terms or in the spiritual overworld. . . .

> He conceived its projection in a stable social order; in this respect he was like the Greeks Plato and Aristotle.

> But, more closely bound to tradition than they, he made possible the ultimate assimilation of Chinese life to the pattern he set, while they did little more than state the theories in terms of which Western men described a stable order they never attained.

Here is the basis of Chinese practicality—theory and practice were close together. Confucian philosophy and ethics, and the sociology of Chinese society were but different facets of the same reality. Here is the basis of its long continuity.

2

The Original Ways of Thought

There were three original ways of thought in China previous to the establishment of the empire in 221 B.C.

Confucianism was the ethic of the aristocratic clans, defining the basic kinship relations within the clan, and the relationship of the members of the various clans at the court of the prince. It was rigid, depended on moral suasion, and was implemented through ceremonial.

Taoism was an individualistic, even anarchistic, reaction against the Confucian insistence on order. It stressed conformity to nature, the following of the Tao, that path which was also the order of the universe. It was chiefly for aristocrats, who were able to withdraw from mundane labors. It was mystical and was implemented by "non-action."

The legalist way of thought was a down-to-earth method of government. It advocated a rule of law that applied equally to all, both nobles and peasants, enforced by the state with punishments for disobedience. This realism furnished the foundation on which was built the structure of the empire.

These are usually spoken of as philosophies. This is misleading. They were primarily practical methods for the ordering of life and not philosophical systems. They are more accurately designated as ways of thought. The philosophical factor was there, but was marginal and largely unorganized. Taoism, because of its attitude of revolt, came closest to philosophy.

Confucianism

Confucianism is best understood as a rationalism of the Chinese social order, as has been indicated above.

It has frequently been defined as religion, ethics, or philosophy.

Such definitions miss the heart of the matter and fail to do justice to the practical character of the Chinese people. It is misleading to abstract or skim off Confucian "philosophy" and deal with it *in vacuo,* disregarding the cultural pattern of which it is a part.

Confucianism moves in the realm of sociology. To this, ethics is closely related, but religion rather less so, and philosophy is still more remote.

It is worth repeating that Chinese society is based on kinship structure, involving the relation of father to son, husband to wife, elder brother to younger. These Confucius and his followers worked out in detail. This was clan ethics. It is this that has given Confucianism its practical character and its stability and power.

Confucius was personally concerned with the political problem and sought office. So he added two relationships outside the clan: prince to minister, and friend to friend.

It was obvious that the many clans had to be related somehow, and the government of the princes in the fourteen hundred states, large and small, bound together the clans within each to a certain extent, and implied relations between the clans and the state. It is typical of Confucianism that these were conceived in terms of personal relations. There is nothing said about the corporate relation of one clan to another, or of the group of clans to the state. The entire emphasis is upon the moral character of the ruler—if he sets a good example, all will follow. In this Confucius was thinking chiefly in terms of the aristocrats, and not of the masses of the peasantry.

Thus Confucianism depended on moral suasion, rather than political organization and structure. As the Greeks did not get politically beyond the city state, Confucius did not get beyond clan ethics and personal relations. Confucius was not interested in theory and he refused to discuss philosophy. He was a religious man according to the standards of his day, but his interest was definitely in this life and he was not willing to divert attention to things beyond.

Whereas Plato in the West envisages an ideal state, and there have been a succession of Utopias, Confucius kept his feet on the ground and dealt in a most practical and commonsense way with the everyday life of his people and sought to bring into it order, stability, and courtesy. In this he was a typical Chinese.

Aristocratic Character of Confucian Benevolence

In Confucianism there are two basic ideas, *jen* and *li,* benevolence and ceremony.

The term *jen,* usually translated benevolence, has been much misunderstood. The ideogram is composed of the two characters for "man" and "two." Thus it means the right relationship of one man to his fellow. A man of *jen* considers others as well as himself. In pre-Confucian times, it appears six times in the Book of Odes, meaning "admirable and kind." It is used a number of times in the Book of History with the same meaning. In these early uses referring to the nobility it in each case indicates their attitude to their inferiors; it is the benevolence or kindness of the superior.

By *jen,* Confucius meant the ideal attitude of the superior to the inferior. It was not the love of equals. This fits perfectly into the five relationships, which also are between superior and inferior, and with the general aristocratic character of Confucianism.

This was implemented by rites and ceremonial.

Mencius

Confucianism developed two main tendencies, the realistic represented by Hsun Tzu and the idealistic represented by Mencius.

The great struggle in ancient ethical philosophy was between inner and outer morality. In Confucianism, outer morality won, taking the form of rites and ceremonial as worked out by Hsun Tzu. Mencius represented the inner morality. His most famous teaching was the goodness of human nature. Man's original nature had four beginnings: commiseration, shame and dislike, modesty and yielding, and sense of right and wrong. These issue in benevolence, righteousness, propriety, and wisdom.

These are inner developments. If logically carried out, they would have developed a new philosophy. But this "would have involved discarding a great part of the inherited culture of the race, and the Confucianists were primarily conservators of this culture, not innovators."

The concept of progress never dawned on any Confucian.

In political philosophy, Mencius held that the people were the most important element in the state, with the spirits of land and grain second and the sovereign third. This was idealistic and put the Confucian school in a dilemma. It supported the Chou institutions and therefore could not attack the principle of hereditary succession. Hence it was unable to formulate its doctrine in a logical way, and could only say "that which is done without man's doing it, is from Heaven." But this was merely theoretical and doctrinaire. Fung comments:

> Most proposed solutions were not realistic enough to be practical. What the rulers needed were not idealistic programs for doing good to their people, but realistic methods for dealing with the new situations faced by the government.

Mencius advocated following the laws of the ancient kings, but what he presented was not a legal code but an idealization of those laws.

His mysticism provided a metaphysical basis for the doctrine of the goodness of human nature.

> Nature is what heaven has given us. Coming to know his own nature, he comes to know heaven, and becomes a citizen of Heaven. Man's nature is thus a part of heaven.

> Man can become one with heaven . . . All things are complete within us. There is no greater delight than to realize this through self-cultivation . . . Wherever the superior man abides, there is a spiritual influence. This flows abroad, above and below, together with heaven and earth.

The moving force—hao jan shih ch'i—"is the spiritual quality of those individuals who have attained this highest state."

The Neo-Confucianists of the Sung dynasty went back to this mysticism of Mencius, and claimed to be in an esoteric succession from him.

Hsun Tzu

Hsun Tzu represents the rationalistic tendency in Confucianism and the victory of outer morality over inner.

Confucianism lacked eminent scholars at this time, and was rejuvenated by Hsun Tzu whose remarkable learning contributed greatly to the development of classical studies during the Former Han dynasty. The first dynastic history describes his times thus:

He hated the governments of his corrupt generation, its dying states and evil princes, who did not follow the Tao but gave their attention to magic and prayers and believed in omens and luck.

It was a generation of low scholars who had no learning. Thinkers such as Chuang Tzu . . . were specious and threw the customs into disorder.

Hsun Tzu carried the Confucian rationalistic tendency to its logical conclusion. He depersonalized the concept of Heaven by taking over the Taoist concept of Tao as universal law and making this the meaning of Heaven. He was the first Confucian thinker to deny spirits; earlier ones had been merely agnostic. He thus began the two thousand years of ridicule of spirits on the part of the Confucian literati. He opposed superstition, disposed of prayer, and attacked physiognomy as a type of fortune telling. He rationalized sacrifice. Divination, however, appears in the classics as a regular government procedure, so he could not attack it too severely.

He rationalized the Li or rites, which constituted the ceremonial and good form which expressed the outer morality of the aristocrats. Li originally meant religious rites. In his time were six: capping at puberty, marriage, funerals, sacrifice, wine ceremony, audience with ruler. These he classified under four types: mourning, sacrifice, court ceremony, methods of courtesy.

Li was custom, law was promulgated by the state. Li was positive. It indicated what was right, what was correct form. Its violation incurred social disapproval. Violation of law was punished by the state. Above all, Li was for aristocrats. Law did not apply to them, but was for the common people only, who were regulated by punishments.

There was only one occupation for a gentleman, government office and position at court. These rituals of courtesy were the chief indoor sport, and were developed in hundreds of petty courts. Hsun Tzu had himself been three times officer for the sacrificial wine offering in the state of Ch'i. His ideas met with the approval of his times and his writings were quoted in the most important works in this field that have been preserved. Three of the thirteen classics are on Li, and give a refined expression to the customary morality of the aristocrats. It had a strong influence on morals. In Chinese eyes courtesy rises to the dignity of religion.

Ritual was easily understood. The new concept of *jen*, benevolence, put forth by Confucius, was a novel idea, and Confucius was many times asked about its meaning.

Hsun Tzu put great emphasis on education. He held that man's nature was evil, but that he had intelligence and could improve himself. Reliance on religion would tend to prevent education and effort, which are superior. He had a high ideal of scholarship. He writes:

> Scholarship means to study with intentness and singleness of purpose . . . The superior man knows that when his knowledge is not complete or refined it is insufficient to be classed as excellent.
>
> These he recites sentence by sentence in order to make them part of himself, seeks to practice them in order to understand them, and puts them into practice and lives as a man of virtue.

The leading Confucian of the Han dynasty was Tung Chung-shu, who played a chief part in giving Confucius the dominant position in the government.

Taoism

Taoism is the other side of the Chinese character. Along with the rigidity of the clan and its relationships fixed by birth was the urge of the individual toward freedom, spontaneity, and even wildness.

Tao and Te

The ancient Chinese regarded the earth as a square block surrounded by water. About it circled the heavenly bodies bringing day and night, seed time and harvest. This movement was the Tao, the order of the universe.

The Tao is not something transcending the world. It is in the world. It is everywhere. It is the whole. In Chuang Tzu's book this is presented by a story.

> "Where is the so-called Tao?" Chuang Tzu was asked.
> "Everywhere."
> "Specify an instance."
> "It is in the ant."
> "How can the Tao be anything so low?"

"It is in the grass."
"How can it be still lower?"
"It is in excrement."
The questioner was silent, and Chuang Tzu went on to explain.
"Your question does not touch the fundamentals of the Tao. You should not specify any particular thing. There is not a single thing without Tao."

Te, usually translated "virtue," is what an individual thing receives from the Tao. Chuang Tzu put it thus:

That which things get in order to live is called Te. The total spontaneity of all things is the Tao. The spontaneity an individual thing receives from the Tao is its Te.

Chuang Tzu

The book by Chuang Tzu had its main influence during the period of disunion following the Han, although he lived and taught during the era of the Warring States, and represents the main current of the Taoist philosophy. Its first chapter is entitled "The Happy Excursion," and begins as follows:

In the Northern Ocean there is a fish, by the name of *kun,* which is many thousand li in size. This fish metamorphoses into a bird by the name of *p'eng* whose back is many thousand li in breadth. When the bird rouses itself and flies, its wings obscure the sky like clouds. When this bird moves itself in the sea, it is preparing to start for the Southern Ocean, the Celestial Lake.

A man named Ch'i Hsieh, who recorded novel occurrences, said: "When the *p'eng* is moving to the Southern Ocean it flaps along the water for three thousand li. Then it ascends on a whirlwind up to a height of ninety thousand li, for a flight of six months' duration.

"We do not know whether the blueness of the sky is its original color, or is simply caused by its infinite height. When the *p'eng* sees the earth from above, just as we see the sky from below, it will stop rising and begin to fly to the south. Without sufficient density, the wind would not be able to support the large wings. Therefore, when the *p'eng* ascends to the height of ninety thousand li, the wind is all beneath it. Then, with the blue sky above, and no obstacle on the way, it mounts upon the wind and starts for the south.

"A cicada and a young dove laugh at the *p'eng,* saying 'When we make an effort, we fly up to the trees. Sometimes, not able to reach it, we fall to the ground midway. What is the use of going up ninety thousand li in order to start for the south?' "

The commentary states that "what each does is proper to its own nature; in this they are the same."

Man too should follow his own nature. This was the ultimate meaning of "non-activity"—*wu-wei*. The commentator Kuo Hsiang said:

> The feet can walk; let them walk.
> The hands can hold; let them hold.
> Hear what is heard by your ears,
> See what is seen by your eyes.
> Let your knowledge stop at what you do not know.
> Let your ability stop at what you cannot do. . . .
> Act . . . within the limit of your nature.

Everything is relative anyway. But all is a part of the Tao. This appears in the chapter "The Autumn Flood" in the Chuang Tzu.

In autumn, when the Yellow River was in flood, the Spirit of the River, who was very proud of his greatness, moved down the river to the sea. There he met the Spirit of the Sea, and realized for the first time that his river, great as it was, was small indeed in comparison with the sea. Yet when, full of admiration, he talked with the Spirit of the Sea, the latter replied that he himself, in his relationship to Heaven and Earth, was nothing more than a single grain lying within a great warehouse. Hence he could only be said to be "small," but not to be "great." At this the River Spirit asked the Sea Spirit: "Are we right then in saying that Heaven and Earth are supremely great and the tip of a hair is supremely small?" The Sea Spirit answered: "What men know is less than what they do not know. The time when they are alive is less than the time when they are not alive . . . How can we know that the tip of a hair is the extreme of smallness, and Heaven and Earth are the extreme of greatness?" And he then went on to define the smallest as that which has no form, and the greatest as that which cannot be enclosed (by anything else).

Taoism and General Ideas

Taoism was primarily interested in cosmology, as appears above. But there was another approach to ultimate reality through the realm of ideas.

This appears in the Lao Tzu book, commonly called the Tao Te Ching. Its opening stanza begins as follows:

> Tao ko tao, fei chang Tao
> Ming ko ming, fei chang ming.
>
> Tao can speak, not unchanging Tao
> Name can name, not unchanging name.

That is, the Tao that can be explained is not the unchanging Tao, and the name that can be named is not the unchanging name.

Here name parallels Tao. The word "ming" appears in modern grammar in the term "ming ssu" meaning "common noun." In this first stanza the word "ming" appears six times, the word "Tao" only three times.

Here the ultimate reality is approached by way of ideas. The stanza says "These two are the same in source, but different in name."

General Ideas and Reality

The thinkers during the Warring States when this was written were struggling with the implications of the general idea, the common noun. Was it merely nominal or real? Were there merely individual horses, or was there a reality corresponding to the word "horse"? If so, it must be some ultimate reality beyond shapes and features.

This School of Names was also called that of the discriminators. Prof. Fung says they were originally lawyers. They were concerned over the relation of names to actualities, and found that actual things were relative and changing, but names were permanent and absolute. These lie behind all shapes and features, and are universals that cannot be objects of experience.

Chuang Tzu was a friend of a leader of this school, and the Taoists inherited these ideas. Indeed they carried them further.

The discriminators reached the idea of the greatest.

"It has nothing beyond itself, and is called the Great Unity."

But the Taoists held that a person who spoke of this Great Oneness was outside it, and its all-embracing unity was therefore lost. So the One was unthinkable and inexpressible.

"The name that can be named is not the unchanging name."

Non-Action

The famous principle of non-action referred not only to the individual Taoist who followed his own nature, but to government also. The Tao Te Ching says in stanza 3:

> The holy man, when he governs, empties the people's hearts but fills their stomachs. He weakens their ambition but strengthens their bones. Always he keeps the people unsophisticated and without desire. He causes that the crafty do not dare to act. When he acts with non-assertion there is nothing ungoverned.

Stanza 18 indicates that the Confucian virtues are merely signs of deterioration, a falling away from the ideal state of nature.

> When the great Tao is obliterated
> We have benevolence and justice.
> When family relations no longer harmonize;
> We have filial piety and paternal devotion.
> When country and clans decay through disorder,
> We have loyalty and allegiance.

Taoist ideas of this sort had a considerable influence on the legalists.

Psychological Aspects of Taoism

The Chinese mind has a Taoist substratum. He is socially Confucian and individually Taoist. Confucianism is a practical prosaic affair of social control guided by accepted rules and expressed through a code of decorum. Taoism upholds a state of nature wherein the free expression of the individual becomes the end and justification of everything.

This freedom is pre-social, while the freedom of the West is the freedom of socially conscious man. It is generalized freedom, whereas in the West it is freedom from something specific, such as freedom of speech or belief. A Chinese writer has characterized Taoism as a "subtle but abiding psychic mood in an educated Chinese."

Political Aspects of Taoism

In practical life, Taoism meant freedom for the individual, anarchy in the sphere of government, and spontaneity in the field of ethics. Or rather a complete dependence on obeying one's impulses supersedes ethical considerations, which have been relegated.

Taoism has an affinity for revolt, and it was no accident that the great majority of secret societies, which have been the hidden instruments of revolt, have been Taoist. But this often takes a negative character in line with Taoist "non-action." The Chinese people have a genius for not doing what they don't want to do.

The Legalists

Toward the end of the Warring States period, there arose a school of thinkers who considered government from the point of view of the ruler of a state rather than that of the people, as had been the case with most previous ones.

These arose in two states whose rulers had held the position of feudal Leader (Pa) over the other feudal lords. The Chou sovereign was hereditary, had priestly functions and held the mandate of Heaven. The Leader, lacking this, had to depend on organization and administrative methods that would work.

The feudal system was going to pieces. The trend of the times was toward rulers having absolute power. Government by customary morality was being replaced by government by law.

At the beginning of the period there had been over a thousand states, large and small, and rule was more personal. In this the peasants ordinarily did not count, but only the many "houses" or clans into which the state was divided. Toward the end of the period, a few larger states had swallowed up the smaller ones, personal rule was no longer possible, and differing local customs had to be unified under law. When numerous small states that had been governed by petty nobles were taken over, the central government took an increased interest in the common man.

As early as 513 B.C. the beginnings of such conditions led one state to inscribe penal laws on bronze tripods which it cast for the purpose.

This was criticized by statesmen of the time and later by Confucius:

> China is going to ruin. It has lost its proper rules . . .
>
> The people will study the tripods. How will they then honor their men

of rank, and what will the nobles do? When there is no distinction of noble and mean, how can a state continue to exist?

The aristocrats were beginning to lose some of their vested interests and special privileges.

Hsun Tzu advocated something more positive:

Deal with the people by authority, and guide them in the Tao . . . explain things by proclamations, and restrain them by punishments.

It was not necessary to follow the past. The times stressed the power of the ruler, government by law, prohibition of private teaching to the contrary.

The legalists rationalized the trend of the times, as Confucius had rationalized the clan structure.

The ideal was that "ruler and minister, superior and inferior, noble and mean, all obey the law." Prof. Fung comments that this is "an ideal which has never yet been actually attained in China."

Taoists and Legalists

The Legalists were greatly influenced by the Taoists. Han Fei Tzu, the foremost legalist, was said to have based his doctrines on Taoist teachings. This seems a strange combination, especially the principle of non-activity. It was worked out in the Chuang Tzu book as follows, and this is important for the periods when government devolved on the Taoists after the fall of the Han.

If superiors have non-action and inferiors also have it they become equal. The inferiors are no longer subjects . . . The superior must practice non-action so as to administer the empire, and his inferiors must practice activity in order to be utilized in the empire.

In other words, the ruler delegates his powers to the members of his government.

LATER DEVELOPMENTS—NEO-TAOISM

It has been related in Part II how Confucian scholars gained control of the bureaucracy of the Han empire, and contributed to its fall by trying to administer an empire on the basis of the personal relations within the clan, or between prince and aristocrats in a petty state.

The fall of the Han empire carried the Confucian officialdom down with it, and left the Confucianists out of office and discredited in a land divided among a score of rival states.

So it fell to the Taoists to assume the lead. As might be expected, they did nothing to retrieve the situation, and a Period of Disunity continued for 369 years, 220–589 A.D., until the empire was again unified under the Sui and T'ang dynasties.

During the Han dynasty China had pushed to the west through Central Asia, and had made contacts with India, Persia, and the Roman Empire. Buddhism was already strong in Central Asia in a modified form. It now penetrated into China, where the dominant neo-Taoism was congenial to its reception, and Confucianism, which might have opposed it, was at a low ebb. Buddhism reached its high point during the first half of the T'ang dynasty.

But, with the reunification of China and the re-establishment of the empire, Confucian officials came to power again and Confucianism reasserted itself. The end result was that Confucianism appropriated certain philosophical aspects of Buddhism and Taoism, and was itself modified into neo-Confucianism. The new ideas were read into certain classics, particularly the Four Books, which took a place beside the original Five Classics. This constituted a new classical orthodoxy that remained dominant until modern times.

Neo-Taoism of the Period of Disunion

Neo-Taoism dominated the first two centuries of the Period of Disunion following the break-up of the Han dynasty. It opposed laws and institutions as artificial, and idealized a state of nature. Ethics were a sign of degeneration.

This comes out in an imaginary conversation with Confucius in the Chuang Tzu book.

"I have made some progress," said Yen Hui.
"What do you mean?" asked Confucius.
"I forget benevolence and righteousness," replied Yen Hui.
"Very well, but that is not perfect," said Confucius.
Another day Yen Hui again saw Confucius, and said: "I have made some progress."
"What do you mean?" asked Confucius.
"I forget ceremony and music," replied Yen Hui.
"Very well, but that is not perfect," said Confucius.
Another day Yen Hui again saw Confucius, and said: "I have made some progress."
"What do you mean?" asked Confucius.
"I forget everything," replied Yen Hui.
Confucius changed his countenance and said: "What do you mean by forgetting everything?"
"I gave up my body," said Yen Hui, "and discarded my knowledge. By thus getting rid of body and mind, I became one with the infinite. This is what I mean by forgetting everything."
"When you are one with the infinite," said Confucius, "you will have no bias. When you are one with the great evolution, you will have no insistence. If you have really attained to this, I beg to follow your steps."

The Taoist Sage

The perfect man of the Taoists was the Taoist counterpart of the Confucian sage. His description in the Chuang Tzu may be compared with that of Confucius given above.

The perfect man is mysterious. Were the great lakes burned up, he would not feel hot. Were the great rivers frozen hard, he would not feel cold. Were the mountains to be riven with thunder, or the seas thrown into waves by a storm, he would not be frightened. Being such, he would mount upon the clouds of heaven, would ride on the sun and moon, and would thus ramble at ease beyond the seas. Neither death nor life can affect him; . . . the sage does not occupy himself with the affairs of the world. He neither seeks gain, nor avoids injury. He has no pleasure in seeking. He does not purposely adhere to Tao. He speaks without speaking. He does not speak when he speaks. Thus he roams beyond the limits of this dusty world.

How could this mysterious state be reached? The Chuang Tzu book gives the process:

There was Pu Liang I, who had the genius of a sage, but not the Tao. I have the Tao, but not the genius. I wished to teach him, so he might really become a sage. To teach the Tao of a sage to a man who has the genius, seems to be an easy matter.

But no, I kept on telling him; after three days, he began to be able to disregard all worldly matters.

After his having disregarded all worldly matters, I kept on telling him; after seven days, he began to be able to disregard all external things.

After his having disregarded all external things, I kept on telling him; after nine days, he began to be able to disregard his own existence.

Having disregarded his own existence, he was enlightened. Having become enlightened, he then was able to gain the vision of the One. Having the vision of the One, he then was able to transcend the distinction of past and present. Having transcended the distinction of past and present, he was then able to enter the realm where life and death are no more. Then, to him, the destructiion of life did not mean death, nor the prolongation of life an addition to the duration of his existence. He would follow anything; he would receive anything. To him, everything was in destruction, everything was in construction. This is called tranquillity in disturbance. Tranquillity in disturbance means perfection.

Such men went on expeditions to seek the isles of the immortals. They became alchemists, and the lives of several emperors were cut short by drinking the elixir of life which they concocted. More recently their descendants persuaded the Empress Dowager that they had a charm so that the Boxers could not be killed by Western bullets.

Shortly afterwards, Tzu Sang Hu died. Before he was buried, Confucius heard of the event, and sent Tzu Kung to take part in the mourning. But

Tzu Kung found that one of the friends composed a song, and the other was playing on the lute. They sang together in unison: "Alas! Sang Hu! Alas! Sang Hu! you have returned to the real, but we still remain here as men, alas!"

Tzu Kung went back and told Confucius, asking him: "What sort of men are those? They have no culture and consider their body as external as themselves. They sing in the presence of the corpse, without a change of countenance. I do not know what to call them. What sort of men are they?"

"They travel outside the human world," said Confucius.

4

LATER DEVELOPMENTS—BUDDHISM

Buddhism entered China in the first century A.D. and gradually acquired influence during the later Han.

The first two centuries (220–400) of the Period of Disunion were dominated by Taoism. During the last two (400–589) Buddhism dominated Chinese thought, and indeed this continued for another four centuries until the early Sung (1000). Prof. Fung states that during these six centuries "Buddhism absorbed the best energies of most philosophically minded Chinese, while the native philosophies suffered comparative eclipse."

This was a major new factor in Chinese life. It was part of a larger process of Indianization, which was also going on in Southeast Asia and Indonesia.

Buddhism and Taoism

But at first it seemed much the same as Neo-Taoism, and as late as the middle of the fifth century a Chinese scholar could write:

From the K'un-lun mountains eastward the term "Great Oneness" is used. From Kashmir westward the term *sambodi* is used. Whether one looks longingly toward "non-being" or cultivates "emptiness," the principle involved is the same.

This led to the use of Taoist ideas to explain Buddhism.

The Biographies of Eminent Buddhist Monks (before 554) tells of the fourth century monk Fa-ya:

His disciples were only versed in non-Buddhist writings—so he equated the contents of the *sutras* with the external writings . . . In this way, external writings and Buddhist *sutras* were alike transmitted, each being expounded in terms of the other.

Beginning of Buddhist Supremacy

The year 400 may be taken as the turning point, marking the beginning of Buddhist supremacy in Chinese thought that was to continue for 600 years.

In 355 the monk Tao-an established a monastery on Mount Heng in northern Shensi, and was the first Chinese who took Buddhism as a religion seriously, and felt it was his duty to propagate it.

To this monastery came Hui-yuan (334–416) who founded the Pure Land Sect, which became the largest and most popular in China and Japan.

In 399 Fa-hsien, famous pilgrim, began his fourteen-year journey to India to bring back Buddhist scriptures.

In 402 the famous monk Kumarajiva, of Indian descent, was brought a captive to the capital Chang-an by the non-Chinese ruler who was an ardent Buddhist. He was provided with a staff for translation. He was among the first who systematically introduced Indian thought into China. Through his scholarly work and his personality he did more than any other to enhance the prestige of Buddhism in China.

Other works had been translated previously, but usually in part, or summarized. This began a series of scholarly translations that have evoked the admiration of later centuries, and have resulted in the Chinese version of the Buddhist scriptures being larger than that in any other language.

About this time there were seven schools of Buddhist thought. Most of these thinkers worked out their own rounded systems of thought incorporating both Chinese and Indian ideas.

One of the most brilliant was Seng-Chao (384–414) who wrote chapters, "On the Immutability of Things" and "The Emptiness of the Unreal." These were a combination of Buddhism and Neo-Taoism. The Buddhism of some of these really came under the heading of Neo-Taoism.

Another contemporary was Tao-Sheng who enunciated the famous theory of instantaneous enlightenment, which foreshadowed Zen.

This eventually replaced philosophy by intuition, and resulted in the destruction of most of the abstruse system of thought, and was the beginning of what the Chinese philosopher Dr. Hu Shih calls the Chinese revolt against Indian philosophy. But that was not to come to a head until 600 years later.

Chinese Sects

The seven schools have been largely forgotten, but by the early part of the T'ang dynasty, the main Chinese Buddhist sects were taking form.

These sects, which were schools of thought and not organized religious bodies, were the results of the Chinese reworking of Indian Buddhism, largely during the 300 years 400–700.

During this period the Chinese accumulated and translated an enormous amount of Buddhist writings that fill fifty-five large volumes in the authoritative Taisho Tripitaka (including Chinese writings). This was largely an unorganized mass of material. Buddhism had changed greatly in India, where there were many sects, and had been reworked in Central Asia.

The Chinese encyclopedic mind sought to establish order in this chaos. This took place along three lines exemplified in six sects.

Three Treatise School

The first and simplest method was to select one scripture or at most two or three, and base a school on their doctrines. This was done by the monk Chi-tsang (549–623) whose literary activity exceeded that of any others of his own time or earlier. He wrote commentaries on three important shastras, resulting in the Three Treatise School.

This method was followed by later sects in China and Japan.

Tien-tai School

The second method was encyclopedic. Here was a mass of sutras, all traditionally from the mouth of the Buddha, that disagreed. This contradiction was solved by classifying them in stages of development, as being taught by the Buddha at earlier or later times, and to hearers at different levels of comprehension. This led to distinctive method and doctrines in this school.

This theory became widely accepted and influential.

Special Sects

The third method was to seek to cut through the mass of details and arrive at the quintessence of Buddhism itself. This resulted in the four sects that were most Chinese. The most drastic, even revolutionary, was *Zen* (Chinese Ch'an), the meditation sect, which was both more and less than a school of thought. *Hwa-yen*: the high point of Chinese Buddhist philosophizing and philosophically the most Chinese. The Mere Ideation Sect, which was philosophically the most Indian, appealed to only a limited circle, and was subjective idealism. The Pure Land Sect, which became the popular faith of the masses, and was a paradise sect.

There were some dozen other sects or schools of thought in China, but closer to the Indian model, and of less importance.

Controversy

This great religious, scholarly and philosophical development did not come about without controversy. Two collections of these polemics by Confucian and Taoist scholars have been preserved. Six main lines of criticism were enumerated: the doctrines of the sutras were wild, vast, and cannot be verified; no one has seen the Buddha, and he does not benefit the country; there was no Buddhist teaching in classical times; it came from barbaric lands; it was unimportant until the contemporary Chin dynasty; the soul is not immortal.

This last aroused intense interest, and the scholarly official Fan Chen (d. 515) wrote a famous Essay on the Extinction of the Soul.

> Buddhism is injurious to government and its monks do harm to custom . . . Creation is a gift of nature . . . Impalpably there is being of itself, and imperceptibly there is no longer being. . . .
>
> Lesser folks should find sweetness in their cultivated acres and superior men should preserve their quiet simplicity . . . Let inferiors present their surplus to superiors . . . the country will remain in order and the ruler will be in his place.

This caused a sensation in the capital, and the ruler assembled learned monks to rebut him.

This indicates the special concern of Confucians with government and the welfare of society, as their chief basis of opposition to Buddhism.

The Buddhist Invention of Printing

About 600 A.D. printing was invented in Chinese Buddhist monasteries in order to multiply the pictures, magic spells, and scriptures, which were believed to have a beneficent magical effect. Printing from wooden blocks made these available to a much larger number of people. It also increased the magical power by repetition. Thus one early scroll contains merely some fifty pictures of the Buddha.

Printing by movable type was developed in China much later, for the cutting of a wooden block for a double page was rapid and cheap, and such blocks were easily stored and could be readily reprinted.

Where previously scholars had merely heard about certain books, they were now able to build up extensive private libraries. Learning increased and scholarship extended. All of this formed the basis for the Chinese Renaissance which came to a climax with the development of neo-Confucianism of the Sung Dynasty in the twelfth century.

Buddhism at High Tide

During the first part of the T'ang, Buddhism in China reached its highest point. But this was merely acquisition and assimilation. The cultural synthesis was delayed until the Sung Dynasty.

There had already been polemic and some persecutions. Confucian scholars and officials came back to power with the reconstituting of the centralized empire, and the 150 years of peace, and the anti-Buddhist tendencies culminated in the persecutions of 845 A.D. from which Chinese Buddhism never recovered.

Transition from Indian to Chinese Buddhism

Doctor Hu Shih, historian of Chinese philosophy, and sometime Chinese ambassador to the United States, outlines the Chinese reaction to Buddhist missions somewhat as follows:

The Chinese mentality is practical and abhors metaphysical speculation.

All the religions and philosophies of ancient China were free from the fantastic imaginativeness, hair-splitting analysis, and gigantic architectonic structure which characterize all religious and philosophical literatures of India. When China was brought face to face with India, China was overwhelmed, dazzled and dumbfounded by the vast output of the religious zeal and genius of the Indian nation. China acknowledged its defeat and was completely conquered.

But after a few centuries of bewilderment and enthusiasm, the Chinese mentality gradually re-asserted itself and began to search for those things which it could really understand and accept.

The forerunner of Chinese Zen was the philosophical monk Tao-seng (died 434), a very learned scholar of great brilliancy and eloquence. He was a revolutionary thinker and is recorded as having made this reflection on the general trend of Buddhist study:

The symbol is to express the idea and is to be discarded when the idea is understood. Words are to explain thought and should cease when the thought is absorbed. Ever since the introduction of Buddhist scriptures to the East, the translators have met with great impediments and the people have clung to the dead letter and few have grasped the all-comprehensive meaning. Only those who can grasp the fish and discard the net are qualified to seek the truth.

The last figure of speech refers to a saying of the Taoist philosopher Chuang-tze who said: "The net is to catch fish. Take the fish and forget the net."

The nihilistic influence of Lao-tze and Chuang-tze has always had an emancipating effect on the Chinese mind, and Tao-seng was the natural product of an age which was one of Taoist revival. His most far-reaching theory was the idea of sudden enlightenment which means that Buddhahood can be achieved through immediate awakening without having to undergo the long and arduous processes of merit-accumulation and dhyana practice (meditation).

The real beginning of Chinese Zennism came toward the last years of the seventh century when there arose in the vicinity of Canton a great teacher, Hui-neng, later known as the Sixth Patriarch. He was an uneducated and almost illiterate monk, who, by sheer force of personality and inspiring eloquence and, above all, by the great simplicity and directness of his spiritual message, succeeded in founding a new sect which was in reality nothing short of a Chinese revolt against Buddhist philosophy.

The Buddha is within you. You have been told to abide by the Buddha, the Law and the Order. But I say unto you: abide by yourself. The Buddha is within you, because the Buddha means the Enlightened One, and enlightenment must come from within yourself. The Law is within you, because the Law means righteousness, and righteousness is within you. And the Sangha is within you, because the Brotherhood means purity, and purity is within you.

For the first time in the history of Chinese Buddhism, Hui-neng revolted against dhyana itself, and in thus overthrowing the principal element in Indian dhyana, he laid the foundation of Chinese Zen.

Chinese Zen was iconoclastic. After it had discarded Indian dhyana practice, it revolted against all prayer and worship. Wu-chu, who died in 766, was famous for his conscious abolition of all rituals and worship of the Buddhist religion. In his school the monks were not allowed to pray, to recite or copy scriptures, or to worship images of the Buddha.

The great persecution of Buddhism in 845 had the effect of purifying the Buddhist religion and elevating the prestige of Zen monks who did not rely upon such externals as rituals and monasteries and who could maintain their convictions in huts or caves. It strengthened the belief that real religion was something apart from the architectural splendor and ritualistic extravagances of the temples and monasteries. It was no accident, therefore, that the great iconoclastic masters arose and taught in the decades immediately following.

One master taught the doctrine of non-activity which harks back to the Taoist philosophy.

My advice to you is, take a rest, have nothing to do. Put on your clothes, eat your food, move your bowels. That is all. No death to fear. No transmigration to dread. No nirvana to achieve. Try to be just an ordinary man having nothing to do. Go and take an early rest! Here in my place, there is not a single truth for you to take home. I myself don't know what Zen is. I am no teacher, knowing nothing at all. I am only an old beggar who begs his food and clothing and daily moves his bowels. What else have I to do?

Another master established the Lintsi School which in the next two centuries became the most powerful school of Zen. He made use of the pedagogical methods of the earlier Zen masters, but his favorite method was that of howling or shouting at his audience.

Methodology

The methodology of Zen has often been misunderstood. There is a clear method behind all the apparent madness for which many Zen masters were famous. The master must not make things easy for the novice; he must not preach to him in too plain language, or in any language at all. One of the great masters once said: "I owe everything to my teacher because he never told me anything."

5

Later Philosophical Developments—Neo-Confucianism and After

Neo-Confucianism was a Confucianizing of Buddhism and Taoism, in which Buddhist ideas were read into selected Confucian classics—the Four Books—which became the new orthodoxy, education and basis of Chinese life.

Beginnings of Neo-Confucianism

The beginnings of Neo-Confucianism have been indicated earlier, and its sources in Buddhism, Taoism and the Taoist religion.

The Confucian scholars Han Yu and Li Ao had attacked Buddhism, which resulted in the persecution of 845 A.D.

Buddhism recovered sufficiently to get out the Tripitika in a printed edition of over 5000 volumes (971–83). Other Buddhist printing went on in various parts of the country.

The reuniting of the country under the Sung dynasty paved the way for Neo-Confucianism. The political unification contributed to a cultural synthesis—this time in the realm of thought and in a wider circle than in the three previous syntheses, for this included Indian as well as Chinese factors.

With the opening century of the Sung dynasty (960–1279) Neo-Confucianism began to take shape as a system of thought.

Cosmology

It began with cosmology, based on a Taoist mystic diagram. This was further elaborated from the appendices of the ancient classic of divination, the Yi Ching.

These contained a mention of the Supreme Ultimate, which produced the Yin and Yang, which in turn produced the five elements, then all things.

Man alone received these in their highest excellence. The method of spiritual cultivation was by quiescence, to have no desires.

The ultimate purpose was to teach men how to reach Confucian sagehood. This paralleled the idea of Buddhahood, but while Buddhahood was cultivated outside society, the Sage functioned within the field of the social relations.

A second system of cosmology grew out of the trigrams originally used in divination, which were now given a philosophical significance. It held that everything involves its own negation, not to bring about something new, but merely to bring it back to the original starting point. The new repeats the old.

A third theory was that of an original ether, which condensed to form concrete things, and dispersed to cause their dissolution, the void being not an absolute vacuum, but this ether in its state of dispersal. All things were constituted of this same ether. Men and all other things were all parts of the one great body. Hence all men should be regarded as brothers.

All three cosmologies arose from the appendices of the Yi Ching.

The Confucian Sage understood this cycle of the ether. He remained within it and led a normal life. The Buddhist tried to be outside the cycle, and thus break the chain of causation and bring life to an end—not merely this life but the series of reincarnations. The Taoist sought life extension—the prolongation of this present human life.

Neo-Confucianism developed two schools: the school of ideas or principles and the school of mind.

School of Ideas

This school developed earlier with Cheng Yi (d. 1108) and Chu Hsi (d. 1200). It became the dominant school.

It goes back to the question of universals with which the School of Names had wrestled during the time of the Warring States. However, it was not descended from the School of Names but from the Yi Appendices of Han times. It took a thousand years for Chinese thinkers to get back to the problem of ideas.

It was based on the idea of Tao in the Yi Appendices, which was the unitary first "that" from which all things in the universe came to be. The Tao was multiple. It thus constituted the principles (li) which governed each separate category of things in the universe. This had a remote resemblance to the *dharma* (elements) of early Buddhism.

This was then related to the ether cosmology. When the ether condenses to form concrete things, why are they different? Because each has its own principle according to which the condensation takes place. Hence principle and ether correspond to form and matter.

The principles are eternal. There are principles for things before the things themselves exist. Prior to the human invention of ships and carts, the principles of ships and carts were already in being.

But for the universe as a whole there must also be an ultimate standard, embracing all the principles, and the highest summation of all of them. This is the Supreme Ultimate. It unites and embraces the principles of heaven and earth and all things.

Fung states that the Supreme Ultimate in Chu Hsi's system corresponds to the Idea of the Good or of God in the systems of Plato and Aristotle respectively, but Chu Hsi's idea is more mystical. He states:

> There is one Supreme Ultimate which is received by the individuals of all things. This one Supreme Ultimate is received by each individual in its entirety and undivided.

School of Mind

The School of Mind was a later development begun by a contemporary of Chu Hsi, Lu Ching-yuen, and completed by Wang Shou-jen three hundred years later.

Both Lu and Wang came to their point of view as the result, of an experience of sudden enlightenment, and placed the emphasis on intuition.

Where Chu Hsi said "the nature is Li," Lu held that "the mind is Li." For Chu Hsi reality consists of two worlds, abstract and concrete. For Lu there is only one, which is mind. They emphasized the term "original mind," originally a Ch'an (Zen) Buddhist term.

An official asked Lu about this, and had to interrupt their conversation to pass judgment in a law case. When he finished, Lu told him:

"Just now in pronouncing your verdict you knew right was right, and wrong was wrong. It was your original mind."

"Is there anything else?" asked the official.

Lu shouted at him.

"What else do you want?"

And he was suddenly enlightened.

Wong Shou-jen (1472–1528) brought this school to its full development. He held that every man has this intuitive knowledge. The important thing was the "extension of intuitive knowledge," not through the Buddhist methods of meditation but by the experience of daily life. When the intuitive knowledge knows a course of action to be right, it must be extended or implemented by doing it at once.

This was a Confucian parallel of Ch'an Buddhism. Mencius had spoken of "establishing the most important." This was now to be accomplished by sudden enlightenment. When this was attained, Confucian teaching became irrelevant. As Lu put it, "the six Classics become merely one's footnotes."

Prof. Fung comments that they became "more Taoistic than the Tao and more Buddhistic than the Buddha." Later under the Manchu dynasty there was a reaction.

Ming

The Ming was a Chinese dynasty and was a period of reconstruction, when China returned to normal boundaries and the implications of Chinese culture were developed. There was a moderate amount of creative activity.

But it was a period specially notable for scholarship which turned out an immense volume of encyclopedias, gazetteers and the like. This was the result of a great advance in education, in which the growing middle class had an increasing part. There were an average of 280 "doctoral" passes per year, a total of 25,000 for the period. There were 200,000 scholars of whom half were officials, in addition to some 80,000 military officials.

Wang Shou-jen brought the Mind School of neo-Confucianism to its fruition, as has been indicated above.

Jesuit missionaries brought the European renaissance to China.

Manchu

The Manchu dynasty produced literature sharply different from previous works. Realism was its basis, experience as contrasted with bookish knowledge based on the classics.

This was carried into classical studies with an emphasis of historical criticism and a critical methodology. There were 179 schools of thought.

Huge reference works were carried to completion under imperial auspices, with 361 editors and a large number of scholars over a period of twenty years. This included 6,109 items under 32 classifications; and contained about three times as much material as the Encyclopaedia Britannica. This was in part a plan of the emperor of a conquering dynasty to keep scholars occupied.

The emperor Ch'ien Lung ordered a literary inquisition that destroyed all books dealing with foreign conquerors that might tend to make Chinese readers discontented with foreign rule.

The Confucian orthodoxy of the Manchu dynasty revolted against neo-Confucianism and attacked it as misrepresenting Confucianism, calling Chu Hsi a Taoist monk and Lu Chin-yuan a Buddhist monk. This was a result of growing cultural and social conservatism.

This led to a conflict between Han Scholarship and Sung Scholarship. The "back to Han" movement emphasized critical scholarship and the actual meaning. They first studied the Confucian school, then turned to Moh Ti and others. There was a trend to Confucian religion.

The Sung Scholarship emphasized the philosophical interpretation of the ancient texts. This had religious implications.

6

The Dynamics of Chinese Thought

The history of Chinese thought reveals certain long-term trends. Some of these have been indicated earlier, but will come out more clearly in a summary.

The establishment of the empire, 221 B.C., marks the main turning-point in the history of Chinese thought.

The transition from the Warring States to the absolutism of the centralized empire was paralleled by the change from the creative thinking of the philosophers to the orthodoxy of the classics.

During the period of disunity, 220–589 A.D., neo-Taoism and the coming of Buddhism and Indian thought led to considerable freedom. But even then, and still more when Confucianism again became dominant during the T'ang, advanced thinking tended to take the form of commentaries on the classics. And in the Sung dynasty synthesis, which was largely in the realm of ideas, Neo-Confucianism was essentially a reading of selected Buddhist and Taoist ideas back into selected classics, thus producing the "Four Books" which became the basis of Confucian orthodoxy.

This classical emphasis has been the basis of much of China's conservatism, and greatly handicapped scholars in dealing with the modern situation, which was something totally different.

From Diviner to Scholar

The first intellectuals were diviners. Archivists were perhaps equally early, but their intellectual activities were more routine and mechanical.

But while divination continued to be used, scholarship gradually established its own standards. The teaching and debates of Confucius and the wandering scholars of his day rationalized and depersonalized the earlier notions, and subjected them to questioning and criticism.

The burning of the books by the First Emperor, and the necessity of piecing them together under the Han resulted in the beginnings of textual criticism and the development of a critical methodology.

Chinese scholars have been indefatigable in piling up commentaries, dictionaries, anthologies, encyclopedias, bibliographies, library catalogues, and essays on every conceivable subject.

Sense of History

The work of the archivists in recording annals, established the Chinese urge to date everything, and this sense of history was greatly enhanced by Confucius, who studied the past as a guide for the present.

Here again the establishment of the empire formed a dividing line and changed the writing of history from day by day chronicles to a systematized account of government, society and institutions. The first dynastic history was written during the Former Han dynasty, and China has today the most extensive documentation of its history of any nation in the world.

Humanistic Trend

Together with critical scholarship and a sense of history was a humanistic trend. Confucius rationalized the Chinese social order. The essence of his teaching was the five relationships. His attention was fixed so intently on these that for him, the supernatural was out of focus.

Agnosticism was followed by scepticism. But no positive religious answer was formulated, which left the door open for the continuance of many superstitions.

The Taoists were more wild and fantastic. But Taoist philosophy developed an abstract and impersonal idea of the Tao as the world-order, and the Taoist religion split off and became the receptacle for superstitions of all kinds.

The Chinese are a religious people, but have left religion largely on this low level.

Education

There is no country in the world where scholarship is held in greater honor.

Confucius, the most typical Chinese, was a teacher, the first to make it a profession and livelihood, and receive pay from his pupils.

Education has always tended to be aristocratic in character, and to be the monopoly of the gentry, but by the time of the Ming dynasty many of the middle class were able to get sufficient education to pass the civil service examinations.

However, it maintained a considerable measure of aristocratic character up to 1948. This was enhanced by the fact that the state could not provide funds for universal education, and above the primary it remained a special privilege. High schools could admit only one in three or four who applied, colleges, one in ten.

The main goal of education was still official position. The graduates were "expectant officials." This, along with ancient tradition and the aristocratic background of many of the students themselves, combined to give students a special pride, a special prestige, and a special influence.

While the graduate awaited official appointment, he taught. As an official he continued to be a scholar. It was the age-long tradition. This landlord-scholar-official class has played its predominant part in the life of the nation.

Utopian Aspect of Sources

In the approach to an understanding of China, the above trends must be kept in mind, and in addition it is necessary to take into account certain aspects of the source materials, particularly for the history of the period before the empire.

We do not have a single document that can be considered first-hand and untampered with. Historians, archeologists, exegetes remain impregnated with traditional piety. They present the objective facts, but also an ideal that precedes history. Our sources have a certain utopian character. They reveal a noble philosophy of history.

Practical Character of Chinese Thought

It has been emphasized above that Confucianism was a rationalization of the structure of Chinese society, and the Legalists rationalized the trend of the times that gave birth to the centralized empire. In these regards Chinese thought was realistic and had its feet firmly planted on the ground. This gave unity and strength to

Chinese culture, and was an important factor in its stability and long historic continuation.

Effect of Classical Emphasis

This factor of stability was enhanced by the emphasis on the classics which held before successive centuries the original and basic clan relationships and Confucian ethic. In education the classics constituted a compact body of knowledge that was memorized, and still is. Education thus aimed to turn out men of character and high ideals rather than specialists in political science or pedagogy. It emphasized memory more than originality. All of this made for conservatism.

Technique of Writing

The earliest known Chinese writing appears on the oracle bones of the Shang period, but must have developed earlier, perhaps even before the beginning of the Hsia period, 1994 B.C.

China has no dead language. There has been a continuous development, and a considerable part of the characters on the oracle bones can be read with little difficulty by modern scholars.

The Chinese written characters may be described as stylized pictographs, or better as ideographs, in that they portray ideas. They vary greatly in complexity, some of them being written with one or two strokes and others requiring as many as thirty. There are some fifty thousand of them. A modern newspaper uses an average of four thousand.

The earliest known characters were written on tortoise shell, the shoulder blades of deer, or other flat bones. Next in antiquity come inscriptions on bronze vessels. Still later narrow strips of wood or bamboo were used, bound together by thongs or cord and folded up something like an accordion. Still later silk came into use.

The writing was incised with a stylus, which doubtless contributed to its terse and cryptic style. Later the brush-pen was used.

At first there were many local variations in the form of the written characters. Upon the establishment of the Empire in 221 B.C., these were standardized, in order to provide literary unification to parallel the political unification.

Paper was invented in 156 A.D. This was cheaper and more convenient and rapidly superseded the other materials in China and gradually spread throughout the world, although it did not reach Europe until over a thousand years later. Printing was invented about 600 A.D. This with the use of paper was one of the great contributions of China.

The use of paper greatly increased the number of books available and therefore promoted the spread of scholarship and the intellectual activities of an increasingly larger group of literati and officials.

Ideographic Basis of Political Unification

Perhaps the greatest of Chinese achievements has been the unification both politically and culturally of one-quarter of the human race.

The chief factor here is that the Chinese written characters convey an idea and are not the transcription of a sound as in the Western languages.

As the area of Chinese political control gradually extended to include more and more barbarian tribes, the process of acculturation was greatly facilitated and speeded up by the fact that Chinese written characters could be immediately used to write all of the words in their vocabularies, pronouncing them first in their own way, but gradually learning the Chinese pronunciation as well. Thus the language itself permitted diversity in unity. Dialects could be written the same but pronounced differently. This enabled peoples of different cultures and dialects to come together and get on together.

It has helped to make the Chinese the most reasonable of peoples.

Inefficiency of Ideographs

The Chinese written characters are very difficult to learn, requiring years of arduous work. This gives them something of the character of a secret code, which enabled a comparatively small group of literati to develop and maintain a practical monopoly of official position, constituting the bureaucracy that has administered the government of China for twenty centuries.

In addition, there is the problem of the special vocabulary of the literary language which was different from the language of ordinary speech. Thus the dog-in-the-street familiarly known as *geo* became *chwan* on the printed page. The verb "is" became the demonstrative pronoun "this." The pronoun meaning "he, she or it" became an adjective meaning "other."

In addition to all this, official communications had to be in a still more highly stylized vocabulary. This gave the literati an additional hold on their monopoly.

Under modern conditions the written character is very inefficient, and it would be much better to change to the Roman characters used in the West. This continues to be opposed by the scholarly class in China, an opposition based to a large extent on the monopoly of learning and the positions of various sorts derived from it, which they still hold.

There is another consideration. These characters are regarded not only as a medium of communication but as a form of art. Many modern Chinese still spend a regular period every day in writing them so as to develop an elegant penmanship. Beautiful calligraphy is much admired, and scrolls by famous writers are hung on the wall the same as pictures in the West, and are even more highly regarded.

In the literary renaissance movement which began about 1918, Dr. Hu Shih and its other leaders began to write in the language of common speech. This constituted a long step in advance, and the practice has come into general use.

The modern newspaper use of four thousand characters has resulted in a streamlined journalistic language, halfway between ordinary speech and the literary language.

The characters are hard to learn and easily forgotten. It is said that English spelling requires a good part of an additional year for its mastery as compared with German. It seems likely that the Chinese character requires an additional year above English. As long as this concerned only the literati who made it their profession and had a monopoly on learning, it did not make so much difference. When universal education is contemplated, the costs of the additional year of teaching runs into a prohibitive figure, not to mention the loss of student time in a country where apprentices leave school early to begin work.

Where speed is of the essence, the Chinese character is still less efficient. It does not lend itself to the modern methods of typewriter or linotype.

Thus in a national conference of a thousand delegates, where it was necessary that reports of the previous day and recommendations of committees which might not have adjourned until late the previous night, be brought before the entire body for action, I edited a daily paper in English that made this possible and put all of this material in printed form into the hands of the delegates as they entered the convention hall at 9:00 o'clock. The parallel Chinese paper which was planned and in charge of an able editor, broke down entirely as it was impossible to get the type-setting done fast enough.

For the same reason, many smaller national conferences were conducted in English if possible, as this permitted a rapid dictating, typing, and copying of recommendations so that the conference could vote on them in written form and know exactly what it was doing. In addition, this constituted a record which could be taken home at once to serve as a basis for immediate action, whereas Chinese minutes and reports would not be available for weeks.

Language as Related to Thought

The nature of the Chinese written language and its limitations have their effect on Chinese thought.

In Chinese the term for "logic" is literally "the study of terms," logical problems having first arisen as problems about terms rather than about judgments. This is partly because it is monosyllabic and uninflected. Relations are expressed either through position or by what are called in Chinese "empty characters," each of which has various meanings and uses, as prepositions, conjunctions, adverbs, or interjections, and are rather vague. Indeed the meaning must be gathered in part from position. Hence the relational aspects of knowledge are obscured by the language structure, especially in the literary language.

Nothing in Chinese corresponds to the sentence as the fundamental element in composition. Its place is taken by the clause or phrase, and phrase after phrase may be strung together. There are, of course, complete thoughts that would make a sentence in English, but Chinese does not force thought into the form of a complete and rounded sentence, but goes on, phrase after phrase, in a less organized manner.

The sentence is a logical form into which the English language compels us to throw our thought. Chinese writing is more like the stream of thought. It does not need to be congealed in sentences; its clauses need not have a subject or a predicate. What would be to us illogical construction may be used with perfect propriety.

PART IV

BREAK-UP AND ATTEMPTS AT SYNTHESIS

A peasant rising in 1774 began the break-up of the Manchu dynasty, and presaged the end which came 135 years later in 1911.

From 1880 to 1949 repeated attempts were made to synthesize old and new—by beginnings of industrialization, restoring a Chinese dynasty, the Boxer rebellion, the establishment of a republic.

The Nationalist Movement, during the years 1927–37, came the closest to a real and lasting synthesis, but Japanese and Communist attacks prevented.

Mao mobilized a peasant army in the interior and attacked the Nationalists from the rear.

The Japanese pressure forced the Nationalists into the interior. This lost them their base, the new industrial and business class along the coast. This class was largely ruined by the war, and this left the Nationalists no foundation on which to rebuild.

The Communists posed as the real resistance to Japan, and forced the Nationalists into a second united front. This legalized their position, safeguarded them from attack, and enabled them to increase their forces so that they outnumbered the Nationalists at the end of the war.

The agreement at Yalta gave Russia control in Manchuria, and made possible the turning over to the Chinese Communists of the great arsenals of the Japanese in Manchuria. This was decisive in bringing about the Nationalist defeat.

1

Break-up and Abortive Attempts at Synthesis

The break-up of the Manchu dynasty was due in large part to the usual forces that operated toward the end of the dynastic cycle—imperial letdown, bureaucratic inefficiency, economic distress.

The fifth synthesis of Chinese history was already overdue.

The descending curve of the dynastic cycle coincided in time with the rising curve of the expansion of the modern world with its imperialism, colonialism and spheres of influence. China was brought into the complex of world forces against its will, particularly after the opium war and the "unequal treaties" of 1842.

The problem of overpopulation had increased in magnitude. New external problems had arisen, for the solution of which Chinese history furnished no precedents—reform of government, industrial revolution, modernization of education, foreign imperialism.

Here was a complex of conflicting forces that rendered abortive a series of attempts at reconstruction and synthesis. These new forces were unknown or only partially understood and were on a scale unprecedentedly vast. In their totality they were beyond the grasp of those who had to grapple with them.

Peasant Revolts

The Manchu dynasty, established 1644, reached its apex under the able Emperor Ch'ien Lung who reigned 1736–1795. The beginning of the decline may be dated as of 1774, the year of the first great peasant revolt, in Shantung. This was followed the next year by one under the White Lotus Society in Honan, which spread to six provinces and was not suppressed until 1802 after heavy fighting. A new rising came under another secret society, the Society of

Heaven's Law in 1813, and there were Mohammedan risings in the northwest in 1825 and 1845.

Then came the great T'ai P'ing rebellion, beginning in Hunan in 1848 and not suppressed until 1864, after it had established its rule over a large part of South China and laid waste several provinces and cost 20,000,000 lives. This too had a religious background, the leader calling himself "Christ's younger brother." A large factor in their defeat was their own lack of effective organization and leadership.

In the north was an uprising under another secret society, 1855–1858, and in the west there were five Mohammedan revolts, 1864–1895. These were all suppressed, but at great cost, and the dynasty was weakened.

Overpopulation

Back of all this was the inexorable pressure of population increase—from 112 million in 1685 to 300 million in 1872. This resulted in a sharp decrease of per capita acreage: (one acre is six mou)

1685	5.48 mou
1776	4.07 "
1872	2.49 "

A major cause was the introduction of new high-yield crops from the West—including corn, sweet potatoes, peanuts. There has been nothing in China of the nature of birth control, for Confucianism advocated large families. The only limitation was food supply, lacking which the weaker children did not survive. The new and greater food supply thus resulted in a sharp population increase.

This was augmented by 150 years of peace under the early Manchu emperors, for war had always been a prime factor in holding down the population.

Property did not go intact to the eldest son, but was divided among all the sons, and the increased population resulted in a fragmentation of holdings, which soon became too small for even a minimum food supply. This cause was not realized by the Manchu government who considered these risings as nationalistic movements against their alien dynasty. It was not realized by the people who blamed the foreign rulers for all these evils.

Foreign Imperialism

The situation in China now became part of the world situation and the pressure on China may be dated from the Treaty of Nanking in 1842, which ceded Hongkong to Britain and opened a number of treaty ports, where foreign concessions flourished under extraterritoriality. One of the reasons for this was the desire of foreign traders to import opium into China as the easiest way to pay for the silk and tea they were buying in quantity. This led to greatly increased use of opium, so that by 1923 the poppy occupied two-thirds of the cultivated land in Yunnan in the winter. This increased the food shortage.

Gentry Reformers

The first attempt at a synthesis came after the T'ai P'ing rebellion and was made by a group of scholar-officials. They too overlooked the problem of overpopulation and aimed at industrialization and military and political reorganization.

Their Confucian training and official experience did not fit them to solve the problem of industrialization. The change-over from the traditional setup to a modern industrial economy involved serious readjustments. It was not merely a question of raw materials, skilled labor and management. It involved the reorganization of fundamental gentry attitudes.

First was the characteristic attitude of government officials. Government enterprises, such as the salt monopoly, were administered by officials selected by the examination system on the basis of classical and literary ability, not for technical training. They were not interested so much in production as in achieving the measure of success that would forward their own official careers. They considered government office the easier or even the only way to acquire great fortune.

Second, family considerations entered in. Technical efficiency was sacrificed to the Confucian virtue of nepotism. Not to give preference to relatives violated basic human relationships. Graft in the Western sense did not appear that way from the Chinese point of view. An official received merely a nominal salary and was expected to make it up. He was not told how much tax to levy, merely how much to remit. Official position was the road to wealth for the official and his clan.

But in modern industry the old considerations of family-first are out of place. The industrial mechanism is interlocking and one inefficient worker can throw production lines out of gear. In its army of workers personal relationships do not count. Only skill and efficiency. There is thus a basic maladjustment and contradiction between nepotism and technical efficiency.

Third, the gentry viewpoint was local. They were not organized for action on a nationwide basis, and their main concern was their own clan. Shih states:

> For centuries the Chinese economic system had not been developed beyond the stage of self-sufficient family units, and enterprise consisted merely of the petty dealings of peasants and handicraftsmen in the local markets and small towns. The vast country households clustered around villages which, in turn, were bound together by kinship ties.
>
> These self-sufficient units kept the whole economic system in an almost static condition and on a very low level. Under these circumstances it was almost impossible to accumulate great wealth.
>
> The kinship system was the dominant institutional pattern and served as the ethical basis. No economic activity could be carried on without regard to reciprocal obligation to one's kinsmen.

Thus a Hanlin scholar petitioned that the part of a railroad passing through his province should be run by the people of the province.

Fourth, the gentry industrial pioneers were naïve in the field of economics, and tended to view it from the point of view of an economy of scarcity in an agricultural society, or of government monopoly administered by officials.

In addition to these gentry attitudes there was the resistance of tradition. This was on three levels: officials, gentry, and the masses. The officials acted through governmental channels. The gentry used the boycott. The masses rioted.

This resistance was generally too much for the merchants, and hence the early industrial leaders of China came from the official class. Thus twelve out of nineteen cotton mills were established 1897–1910 by officials and only two by merchants and small gentry.

Thus the attempt at a synthesis that would save the situation by industrialization did not get very far. The gentry were disqualified by the limitation of their past, and the growing middle class of merchants was not yet strong enough. Confucian attitudes would not fit the requirements of modern industry.

The Hundred Days Reform

On the political side the scholar-official reformers were reinforced by a revolutionary movement, largely financed from overseas and led by K'ang Yu-Wei, which constituted a second attempt at a synthesis. This culminated in the Hundred Days Reform from June 11, 1898, during which the emperor, under the influence of a group led by K'ang, issued reform decrees by the dozen, aimed at a political modernization of the government. This was betrayed by Yuan Shih-kai, and the emperor was imprisoned by the Empress Dowager, who resumed the supreme authority.

The Boxer Uprising

The third attempt at a synthesis was the Boxer Uprising, a throwback to primitive superstition embodied in Taoist secret societies, and authorized by the Empress Dowager. It failed.

The scholar-officials, the monarchist reformers, and the Empress Dowager had now tried their hands at meeting the situation. Something more drastic was indicated. These were attempts to bring the new forces into a synthesis based on the old pattern, chiefly Confucian. But this was too rigid, and not easily adaptable to modern conditions.

The Japanese Example

The scholar-official reformers were greatly impressed by the success of Japan after 1868 in building a strong modern state. But Japan was small and compact, and it was only a partial, German-style, technical and military modernization, implemented by an efficient school system. Then the Meiji Emperor took the lead in modernization, and had the prestige of divinity, whereas in China the dogma of the "Mandate of Heaven" opened the way for revolution. Furthermore, the Chinese gentry were merely scholar-bureaucrats, and lacked the military strength of the Japanese daimyo and samurai. The Chinese word now used for the literati means "knight," but has long since lost its military aspect.

So the Japanese example did not fit the Chinese situation.

The Republic

The fourth attempt at bringing about a synthesis was made by Sun Yat-sen who found his inspiration in America, and aimed to turn China into a republic.

Sun was not primarily an intellectual and was influenced by what he saw of the American way of life rather than by theories about it. However, in 1905, in his Three People's Principles, which covered nationalism, democracy, and the people's livelihood, he presented a formulation that included the economic problem and a considerable measure of socialism, but in a rather general and theoretical way. But it was not generally accepted until the middle 1920's and remained vague and ineffectual until implemented by the Nationalist Movement.

Secret Societies

It has been pointed out above that the only basis for concerted action arising from among the people was through secret societies. These were extensively utilized by Sun Yat-sen. Those in America and the South Seas provided the money and are estimated to have contributed over ten million dollars. Those in China were brought together in an underground revolutionary organization which served as the basis for some ten abortive attempts at revolution.

Secret societies had turned to political action when the rule of the alien Mongol dynasty led to underground movements that were a considerable factor in its overthrow and the re-establishment of a Chinese dynasty, the Ming. Under the alien Manchu dynasty they again became secret revolutionary parties, and by 1761 were so strong that the emperor attempted to repress them and issued an edict decreeing decapitation for any one found to be a member. The T'ai-p'ings were in this succession. They had an oath of blood brotherhood:

> Henceforth I am one with the family of Hung. Its friends are my friends, its foes my foes. Where the brothers lead I will follow.

Hung was the name of the first Ming emperor, and became a symbol of the restoration of a Chinese dynasty. When the T'ai-p'ing leader became emperor he took the name Hung.

Sun Yat-sen was also in this succession. He always said his father was a Christian. He probably was a T'ai-p'ing Christian.

The most important and widespread of these secret societies was the Hung League. Two incidents testify to the significance of this name. When Sun Yat-sen later turned over the presidency to Yuan Shih-kai, his last official act was a ceremonial visit to the tomb of the first Ming emperor in Nanking. This showed his respect for the Hung League, and this visit was the symbol of the realization of their objective. Again, when Yuan had himself proclaimed emperor, he called his new dynasty Hung Hsien. This was to gain the support of the Hung League.

Revolt from the South

It is to be noted that Sun's revolution, and the Nationalist Movement later, began in South China, although there had been a succession of peasant uprisings in the north for over a hundred years as indicated above.

This is related to the long-standing differences between north and south, and to the fact that the south was more recently and less completely sinicized. This appeared in the Manchu division of the population into four classes: Manchus, peoples of northwest China and Central Asia, North Chinese, and South Chinese. The North Chinese had been the first to be conquered and had offered the least resistance, perhaps because during the period of disunion (220–589) some fifteen out of seventeen dynasties that ruled North China had been alien, and during the Southern Sung Dynasty all North China had been ruled by Tartars. During such periods large numbers of the original Chinese families had fled south. This was true of a large number of Ming patriots also.

This difference was accentuated by the fact that large numbers from the south had gone overseas, and were in touch with western governmental and industrial conditions, and were in a position to supply both revolutionary ideas and money to put them into effect.

Another difference appeared when, about 1915, Chiang Kai-shek went on a secret mission to North China with the object of bringing

North China into the Republic, and found that the secret societies had never been organized in Manchuria, and there was little chance of stirring up revolt among soldiers or people.

After one of the early revolts which he engineered in Canton in 1895 had ended in fiasco, Sun began to realize that it would take a long time. So during the years that followed, one of his close associates traveled all over South China, meeting with leaders of branches of the Hung League. Sun stated the case thus:

> In China the job of spreading revolutionary propaganda is even more difficult than among the overseas Chinese. Outside the members of the secret societies, no one in China will listen to anti-Manchu or revolutionary speeches.

The Hung League included the lower classes. K'ang Yu-wei, who was still agitating for the restoration of a Chinese dynasty, scorned the uneducated and would have nothing to do with the Hung League.

But all Sun's attempts, through uprisings at one city or another, failed, largely through the inexperience of those who led them, who did not know how to plan and organize the seizure of power. They were largely local and isolated. But he kept on trying, chiefly through raising funds abroad to finance yet another effort, and his underground organization spread more widely.

End of the Empire

The Manchu dynasty was now in a virtual condition of collapse, but continued in a state of inertia, waiting for some one to give the final push. This came from a local situation in the centrally located city of Wuchang, and this time quickly spread to a number of other centers.

Thus, a couple of weeks later, Chiang Kai-shek led a band of a hundred two "dare-to-dies" organized by the Hung League in Hangchow, captured the governor's yamen, and took over Hangchow for the revolution. He then got an army together in Shanghai, under Ch'en Chi-mei as commander-in-chief, which consisted largely of members of a branch of the Hung League, known as the Blues.

Just as in business the scholar-officials were locally minded, so in political matters there was no national movement. The revolution was more of a concatenation of fortuitous circumstances, and in the end the final push came from a local situation, when regional interests opposed centralized control over a railway; Rostow states:

> The dynasty fell only because the reformers' purpose briefly converged with the interests of regional groups who had become powerful through the dilution or destruction of the power of the central dynastic rule over their areas.

So the Chinese empire, established 211 B.C. came to an end in 1911, after 2,132 years.

The Republic

The Republic of China, was proclaimed on February 12, 1912, with Sun as president.

Now that the revolution was accomplished, Sun changed the revolutionary name of his organization, Tung Meng Hui, to Kuomintang, National Peoples Party, usually designated as the Nationalists. This party, while no longer secret in the former fashion, still retained many of its exclusive characteristics, and was not an organization to which any one could adhere on his own initiative as is the case with American political parties.

Frustrated Revolutionaries

The overthrow of the Manchus did not bring the hoped-for result. China's ills were more deep-seated than merely the oppression of an alien rule—which indeed had become largely Chinese.

The Republic, too, was a disappointment. It merely changed the signboard outside government offices. Inside, the same staffs carried on much as before. Officials trained in the technique of democratic government simply were not available, except for a few key positions. Progress was inevitably slow.

For example: an order to take part in a provincial school census came to the district magistrate in the interior city where I was then living. He was a well-meaning official trained in the old school, with a smattering of modern education and a slight knowledge of German, who owed his position to an uncle in the provincial government. He gave the census-takers a sketchy training and sent them forth.

The villagers were suspicious of all government action, which usually meant trouble for them. Then the rumor started and spread through the province like wildfire that the names of the children taken in the census were to be deposited in the foundation piers of the proposed railway bridge over the big river, whereupon the children would shortly die and their souls go to reside in their names, thus ensuring the lasting stability of the bridge—a superstition common to both China and the West. Census-takers were attacked. Schools were wrecked or burned so that a considerable portion of the schools in the province were unable to open that fall.

Our magistrate sought resolutely to carry the census through and went in person to enlighten and reassure the villagers, or if they proved obdurate, to arrest the ringleaders and restore order. But the villagers were beyond any possibility of listening to reason, and arose in desperate defense of the lives of their children and fell upon the magistrate himself, smashed his official sedan-chair, and beat him to the ground, so that his escort had the greatest difficulty in rescuing him and making a hurried retreat. The census lapsed into chaos.

This was merely a minor matter of routine. More important problems presented greater difficulties.

The Party Lacked an Army

A strong national government would have made a great difference, but the central government of the new Republic of China was hopelessly weak. In the emphasis upon the civilian bureauracy of scholar-officials that had run the government of the centralized empire, it was overlooked that a dynasty had always been established by force, and could maintain itself only so long as it could keep an army in being at the capital that could impose its will.

But the Republic had been established by what was merely a political party that depended on democratic theory—a party that had no army. Thus it came about that Sun, duly elected president, stepped aside in favor of Yuan Shih-kai, the general in control of the armed forces in the capital.

Politics gave way to military force, and that phase of the revolution was finished.

Sun's revolution failed for lack of organization. The army was not controlled by a disciplined political organization loyal to Sun Yat-sen's party or its broad aims. This lack of organization goes back to the unicellular clan structure of Chinese society, with its narrow localism, enhanced by the Taoist anarchy and non-action. This lack of organization had been a large factor in the fall of the T'ai-p'ings. It was to plague the Nationalists.

War Lords

Yuan took over as president, but very soon began to maneuver to make himself emperor and establish a new dynasty. This represents a fifth attempt at a synthesis, and was again a throwback to the earlier pattern. However, the sentiment of the country was against it, and his attempt failed.

When Yuan died in 1916, no successor was strong enough to dominate the whole country, and power fell into the hands of war lords, each controlling as much territory as he could. This was the traditional localism and regionalism, more rampant for lack of an empire to tie it together.

This weakness was exploited by "foreign imperialism," especially by Japan, who took advantage of the confusion of the world war to make serious encroachments. This touched off a student movement in 1919 and boycott of Japanese goods that roused the national anger and added to the national frustration. No one else did anything. The war lords continued to bicker. China continued to drift.

2

The Nationalist Synthesis

After Yuan's death in 1916, a succession of war lords rose and fell in various areas, and a figurehead government went through the motions in Peking. So Sun Yat-sen decided that it was necessary to begin over again in the south, and set up a government in Canton with the object of eventually uniting China as a whole.

He also reorganized the Kuomintang on much the same lines as his previous revolutionary secret societies, but with the personal oath not so strong, and fewer restrictions on membership than formerly.

The Kuomintang represented the new development of business and industrialization. Taylor characterizes it thus:

> The KMT represented the political and economic interests of the one new social class in China, the middle class, which had grown up under the impact of western imperialism and secured a share of political power in 1928. This middle class was always tied in with the Chinese scholar gentry officialdom . . . by 1937 . . . the middle class had made considerable inroads on Chinese traditional society.

This was the class that had been modernizing most rapidly and making the most progress. It was the essential factor in any synthesis.

However, the fact that it was a middle-class party led to emphasis on urban and industrial problems, and mitigated against an understanding of the agrarian situation, and the formation of a sufficiently drastic program to deal with it.

The Canton Government

The new Canton government controlled only a single province, but made progress. Sun and his associates now came to realize that an army of their own was necessary and established the Whompoa Military Academy with Chiang Kai-shek at the head.

This was the real beginning of the Nationalist Movement, which was another attempt at a synthesis. For a while the Nationalist Movement showed great promise, and would probably have succeeded but for the tragic pressure of world events. This, of course, is hindsight.

A large part of the revenue of the Central Government came from the customs receipts at the various treaty ports. Sun's government in Canton had no money, while customs income continued to be remitted to the figurehead government in Peking. So Sun tried to seize the Canton customs house. But this income secured foreign loans and the foreign powers intervened. He tried to get the needed funds through a loan from the United States. But in vain.

It was at this point that Sun lost faith in the Western democracies and turned to Russia.

Communist Beginnings in China

Democracy had not gotten off to a good start in China, but became associated in the minds of the people with instability, war lordism, and a growing feeling of frustration.

This was particularly the case with the intellectuals who had taken an important part in the Revolution. They were more conscious than any other group of the impact of the West, and resented it the more bitterly because of inherited pride in their long cultural heritage and centuries-old feeling of superiority.

A new national spirit was in the making. Love of country was reinforced by the demands of their own pride that China be able to stand on its own feet, "beat down foreign imperialism," and face the world on a basis of equality.

But they faced only further national indignities, and became disillusioned over the way one national government after another was taken into camp by the old bureaucratic crowd at Peking, who were the only ones who knew how to run the national government, and continued to do so in the time-honored fashion, while the regional war lords continued to rule their territories as they pleased, and all were powerless to resist Japanese aggression.

It was the students who started an anti-Japanese movement on May 4, 1919, and took the lead in boycotting Japanese goods.

Up to this time Chinese intellectuals had paid little attention to Marxism. Now in their frustration, they were immensely impressed by the success of Lenin in seizing power and organizing the government. Perhaps here was the formula they needed. Its positive plan of action was in sharp contrast with the laissez-faire democracy, free individualism, slow process of education, and Christian dynamic that they had learned from the West. It was getting results in Russia.

So an outstanding reformer, Ch'en Tu-hsiu, set up a group for Marxist study in Peking in 1918. It is significant that he was an influential dean in Peking University, the headquarters of the Literary Renaissance, where the student movement originated in 1919. He attended a small conference of a varied group of intellectuals in Shanghai in 1920, which led to the secret organization of the Communist Party in Shanghai in 1921, and his election as chairman of its Central Committee.

They favored cooperation with the Kuomintang, and emissaries from Russia took the same line which led to talks between Sun and the Russian Joffe.

Kuomintang at Low Ebb

In 1922 the fortunes of Sun and his party were at a low ebb. He was a refugee in Shanghai, expelled from his capital in Canton by the local war lord. His party had no firm support from either the masses or an armed force of its own.

However, the Kuomintang was still, under all the circumstances, the best instrument for the completion of the revolution, and had great potential strength growing out of the revolutionary tradition and prestige of Sun himself. This the Communists recognized.

There were two fundamental needs, organization and military aid. The Russians could give both.

Here the comment of Brandt, Schwartz and Fairbank goes to the point:

> It was precisely because the KMT was organizationally infantile that the Communists undertook to make it "the central force of the national revolution."

For if the organizational apparatus, the mass basis, of the new KMT came under their control, its role of revolutionary leadership would fall to them also.

Russia sent advisers at Sun's invitation, and the Kuomintang was reorganized on Russian lines. Chiang Kai-shek was sent to Russia to observe and learn.

First United Front

The Communist Party now officially joined with the Kuomintang in a United Front. The Communist Party, significantly, was not abolished, but worked vigorously within the KMT as its left wing, secretly looking forward to gaining complete control.

Chiang Kai-shek, the KMT leader after the death of Sun Yat-sen in 1925, began the Northern Expedition in 1926. By the middle of 1927, the Nationalist Government was established in Nanking, after crushing communist unions in Shanghai and dismissing the Russian advisers.

The first United Front thus came to an end.

Chiang Kai-shek took the lead in dismissing the Russians and other communists, and went on to establish his government without them. It is to be noted that at this time began the propaganda against him—personalities, charges of personal graft and inefficiency—that has continued with increasing virulence to the present, and has taken in and misled many. There has been plenty to criticize, but in the judgment of this writer it has been grossly exaggerated.

This postponed the communist control of China for twenty years.

National Unification Through Compromise

At this point the Northern Expedition ended, and the rest of China was brought under nominal Nationalist control through negotiations.

There was a sound reason for this, for the new government aimed to reorganize the provinces it controlled, especially along the lines of financial efficiency that had proved so successful at Canton, and thus make a demonstration that would bring the others into their orbit. The alternative was prolonged civil war with the war lords who had powerful private armies and controlled the rest of the country.

This seemed statesmanlike at the time, but actually left the war lords in power. The Nationalist Government controlled only eight provinces out of twenty-eight. Incidentally, the Nationalists got the blame for the corruption and inefficiency of the war lord regimes.

The Nationalist Government

The problems facing the Nationalist Government were almost insuperable and called for a long-term readjustment. But they were given only four years of peace from their establishment in Nanking in 1927.

They turned to western technology, American education, and in part to Christianity. Taking into account the problems they inherited, the massive nature of the task, and the lack of trained personnel to man the machinery of government, they made far greater progress than they have been given credit for. The majority of government positions—except at top levels—had of necessity to be filled with old-style officials, who went on in the same old way.

It was a time of high endeavor and real advance. So much so that it seemed the part of wisdom to Japan to strike before China got too strong, and in 1931, they invaded Manchuria and attacked Shanghai.

That same year the Chinese Soviet Republic was proclaimed, comprising six districts on the border between Kiangsi and Fukien.

The Nationalist Government, harassed on two sides, struggled on until Japan began full war in 1937, and the government had to move to Chungking, in territory controlled by war lords, who did not want it there and had never given it more than nominal allegiance.

Contrasting Policies

The policies of America and Russia at this time were in sharp contrast.

The Russian method was that of sending advisers, and organizing and directing the Chinese Government, the party, and the military, from the inside.

The attitude of the United States was one of maintaining the "open door" and the integrity of China, so that the Chinese might be free for the slow process of developing democracy themselves, which American friendship sought to encourage.

Americans were particularly interested in the power of education and religion to bring about, from within, that transformation of the individual on which democracy in the long run must depend.

Thirteen Christian colleges and universities (largely American) enrolled one-eighth of all students at the college level in China. The 250 Christian high schools had one-tenth of all high school pupils. Some 250 Christian hospitals treated 2,000,000 persons annually. There were some 8,000 Protestant churches and 7,000 regular preaching places, with over half a million members. Catholics counted some two and a half million. Protestants were only one-tenth of one per cent of the population, but their influence was out of all proportion to their number. One earlier government had a majority of cabinet ministers who were Christian.

The American system of education was adopted. Chinese students flocked to American universities, and American "returned students" began to replace the Japanese "returned students" in important positions.

But the situation was too complex, and even Western practice as a whole is characterized by Rostow as a "confusing mixture of aggression, practical self-interest, and authentic missionary humanitarianism."

Also, those in China who advocated reform had their attention diverted from the basic problem by the issue of what came to be known as "foreign imperialism." China had suffered a series of encroachments and humiliations, which were a terrible blow to the national dignity and to the pride of the scholar-officials.

The Financial Factor

The complexity of the problems facing the Nationalists will appear more clearly from an examination of the financial factor.

The Nationalist Government which was established at Nanking in 1927 possessed the two main requisites for a stable synthesis, an army able to crush revolt and maintain order, led by Chiang Kai-shek, and a modern financial foundation, developed by T. V. Soong.

The new and essential factor was the financial structure.

In Canton, T. V. Soong, on the basis of his Harvard training in business administration, had reorganized things. Hauser states it thus:

> He raised the value of the Canton bank notes from 40 to 100. He brought the provincial revenue from one shabby million up to ten million dollars. In less than two years he multiplied the government's income by twelve. He unified the tax system, he hired spies to prevent corruption. He became indispensable and most unpopular.

He developed the first budget in modern China that did not lean heavily on the land tax.

Chiang Kai-shek and T. V. Soong rose together. Their tasks were complementary. And as the northern expedition took over one province after another, T. V. Soong reorganized their finances on the Canton model. Later, Chiang's break with communism gained the confidence of the Chinese business and banking circles in Shanghai, and enabled Soong to raise a loan for the new government—the first government loan exclusively from Chinese sources.

This financial reconstruction was the real essence of the revolution. Only thus could China make an adjustment to the modern world that would be stable and provide a solid basis that would give the government a chance to deal one by one with the other problems. And a stable government, able to maintain peace and order was the first requisite.

Financial Limitations

The importance of the financial factor cannot be grasped merely by a study of national financial statistics or by their comparison with those of other lands. It is necessary to break them down and interpret them in the light of local situations in China.

The easiest way to tap the new money generated by the new industrialization and commerce was to seize a customs house in a treaty port. This was regularly done by war lord adventurers. But their scope was limited to a relatively narrow circle by the slowness, difficulty, and high cost of transportation. This was true of war lords everywhere, and it was rarely that a war lord could control more than a single province, usually less. The reason was that they could not finance it.

In the old days granaries had sufficed. Soldiers fought with bows and arrows, swords and spears. They traveled light. All that was necessary was to feed them. Now rifles, machine-guns, artillery, and ammunition were necessary. These cost money, and still more money for their transport, especially over any considerable distances. So war lords in west China made the farmers grow opium and trafficked in it. Others collected taxes for tens of years in advance. Even so, they could seldom control as much as a province.

Taxes were incredibly low by Western standards. About 1915 I paid taxes year by year on a chapel with a forty-foot frontage on a main street just outside the gate in the city wall of an interior city of 20,000. The amount was two cents per year.

About 1922 I paid taxes of ten dollars a year on a six-acre high-school campus fronting on one of the main streets of Hangchow, a progressive provincial capital of half a million. The school received no tax exemption. But there was no city water, no sewage system, and the night-soil was carried through the streets in "honey buckets" that stank to heaven. There were only volunteer fire companies. Once our students built a big bonfire to celebrate a football victory. That had never happened before, and we collected six fire companies.

A man came sprinting up with a bamboo ladder over his shoulder and the sweat flying in every direction. He was the hook and ladder department. Two men came trotting along with a big tub suspended from a pole between them on which a pump was mounted, cranked by hand. This was the fire-engine. It was followed by a contingent with buckets hung at each end of their carrying poles. These brought water from the nearest canal and poured it into the engine tub.

This sort of thing was all that the city could afford. The places of business that lined its miles of streets were, with few exceptions, small retail shops or small-scale makers of various wares on a handicraft basis.

Such an economy simply could not pay the taxes necessary to support a modern government.

There is a psychological corollary to be noted in passing. Modern government and its cost in taxes was quite beyond the imagination of the people of that time and place. When the government attempted to approach this, the people reacted according to the only standards they knew, and were sure some tremendous government graft must be involved.

Nationalist Progress

Such were the problems that had to be faced. It was recognized by all concerned that this was necessarily a slow process, and would require a generation or two. Given a large per cent of officials trained in the old ways, it was inevitable that there would be a considerable carryover of inefficiency and corruption. Rostow makes an impressive statement of the "important, and now often forgotten, progress over the decade 1927–1937." He summarized thus:

> Major advances were made in reorganizing relations between China and the foreign powers. . . .
>
> A substantial group of able . . . administrators brought an unprecedented degree of competence and order to the organization of national affairs . . . created a unified national currency . . . proved capable of financing large civil and military operations.
>
> Progress was made in agriculture, industry, transportation, and public health. . . . The underlying social revolution in method of education, position of women, and in social life and culture generally went forward, especially in the cities.
>
> This was the essential synthesis that had to be made—the old China with the new world of the industrial revolution—and they were making it.

With this judgment, Pritchard agrees as follows:

> During the ten years 1928–37 . . . the movement possessed real vitality, and many reforms and projects were instituted which possessed real merit, and which if given time to mature, might have resulted in a new and stable society.

But they were not given time.

3

Mao Mobilizes Rural Riffraff

By February, 1927, sixteen years after the establishment of the Republic, and after five abortive attempts at a synthesis, the Nationalist Movement had entered into a united front with the Chinese Communist Party, had launched the northern expedition which conquered South China, and had established itself in the strategic center of Wuhan which commanded the Yangtze valley. It was now about to receive the submission of the war lords to the north and northwest and thus unify all China—nominally at least.

Thus, at long last, it began to look as if the revolution were really getting somewhere—as if a synthesis had been brought about and only needed to be consolidated.

Disruptive Forces

But disruptive forces were at work from four directions. Japanese aggression had been intensifying and was soon to develop into a military attack that eventually led to open war. Russia was directing the policy of the New Chinese Communist Party along orthodox Russian lines, as was exposed by the discovery in 1927 of secret documents in the Russian embassy in Peking, including orders to secret agents, and which was one of the factors that led Chiang to break with the Communists a few months later.

Workers' strikes and peasant movements continued. One led by the Communist Ping Pai in Kwangtung, beginning in 1921, had 134,000 members in Peasant Associations by 1924, and staged an unsuccessful uprising in 1928.

The fourth disruptive force was that of adventurers and plotters for power, like Yuan Shih-kai and the numerous war lords who followed him. This was the age of Hitler, Mussolini, and Stalin. But this adventurer type had long been a familiar figure in Chinese history.

Professional Communist Revolutionaries

The old adventurer type now took a new form, that of the professional revolutionary. Taylor states it thus:

> The Chinese Communist Party—like all Communist Parties—arose as a small group of professional revolutionaries . . . their common objective was the seizure of power.

They were self-appointed, and represented only themselves—or Moscow—not any section of the Chinese people. To quote Taylor again:

> Those who have urged that the CCP was leading the revolution in the same sense as the KMT . . . have based their argument on a false premise.
>
> The Communists in China, as in Russia, came into power as manipulators of social forces, rather than as representatives of social groups. As professional revolutionaries, they are artists in the creation of social chaos for the purpose of acquiring political power . . .
>
> They cannot be understood . . . unless it is assumed that we are watching a group of self-conscious, highly disciplined men in their search for total power.

One of these was Mao Tse-tung.

Hijacking the Revolution

It was not their revolution—it had preceded the Bolshevik revolution in Russia. They simply hijacked the revolution that had been started and carried on by others. Steiner puts it very moderately as follows.

> Historically the CCP captured the revolutionary forces first unleased between 1898 and 1911 by such "bourgeois" agitators as Liang Ch'i-ch'iao, K'ang Yu-wei, and Sun Yat-sen, and converted them to the service of the Marxist-Leninist world revolution.

Or in the words of another group of authorities on the situation (Brandt, Schwartz and Fairbank):

Leninism is more than a dogma; it is also a way of seizing or holding power under any particular conditions.

This was carried out along two lines. One was the reorganization by Russian advisers and along Russian lines of Sun Yat-sen's Canton government, party, and army, as outlined above. The other was Mao Tse-tung's mobilization of the poorer peasantry in Hunan.

Mao's Report on the Peasant Movement

This is no simple tale of "agrarian reformers," as the world has been tricked into believing. It will be best to begin with Mao's own words, written in February, 1927, his "Report on an Investigation of the Peasant Movement in Hunan," which was published in three Chinese journals; it is the most authoritative statement possible.

This report is in two parts: the agrarian revolution and the revolutionary vanguard. The following excerpts from Brandt, Schwartz, and Fairbank indicate its character:

1. Agrarian Revolution.

The Hunan peasant movement . . . can be divided into two stages: the first being that of organization from January to September, 1926 . . . Within this stage there was a secret period . . . and an open period . . . The total membership of the Peasant Associations did not exceed 300,000 or 400,000.

The second or revolutionary stage lasted from October (1926) to January of this year (1927) . . . The membership . . . jumped to 2,000,000.

After the peasants organized themselves action ensued . . . This attack was like a hurricane . . . the Peasant Associations became the only organizations of power . . . It is the rising up of the democratic forces in the countryside to overthrow the feudal forces in the villages, which is the true goal of the national revolution. Sun Yat-sen devoted forty years to the national revolution; what he wanted but failed to achieve has been accomplished by the peasants in a few months.

Another group says: "Peasant Associations should be organized, but their actions are too excessive."

The peasants in the villages have indeed been disorderly. The power of the Peasant Associations being supreme, the landlords are prohibited from speaking up and their prestige is wiped out. This is like stepping on the landlord after striking him down . . .

Some people forced their way into the homes of t'u-hao (bosses) and bad gentry . . . and killed their pigs and commandeered their grain. The ivory beds of the daughters and daughters-in-law of the t'u-hao and bad gentry were stepped upon by the dirty feet of the peasants. On the slightest provocation men were paraded down the streets, wearing tall paper hats [such as are worn by criminals en route to punishment].

"Vile gentry! Now comes your day!"

Actions were unrestrained; things were turned upside down, and terror swept some of the villages.

This is what some people call "excesses" . . . "unspeakable." This kind of comment appears superficially correct, but actually it is erroneous.

First, the above mentioned incidents were the result of oppression . . . Second, revolution is not a dinner-party, nor literary composition, nor painting, nor embroidering . . . It cannot be done so delicately, so leisurely, so gentlemanly . . . Revolution . . . is the violent action of one class overthrowing the power of another.

There must be a revolutionary tidal wave in the countryside in order to mobilize tens of thousands of peasants and weld them into this great force.

In the second (revolutionary) stage of the people's movement, such acts are very necessary. All excesses in the second stage have a revolutionary significance. In fine, every village should be in a state of terror for a brief period.

2. The Revolutionary Vanguard

But is this revolutionary mission . . . carried out by all the peasantry? No. The peasantry is divided into three subclasses.

Rich, middle, and poor . . . rich peasants (those with cash and grain surpluses) . . . middle peasants (those having no surplus cash or grain, nor debts, but barely maintaining a living).

Only one group . . . has fought hard and relentlessly from the very start: the poor peasants. Out of the secret into the open stage, it was they who fought, who organized, who did the revolutionary work. They alone were the deadly enemies of the bosses and the bad gentry . . . They alone were capable of doing the destructive work.

It is true that the poor peasants have nothing to lose. They are the outcasts or semi-outcasts of the village, and some of them are literally without a single tile above and without a strip of land below . . . the poor peasants constituted 70 per cent, middle 20 per cent, and the rich peasants 10 per cent . . . The poor peasants can be further classified as poor and very poor. The very poor—20 out of the 70 per cent—are entirely without occupation, having neither land nor capital; with nothing to live on, they have to become soldiers, hired hands, beggars, or bandits. The remaining 50 per cent constitute the poor who are partially without occupation, but who have a little land and capital, though not enough to meet their expenses. Thus they suffer all year long . . .

The poor peasants (especially the very poor) secured the leadership of the Peasant Associations because they were the most revolutionary. During the first and second stages the chairmen and committee members . . . of village Peasant Associations were almost entirely poor peasants.

This leadership by the poor peasants is very essential. Without the poor peasants, there will be no revolution. [Mao's italics.]

Terror

In the above, Mao first portrays the course of the Hunan Peasant Movement. It began with a six-month secret stage of organization of peasant associations. After the peasants organized themselves, action ensued. The attack was like a hurricane. It ended with terror, which Mao defended:

Every village should be in a state of terror for a brief period; otherwise, counter-revolutionary activities in the villages cannot be suppressed, and the gentry's power cannot be overthrown.

This, Mao proclaimed, was the real revolution.

Sun Yat-sen devoted forty years to the national revolution; what he wanted but failed to achieve has been accomplished by the peasants in a few months.

The peasants have fulfilled a long unfulfilled revolutionary mission, performing the major task in the national revolution.

In the second part of his report he considered its leadership. Those in the vanguard were not the peasantry as a whole, but were the men lowest down, floating population, riffraff. Mao described them as follows:

Who used to go around in worn-out shoes, carry broken umbrellas, wear blue gowns, and gamble. In brief, all those who used to be despised and trodden down by the gentry, who had no social standing, and were deprived of their right to speak.

Basis of Mao's Power

As Lenin used the proletariat to seize power, Mao used this rural element. Mao's own words are repeated for emphasis.

But is this revolutionary mission . . . carried out by all the peasants? No.

Only one group . . . has fought . . . from the very start: the poor peasants. Out of the secret into the open stage, it was they who fought, who organized, who did the revolutionary work . . . They alone were capable of doing the destructive work.

The poor peasants have nothing to lose. They are the outcasts . . . of the village, and some of them are literally without a strip of land.

The very poor . . . are entirely without occupation, having neither land nor capital; with nothing to live on, they have to become soldiers, hired hands, beggars or bandits.

These very poor elements of the poor peasantry not only made up the rank and file of the peasant movement. They were its leaders:

The poor peasants (especially the very poor) secured the leadership of the Peasant Association because they were the most revolutionary.

The chairmen and committee members of the lowest units of the Peasant Associations (village Peasant Associations) were almost entirely poor peasants. [In the village Peasant Associations of Hengshan, fifty per cent of the cadres came from the very poor peasant class, forty per cent from the poor peasant class, and ten per cent from poor educated elements.]

This leadership by the poor peasants is very essential. Without the poor peasants, there will be no revolution. (Mao's italics.)

Mao grasped the "revolutionary potential of the peasantry" as Rostow points out, and:

Stressed the violent feelings which could be generated among the poorer peasantry against the rural gentry . . . Mao gave full play to the emotions that could be released among the poorer peasants by the land-distribution process.

Here was the basis of Mao's power, and it was on this basis that he later became the undisputed leader of the Communist Party and still later master of all China.

Leaving the Moscow Line

However, at this time in 1927, this went dead against the orthodox Moscow line of basing the revolution on the proletariat of city workers, and this line was then being followed by the party in China under orders from Moscow. A few months later Mao was accordingly dismissed from the Politburo and from the Party Front Committee.

Mao's report, as above, is therefore so basic for an understanding of Communism in China that it calls for the most careful study of its background and implications.

This report must be viewed against the background of the situation in 1927.

It was now sixteen years since the revolution, and China had not gotten anywhere. There was anger over external aggression and frustration over internal weakness. Proposed solutions had run the gamut of theory and practice in the West, but no one had yet achieved the right formula for China.

Second, Mao and his Peasant Associations were in the turbulent province of Hunan where the T'ai-p'ing Rebellion had ruled from 1848 to 1865, and had come close to gaining all China. Peasant uprisings were under way in several adjoining provinces, often led by Communists.

Third, it is reported that when Mao was still in the hinterland plotting for power, his favorite reading was the popular novel, *All Men Are Brothers.* This famous novel deals with bandits at the time of the Sung dynasty who fought the forces of law and order because of injustices they felt they had suffered.

This provided a pattern and ideological background of a purely Chinese variety.

Mao had at hand in Hunan all the various elements that figure in the novel—not only the poor, but, as he mentions in his report cited above, "hired hands, beggars, and bandits." And doubtless rural riffraff, petty gangsters, and other vagrant elements in what is known as the floating population.

Mao's autobiography gives some details along this line. He tells of the beginnings of the Red Army in September, 1927, which he was organizing:

> The army, leading the peasant uprising, moved southward through Hunan. It had to break its way through thousands of Kuomintang troops and fought many battles with many reverses . . . When the little band climbed up Chingkanshan they numbered in all only about one thousand . . .
>
> Two former bandit leaders near Chingkanshan, Wong and Yuan . . . joined the Red Army in the winter of 1927. This increased the strength to about three regiments. Wang and Yuan were each made regimental commanders and I was army commander.
>
> These two men, although former bandits, had thrown in their forces with the Nationalist Revolution, and were now ready to fight against the reaction. While I remained on Chingkanshan they were faithful Communists . . . Later on, when they were left alone on Chingkanshan, they returned to their bandit habits.

Floating Population

To understand this situation it is necessary to recur to the population study previously cited which, over a four-year period, indicated a considerable floating population.

One result was the formation of local gangs of ne'er-do-wells, secret societies and, when things got worse, of full-scale banditry. It was easy for Mao to recruit a peasant army in Hunan from these elements.

The method was simple. They approached landless men and farm laborers out of a job who had nothing to lose, and local gangsters, who were ready for anything.

Even in fairly good times local gangs were to be found in most localities, as I learned by experience when I lived for four years in the far interior, 1912 to 1916. There I ran into gangs in two of the country parishes under my supervision, where I had personal contacts with some four hundred members, and a larger number of their relatives and friends. The local Chinese pastors had constant trouble with gangs of young hoodlums and ne'er-do-wells, one of which was known as the Forty Good-for-Nothings.

The Forty Good-for-Nothings . . . do no work, but gamble, and beat the bamboo carrying-pole, as Chinese say—that is get money by trickery and extortion.

The operations of another gang were described by several men who were "leaders in the village, several of them being particularly bold and enterprising."

"We are afraid of Scholar Moh and his gang," one of them reluctantly replied.

One told how Moh, with several of his gang to prevent interference, had come and picked his fruit. Another told how Moh had picked his mulberry leaves. Still another told how the gang had come and carried off part of his fodder. Another explained how Moh . . . had gotten the concession of a large piece of land which was granted for operating a ferry . . . He had cultivated the land and reaped the crops, but had not maintained the ferry, and the village had suffered in consequence but had not dared to do anything.

The sociological background of this was indicated as follows:

In no country is more importance attached to propriety and what is right and fitting than in China, but the intensely practical character of the people leads to the paradox that the man most generally admired by the populace is the one who can get away with it.

My American missionary predecessor was badly beaten up by Scholar Moh and his gang when he tried to put a stop to some of their skulduggery. This was taken up by the American Consul, but nothing could be done about it, for no one dared to testify against the gang. On four occasions, I personally escaped violence by a hair's breadth.

Not Primarily Land Reform

The myth of agrarian reformers is far from the truth. Here Rostow's conclusion is to the point:

In general, outright tenancy . . . was not so prevalent as it is generally believed. In 1947 only about ⅓ of the farm population were tenants, ¼ part owners, and about 40 to 45 per cent were full owners.

Therefore agrarian unrest in China was primarily compounded of . . .

pressure of population and low productivity rather than the extent of tenancy.

Mao enrolled the landless, the restless, the adventurous, the rascals. He won them by giving them houses, property and land taken from the landlords and rich peasants. Banditry was baptized as superdemocracy. These miscellaneous elements now discovered that they were the apostles of the Communist millennium. They were ready to fight like tigers to defend their loot—and from the highest motives. As Mao put it:

> The poor (especially the very poor) secured the leadership . . . because they were the most revolutionary . . . They alone were capable of doing the destructive work . . . Without the poor peasants there will be no revolution.

It is only when Mao's accomplishment is seen against this background that its true character appears.

But it worked.

Mao had begun organizing the Peasant Associations in Hunan in May, 1925. By January, 1927 he had 2,000,000 members, and wrote the report quoted above. In November he set up a Soviet regime in Ch'a-lin, Hunan. In January, 1928 Chu Teh headed the "South Hunan Uprising," and in May he and Mao joined forces at a bandit stronghold in south Hunan to form the Fourth Red Army. In December, 1930, the first KMT offensive against them was stopped in a month. In 1931 they set up a soviet in Kiangsi.

4

THE SECOND UNITED FRONT

One of the slogans used by the Nationalist Movement to rouse popular support was "Beat down foreign imperialism," and the new Nationalist Government was under pressure to make good. This was a formidable and delicate task.

"Show us what you can do," editorialized the *Shanghai North China Daily News,* speaking for the British interests. "Take all the time you please . . . We know you can pull down; prove to us also that you can build up."

The Nationalist Government did not wait, but increased the pressure for the abolition of extraterritoriality, and the Western powers unwillingly prepared to yield as gracefully as possible.

Not so Japan.

War with Japan

Japan had invested a billion yen in China, and the China trade was one-third of Japan's foreign commerce, mostly passing through Shanghai where the Japanese population had grown to 30,000. They had thirty cotton mills in Shanghai, and the five British mills were hard put to it to compete with them. They had a fleet of twenty-seven ships carrying Japanese goods from Shanghai up the Yangtze into the interior.

The Nationalists were pushing things too fast, and then Japan had her own plans with regard to China. So in September 1931 came the Manchuria incident, and in January 1932 the Shanghai situation blew up, and a considerable part of Shanghai was devastated by the Japanese. This was the prelude to war, which came in 1937.

The Kiangsi Soviet

Meantime the Communists had not been idle, but had continued their quest for power. They staged uprisings in various places in Hunan, Kwangtung, and Fukien, and tried to seize various cities, including Changsha and Canton.

These movements came to a climax in 1931 when a Communist Soviet Republic was proclaimed, consisting of six districts in the mountains of the Kiangsi-Fukien border. Its laws followed the Russian model almost word for word. Its program was land redistribution which was carried out with violence.

The Nationalists now had the Japanese in front and the Communists at their backs.

In 1932 this Chinese Soviet Republic declared war on Japan and called on all groups and classes to resist Japanese aggression. From that time on they harped on the theme that they were really the ones who were resisting Japan, and led a large section of the population in China—and abroad—to believe this.

By 1934 the Red Army in Kiangsi had grown to 180,000 and it took Chiang four years and five campaigns to dislodge them.

In November 1935 some 100,000 of them broke away and began the long march of 6,000 miles to a new base at Yennan in the northwest. Some 20,000 of them got there.

Meantime, under Japanese pressure, the national defense became of supreme importance, and in 1936 Chiang was forced to agree to a second United Front, due largely to the Communist success in representing themselves as an important factor in resistance.

In 1937 Japan unleashed a full-scale attack, and after a gallant but ill-advised attempt to hold Shanghai, the Nationalist Government withdrew, first to Hankow, later to Chungking.

Nationalist Government in Wartime

During the long hard years of war, the Nationalists maintained a government in being in Chungking which was a symbol of hope to the occupied areas, and tied down nearly a million Japanese troops who might have made a lot of trouble elsewhere.

The Nationalists faced two great disadvantages. They had lost their base in the coastal region where their chief strength and backing came from the more modernized and democratic commercial class. And they were in war lord territory which they had never really controlled, and where they were not wanted. The Nationalists were not geared to subsist on a rural basis, or rather on what was left after the war lords had taken theirs.

On top of this was the weariness and exhaustion of refugee war conditions. I was there and lost thirty pounds.

Second United Front

This united front was widely hailed as greatly strengthening the resistance to Japanese aggression, for the Communists have been able to pose as an important factor in the war of resistance, and also gained prestige when the Eighth Route Army won the first major victory over the Japanese at P'ing-hsing-kwan. They also succeeded in capitalizing on the patriotism of the country to discredit Chiang for his more cautious policy of not going all out in a great campaign against Japan.

Actually the chief advantage accrued to the Communists for it secured them from attack, and enabled them to exploit the war situation to their own advantage, which they did under the cover of guerrilla action against the Japanese. In 1937 they occupied some 30,000 square miles in the northwest with a population of two million. By 1945 this had grown to 300,000 square miles and 95 million people. Their army grew from 20,000 to 900,000. We know now that during this time Mao never committed his forces to a real battle with the Japanese where they might have been destroyed.

Guerrilla War Masks Seizure of Power

The united front legalized the position of the Communists and gave them a free hand to build up control under cover of guerrilla operations. It was really a truce rather than a united front.

The Communists thus came to supreme power by means of their special type of guerrilla tactics. These deserve detailed examination. The first step was the organization of militia in every village. The second was the development of Communist-type local government organs.

Organization of Rural Militia

The militia are under the direct control of the local Communist Party organs. Under the military districts and sub-districts, the rural villages form militia companies under a company leader and a political commissar. The members are taken in individually. They are introduced by the peasants' unions and must be passed on at meetings of members of the militia corps. In addition, their admission must be sanctioned and their names kept on record by organs of higher rank.

The political power of the Chinese Communists is founded in the first instance on the rural villages as bases and spreads therefrom to the cities and towns.

They exercise greater care in the selection of members in the urban districts than in the rural villages. In the cities there are more educated persons who are not easily susceptible to the treachery and designs of the Communists.

Discipline

Much emphasis was placed on discipline. The first rule was to "talk in an affable tone," and they were specially admonished not to engage in fights or quarrels but always to present an affable countenance. This paid off later, and much of the favorable impression they made everywhere when they first took over a locality was due to their discipline and politeness.

Production and Labor

The rural militia, as civilian armed forces, spent most of their time in production, and were in duty bound to accept orders from the Government in tasks of a public nature (such as building dykes and river embankments, escorting the despatch of public grain to public granary, and farm duties on others' behalf). This work is recorded and credits are given each month.

Guerrilla Tactics

The militia furnished a special type of help in battle operations, whereby the Japanese enemy found himself inside their guerrilla network. Frontally he was resisted by the field army corps, but the battle front was everywhere and his opponents were all round him.

The militia developed special tactics. These included (1) land-mines, (2) scorched earth policy (3) sabotage in the enemy's rear, (4) "tunnel warfare," (5) "sparrow strategy" or widespread dispersal of small units, (6) psychological warfare.

Sabotage was on a huge scale. In the autumn of 1940, in the middle part of Hopei Province, no less than 350,000 peasants engaged in sabotage and demolition work. In 1942 militiamen in the northwestern part of Shansi Province cut and collected over 13,000 pounds of telegraph wires and burned over 20 bridges.

Tunnel warfare involved dugouts linked by networks of tunnels and by miles of tunnels connecting villages. The total labor strength of entire villages was mobilized for months. This enabled whole villages to disappear on the approach of the Japanese, and to pop out in unexpected places to harass them. They thus avoided a frontal clash with the better equipped Japanese.

This method was used in 1952 in Korea. A propaganda statement put it thus:

> During the year the Chinese Volunteers have excavated tunnels piercing and linking thousands of hills and mountains on the Korean front. In so doing they have performed a miracle hithertofore unknown . . .

Enormous man-power was employed for they commanded vast human resources. The military analogy of this was the "human sea" tactics on the battle front, using human mass attacks to overcome superior fire-power.

Espionage was a constant activity of these half-civilian, half-military forces who were everywhere and were in close touch with the populace. They excelled especially in gathering intelligence while keeping their own movements secret. President Chiang, referring painfully to this at a later time, had the following to say:

> I have examined the cause why so many of our high military commanders fell into the hands of the enemy and so many of our armed units met reverses . . . I have come to the conclusion that this was not due to the superior fighting power of the bandit forces but rather to their excellent intelligence system.

Guerrilla Warfare Built Local Government

The second step of the guerrilla fighters was to take advantage of the confusion of warfare and of their military control to build up their own local government organizations.

These began as guerrilla bases. The guerilla units had no organization furnishing them with provisions or replenishments but lived off the country, depending on the sympathy and help of the local populace. Guerrilla bases were therefore necessary. Mao Tse-tung stated it thus:

> Guerrilla warfare behind enemy lines cannot be sustained without the existence of operation bases.
>
> Guerrilla areas may be converted into operation bases through annihilating or defeating in battle large numbers of the enemy, overthrowing the puppet political authority.
>
> Mobilizing the populace to give vent to their spirit of activism, formation of civic organs, development and growth of the armed strength of the people, and establishment of the people's own political authority and power.

These last were merely what the Communists had already been doing in organizing soviets. Mao added further details.

> Likewise there are to be organized civic bodies of various natures such as those belonging to workers, peasants, youths, women, children, merchants, or members of the independent professions . . .
>
> These struggles should serve as the basis for mobilisation of the populace in order to consolidate or build up political authority in the localities.

Thus at the end of the war they had not only military control, but had developed their own organs of "political authority."

Their ultimate objective was to achieve one-party dictatorship. Democratic methods were not employed. They were not considered suitable to Chinese conditions and the Chinese people were not ready for them. Hence, military force must be used and a militia force was trained up who were active in spirit and willing to play a leading role.

The regular armed forces had war duties and could not be stationed long at any one place. Local militia units could stay put in their localities and serve as tools in the class struggle. Thus the Communists won political control.

Militia Expansion

The Communists took full advantage of the opportunity offered by the anti-Japanese War to create for themselves a huge organization of militia. They thus greatly increased their reserve strength, solved the difficult problem of replenishment of man-power and enlarged the areas forming their bases. This represented an important turning point in the growth of their military power, as witness a report by Chu Teh at the 7th Party Congress of the Communist Party of China in 1945:

> The enormous force of militia corps in the liberated areas is something we never had before. We have now learned the technique of organizing militia corps. The significance and importance of this accomplishment are beyond imagination.
>
> Militia corps, once formed, can cooperate with the regular armed forces in battle. They may separately shoulder battle tasks. They also play an important role protecting the production campaigns of the populace. . . .
>
> In various localities arrangements have been made to link together militia corps for joint protection and battle assignments. Herein may be seen the beginning of militia corps gradually evolving into and becoming regular armed forces of the localities.
>
> At the same time the militia corps and self-protection units also take part in general production activities. This enables war prosecution and production activities to be linked together and become coordinated. . . .

By 1947, during the period of open rebellion against the Nationalist Government, the Communist militia increased to an estimated total of 5,000,000. Still later, after the Communists gained control in 1949, they issued a directive concerning the militia which included the following:

> To effect in a planned and systematic manner consolidation and development of the militia system, in coordination with such popular campaigns as land reform, and suppression of banditry. In the build-up work of the militia corps stress would be laid on the rural villages. The general objec-

tive should be to attain, during the next two to three years, a figure equivalent to five per cent of the entire population of the country, or a total of 23,750,000 men.

Other Applications of United Front Strategy

The use of the united front stratagem is thus revealed as the chief factor in the build-up that enabled the Communists to seize sufficient power to enable them to begin all-out civil war in 1947 with a good prospect of success.

When the Communists won the civil war, the same united front strategy was later used with the war lords. They were to have a place as allies. But soon they transferred to other commands. Then many of their armies were sent to Korea—the Communists did not trust them.

The Chinese Communists continued to use the united front as their favorite and most effective stratagem. They used it to hoodwink the American government, which sent General Marshall to bring about a cooperation that the Communists never had the slightest intention of entering into. They are using it now in the international field. It even fooled most of the Chinese intellectuals.

5

UNCERTAIN INTELLECTUALS

The Chinese have been described above as a culture group rather than a conquering state, and Chinese expansion as a process of sinification even more than military conquest.

The dynasties of the empire had been founded by force of arms, but were governed by an elite class of scholar-officials. This was in accord with and grew out of the Confucian ideal.

The Communists therefore had to secure the cooperation of a sufficient number of intellectuals in order to govern. This they have succeeded in doing. It is necessary to analyze how this came about.

Chinese Intellectuals as of the 1920's

Chinese intellectuals had been a unified group, held to a uniform classical scholarship implemented by the government examination system.

This scholastic and political system now failed them. Politically, the old examination system was scrapped and their classical learning no longer opened the way to a career. Practically, Confucianism had been closely related to the ancient structure of Chinese society, and did not fit the new industrialized, international order that was forced upon them. It even prevented progress, as in the case of the early scholar-official industrialists.

They were scholars in search of a new scholarship—one that would fit the modern situation as Confucianism had fitted its own day. So, as recounted above, they made abortive attempts at a synthesis.

New Learning

Meanwhile modern universities with partly Western curricula, were being established in China, and modern books were being translated. Chinese scholars began to think and write along new lines. Many had lost faith in the old learning, yet they could not rid themselves of it. It conditioned their thinking. They remained Chinese, and sought a solution in line with their justifiable pride in the long history and greatness of Chinese culture.

But great numbers went abroad to study. First they turned to Japan. It was nearer and cheaper. It was easier, for the Japanese language was half made up of Chinese characters and could be learned more quickly. Japan was an oriental nation that was already making use of Western methods to solve eastern problems. The Western learning in its Japanese version was, so to speak, predigested. So some 20,000 Chinese students studied in Japanese universities over a period of years, and came back to jobs in government, universities, business. What they got, in addition to various lines of technical training, was a Japanese version of Western science, culture and philosophy.

Then the tide shifted to America, in smaller numbers but still some thousands, where they went to learn business, education, science, democracy. But in a more individualistic, less integrated, laissez-faire, liberal fashion. When they returned, they found the Japanese returned students intrenched in all the best positions, which they had no intention of relinquishing. Cliques and rivalries developed.

Later, a thousand or so went to France on a labor-scholarship basis which was attractive and required little money. About the same time they began to go to Russia, so that by 1949 there were 10,000 graduates of the Communist training college for Chinese in Moscow. And all the time they had been going in lesser numbers to England, Germany, and elsewhere.

These many varieties of "returned students," together with those who had to stay at home in universities in China, resulted in a fragmentation of the Chinese scholar class that did not help them to get together to work out any practical synthesis.

Alternative Solutions

The old language did not easily lend itself to the expression of all these new and strange ideas, so they had to talk about them in Japanese, English, French, German. But it was not merely the languages that were different. The cultural, national, and historic backgrounds were still more diverse. They now had access to Western ideas and techniques in bewildering variety, and they had no one to tell them which to choose.

It is difficult, perhaps impossible, for Americans to realize the extent of the uncertainty in the minds of thinking Chinese in the 1920's, as they faced their country's future. For them the vast edifice of Chinese scholarship no longer provided sure guidance amid the unprecedented conditions in which they now found themselves. Nor had the new theories worked much better.

They had nothing to correspond to the century of Japanese historical scholarship that had paved the way for the Restoration, the emperor system, and the messianic drive for world conquest.

On the contrary, instead of the Japanese drive, China had more of a cultural drift, as befitted a people that were more of a cultural entity than a military state. It will be remembered that the area of sinification had expanded slowly for over two thousand years, and had not yet reached some 20,000,000 hill tribes in the southwest.

Now they had to make a choice from the great variety of Western ideas and systems, and fit them into a workable synthesis with the traditional Chinese culture.

They had the greatest freedom of choice of any nation in Asia, but their lack of guidance was by no means an advantage under all the circumstances.

India had been conquered by England, and Indian universities and government officials followed English learning and English law and civil administration. Japan had voluntarily adopted the German system as the highest and the most congenial. German philosophy and science ruled in Japanese universities. Japanese students—and perhaps twenty thousand Chinese students—received a basically German university training and a German acculturation. The Philippines had a Spanish and American background. In China, American influence consisted of little more than a tradition of friendship, the impact of missionary and business interests, and protestations of good will. China and America were both slow-moving laissez-faire cultures. They understood each other and got on well together. But the tempo of the times was too fast.

The Chinese intellectuals of the 1920's had the world to choose from. There was no fixed norm of modern government in the West. There was a welter of conflicting doctrinaire theories. Which should they adopt?

Miscellaneous Western Solutions

All this diversity had its roots in the development of modern philosophy in the West, and to this it is necessary to turn for a brief summary, as a basis for understanding what happened in China in this connection.

In the allied fields of government and economics, the outstanding solutions were those worked out by England, Russia, and America.

Liberalism originated in England and Holland. It was first comprehensively stated by the English philosopher Locke (1636–1704), the most influential of modern philosophers. It was Protestant and religiously tolerant. It favored the middle class, and democracy tempered by the rights of property, especially when accumulated by the labor of the individual. It was optimistic and individualistic but not dogmatic. It was further developed in England with a characteristic British emphasis on the practical, the utilitarian. The Empiricism of Locke, which holds that our knowledge (with the possible exception of logic and mathematics) is derived from experience, never prevailed in German universities. They were the habitat of the fabled German professor who lights his pipe, goes into the silence, and excogitates a whole new system of philosophy from his own inner consciousness.

The movement of German philosophy that started with Kant culminated in Hegel (1770–1831), and it was his dialectical method that became a fundamental ingredient in the basic Marxist dogma of "dialectical materialism." Marx's philosophy of history is a blend of Hegel and British economics. The world develops according to a dialectical formula. But the motive force is not Hegel's "mystical entity called Spirit," but materialism which in practice takes the form of economics, especially the "mode of production," and, to a lesser degree, distribution.

Hegel and Marx were followed by other writers in the field of the philosophy of history, like Spengler and Weber. They used technical terms whose Hegelian and post-Hegelian background was not familiar to students in the English speaking lands—such as

"Asiatic society," "oriental despotism," "slave society," "feudalism." Such philosophies of history were not only doctrinaire, but dogmatic, pre-ordained. They made an apocalyptic appeal.

This trend produced Lenin and Stalin. But its development was not due solely to the inherent movement of ideas. It was greatly influenced by external circumstances.

Impact on Asia

Most of this was translated from German into Japanese—including much that was unknown in English. It was diligently studied in Japanese universities, where it had the authority and prestige that went with everything German. The thousands of Chinese students who went to Japan imbibed this likewise. Americans were not aware of this.

Here then were the chief solutions for the consideration of the Chinese intellectuals in 1931: Russia exemplified communism, drastically modern, dogmatic, apocalyptic, successful, ruthlessly aggressive; England exemplified a laissez-faire liberalism, which was involved in serious practical difficulties, socialistic indeed, but not thorough-going socialism, only a British compromise; America embodied a liberalism that had changed little since the ideas of Locke had been written into the American constitution 150 years earlier.

These were only the main solutions which had been actually adopted in practice. Other theories abounded. The century had begun with an optimistic belief in progress, which the First World War had only dimmed. Economic democracy was still to be achieved. There were theories for the solution of every problem. They made a tremendous appeal to the idealists and generous-minded in all lands, who believed in them like a religion. Mere democracy, as in America, or even socialism as in England, was old stuff.

To the Chinese intellectual, lacking any experiential test, they all seemed good. There was some Chinese intellectual to espouse nearly every one.

The New Philosophy of History

They faced a second question. Would the new social theory fit the old Chinese culture?

This was answered by inverting the question. Could Chinese history be made to fit into the schematism of the new philosophy of history? For the outstanding characteristic of all these philosophies of history was a "scheme of successive stages of economic development."

The Hegelian conception included in Marxism was that of an "eternal principle of human development moving, in universal and identifiable stages toward ultimate perfection." Marx held the conception of four stages (or modes of production): Asiatic, ancient, feudal, capitalistic.

Chinese thought came under this influence in the second quarter of the century because of the appeal in academic circles of the German sociological theories. This led to a discussion during the early 1930's known as the "Chinese Society Controversy." The pioneer Chinese work was Tao Hsi-sheng's *Analysis of the History of Chinese Society* in 1924, and the Chinese decided that Chinese history was not something in a class by itself, but paralleled the history of the West—that is, went through the same stages. The problem then was to fit Chinese society into the stages of economic development. This was accomplished by declaring that Chinese society was in the feudal stage.

Mao's Conversion

Mao Tse-tung, in his autobiography, describes his own personal development that parallels the situation outlined above. He describes himself at the time of his graduation from the Hunan Provincial First Normal School in 1918 at the age of 25:

> At this time my mind was a curious mixture of ideas of liberalism, democratic reformism, and Utopian Socialism. I had somewhat vague passions about "nineteenth century democracy," Utopianism, and old-fashioned liberalism, and I was definitely anti-militarist and anti-imperialist.

During the following two years he did much reading in the library of the Peking National University where he was employed. This led him to communism. He describes his conversion thus:

> Three books especially deeply carved my mind, and built up in me a faith in Marxism, from which, once I had accepted it as the correct interpretation of history, I did not afterward waver. . . .

By the summer of 1920 I had become, in theory and to some extent in action, a Marxist, and from that time on I considered myself a Marxist.

Here Mao ascribes his conversion to Marxism to the fact that he "accepted it as the correct interpretation of history."

In that he was perhaps typical of the Chinese Communist intellectual convert.

In similar fashion, this whole question interested scholars in many fields in addition to history—archeology, ethnology, philology and other related studies, and brought them into the Communist orbit.

Thus the Communist philosophy of history coincided in time with the Chinese interest in the field of Chinese history, and made it easy for the two to merge, and the field of Chinese history became the chief means on the intellectual and educational side in securing the passive or even active support of an increasing number of the educated class.

It was this class, particularly the students, who became members of student movements and similar organizations that have been the chief source of communist cadres, far more than the proletariat or peasantry.

This was summed up by Brandt, Schwartz and Fairbank, writing in 1950, as follows:

The need for a new universal view of human history had become urgent in Modern China. The efforts to remake Confucianism, in the period of the 1898 reforms, and the efforts to synthesize Chinese and Western principles, made by scholars like Liang Ch'i-ch'ao and politicians like Sun Yat-sen, had all proved inadequate.

Caught in the transition between old and new, East and West, China has had some of the characteristics of an ideological vacuum and others of an ideological melting-pot.

The resulting intellectual confusion has inhibited political unification.

Practical Considerations vs. Ideology

It would be a mistake to consider this intellectual aspect of communism as the cause, or even a large contributing factor in the communist conquest of China. Kirby puts it thus:

Communism established itself in China in circumstances fundamentally artificial and abnormal. Even less than in the case of Russia was communism here the result of normal historic evolution, and even more was it the fortuitous outcome of war, invasion, disaster, and decay.

Nothing in China's experience was of much use in this connection. The very stability of Chinese society which had endured for forty centuries unfitted them for change and for grappling with so novel and complex a situation. The intellectuals, who had always been China's leaders in the past, now spoke with many voices and from many points of view.

This situation was exemplified in the diverse group that came together in Shanghai in 1920, and the next year secretly organized the Communist Party. They had two things in common. One was the feeling of frustration over the failure of the various partial solutions that had been tried. The other was that both the Russian and the Japanese training stemmed from the German philosophy that was basic for Marxism. The French-returned students had imbibed similar brands of radicalism. And in the England and America of those days, socialist and even communist ideas were by no means rare in intellectual and political circles.

They were able to get together on one thing—the Communist preordained interpretation of history.

But practical considerations have been determinative rather than ideology. Frustrated reformers who found Western democracy too slow and too mild were thrilled by Lenin's success and began to study and imitate it. Sun Yat-sen turned to Russia for needed help he could not get elsewhere and was happy to get their support in the first United Front in 1923. Mao went contrary to the Russian pattern when he based his bid for power on the peasants. His agreement with Russia in 1950 was probably the only way of getting control of Manchuria, then in Russian hands.

The intellectual aspect was a concomitant, not a first cause. But it was most useful in enlisting needed workers at a higher level.

Non-Chinese Roots of Communist Ideology

Communism in China was not the child of the Chinese intellectual development, but an importation. Several considerations bear this out.

The Renaissance Movement which reached a high point in Peking about 1918, moved largely in the field of language and literature—

the use of the spoken language in literary work, and a renaissance of Chinese scholarship. It was led by men from families with a long lineage of distinguished scholars. Their reaction to the revolution and the problem of modernization was academic. This left a partial political vacuum.

The leadership of the revolution came from Sun whose father was a tenant farmer and from Mao who was the son of a well-to-do peasant. Sun was a convert to the American way of life, and Mao to a German philosophy of history in its Marxist-Leninist form. Mao's originality was in the field of realistic statesmanship rather than of doctrinaire theory, especially in seizing power.

Cooperation of Intellectuals

Great numbers of Chinese intellectuals have fled to Formosa, Hong Kong and other places, but a majority of educated persons necessarily remained in China, and are today cooperating with the Communists. Brandt, Schwartz and Fairbank state the problem as of 1950:

> For Americans the most interesting problem is that of the relation of the CCP and the non-Communist intellectuals in China. The chief fruit of the American investment in missionary education and humanitarian good works in China during the last century has been the modern-minded Western-trained academic and professional personnel who still form a major portion of the Chinese upper class.
>
> Their present position and future prospects should be both instructive and of melancholy interest to us.
>
> The fate of these intellectuals, and of their formerly pro-Western or "liberal" political views, has an important bearing on the efficacy of the traditional Western ideology in its modern application to Asia.
>
> How were the Communists able to gain the cooperation of many who had risked everything rather than collaborate with Japanese invaders?

Their strategy was that of the united front. It is noted also that up to the present there has been no purge in the upper party ranks comparable to those in Russia, which gave the united front something of a semblance of reality.

Mao's New Democracy

A decisive part in winning the cooperation of intellectuals was played by the publication of Mao's "New Democracy" in 1940. This expatiated upon the united front and was designed to make a wide appeal. Communist China was not to be a proletarian dictatorship like the Soviet Union, but a joint dictatorship of the several revolutionary classes, with a place for capitalists and non-Communist parties. It was based on Sun Yat-sen rather than Lenin. It did include complete socialization as its ultimate goal. But this was overlooked by many Chinese (and Americans) whose attention was caught by the Communist attitude of tolerance and large promises to various classes of better times.

It is necessary to give credit for generous motives and high ideals to many non-Communists who accepted this and who cooperated in the earlier stages.

Many who were dedicated to progress and reform have found a place to serve in the vigorous Communist program of railway building, conservancy, industrialization and planned economy "for the people." Many Christians have cooperated, hoping for the best, and trusting that Christianity could modify Communism, which they felt sure would become far different in China.

The principal of a Christian girls' high school asked one of the teachers who was one of the committee of party members who really ran the school, how it was that she was always so happy in spite of all the rigid restrictions and controls.

"Do we not have the Christian hymn," she replied, " 'Make me a captive, Lord, and then I shall be free'?"

The principal commented that this young woman seemed indeed to have found her freedom in this fashion. She, however, was one of those who were in power.

Totalitarian Youth

This was the age of Hitler youth, and all of their kind. Chinese Communism seems to have made a similar appeal, especially to students.

It was a short step from anger and frustration to fanaticism, particularly when they were told Communism held the answer, and the power was put into their youthful hands to bring it to pass.

Position and power and an idealist messianic evangelism made a heady mixture for thousands of high-school students. China had always been governed by a self-appointed elite. Now they were it. This was not lessened by the special privileges that went with it. They acquired a vested interest in privilege and position and power, just as militia members did in the land when the landlords were liquidated.

6

The Nationalist Defeat

The sudden end of the war in 1945 caught the Nationalists at a great disadvantage, and a number of factors combined to bring about their defeat.

The initial loss grew out of the fact that the Nationalist government and most of its forces were in the far west, whereas the Communists were on the spot to take over Japanese arms and supplies. This was particularly the case in Manchuria, where the Yalta agreement had put the Russians in control. Here was the great arsenal and supply base of the Japanese armies on the mainland. Russia was able to see that this vast armament was denied to the Nationalists and got into Communist hands. This was one of the deciding factors.

The United States air force flew large numbers of Nationalist officers to North China and East China to receive the Japanese surrender. But this was largely a token take-over, and was more a political and propaganda move than a transfer of real control. The Nationalists were too few.

A little later, a national secretary who had traveled extensively in North China came to Shanghai and made a confidential report. He summed it up by quoting a popular saying that he had found current everywhere.

"China has two friends. One gives everything. The other takes everything."

"If the people feel like that," we asked him, "why do they let a Communist minority lead them around by the nose?"

"The people were completely disarmed by the Japanese," he explained. "The Communists are the only ones who have any weapons. No one can resist them."

Low Nationalist Morale

A second factor was that the Nationalist government was at a low ebb, and was worn out by eight years as a refugee government. It now had to undergo the delays and confusion of moving back from the remote western hinterland to the coast, with no railway available, and only very limited shipping and bus facilities.

An inevitable period of delay and demoralization ensued and continued month after month, in spite of everything that the discouraged refugees could do.

When they did get back, there was a psychological adjustment to be made. People in Free China and those in the occupied regions had grown apart. Those who had stayed were looked on as collaborators. They in turn felt that those who had gone to Free China had merely run away.

In spite of all this, the government, returned to Nanking, attacked its problems with unexpected vigor. They extemporized offices and started in on the immense task of rehabilitation and reconstruction.

An Exhausted Country

A third factor was that the country had been devastated and disorganized after the Japanese occupation. Boats, large and small, had been carried off, and river and canal traffic was the most essential factor in transportation. Railroads and buses had partly broken down. Roads were in bad shape. Goods could not be moved. When we returned to Shanghai the electric power company was advertising in the papers, urging customers to use as little as possible, for fear the power plant would break down.

It took the efficient mayor of Shanghai weeks to clear the streets and alleys of squatters who had built matting huts and were camping there. People slept in doorways. It took weeks to clear the halls of our own office building of the people who had moved in and were living there. It took months to get back the office next to mine in our suite, which had been simply appropriated while we were away.

"Go ahead and sue," they told me. "The courts are overburdened and it will be two years before the case comes up. Meanwhile we will be right here. We can't find any place to move to."

Similar problems beset every department of government, every aspect of life. Nothing could be done in a hurry.

In such a situation all that any honest government could offer was a long hard period of gradual reconstruction.

But they were not given the time.

The Lost Nationalist Base

What all this added up to was that the middle class was largely destroyed, together with the industrial plants, most of the transportation facilities, the business houses, and the banks on which they depended.

This was the class that the Kuomintang had represented, and the basis of the power of the Nationalist Government. This was a decisive factor. Taylor describes the situation as follows:

> The chief and most decisive loss to the KMT was the special role and position of the middle class which had been so powerful in the years before the war. The KMT had set up the first modern government in Chinese history that did not draw on land taxes for financial support.
>
> When . . . as a result of the war . . . it was compelled to return to land taxes as its chief source of revenue, it came to depend once more for social and political support upon the oldest and least reconstructed part of Chinese society.
>
> Such a change made a vast difference to the political outlook and program of the Nationalist government.

Taylor places the Communist success in "sharp contrast to the attempts made by the KMT to revitalize the party both before and during the war."

The middle class that made up the constituency of the KMT was largely gone. A large part of them had been uprooted and fled to the west, and returned to find their business and properties looted and wrecked by Japanese militarists. Those who remained fared little better. The Nationalist Government had lost most of the foundation on which it had been built. There was little left to be revitalized.

Taylor estimates that "the restoration of China to its 1937 condition would have required two generations of peace . . . the collaboration of friendly powers with technical and financial assistance."

Then came the final blow to the middle class. Inflation had mounted as part of the general situation. The Nationalist Government made a desperate effort to control it and called on the people to turn in gold and securities in exchange for the new national currency. The people responded heroically, but the effort failed, and the inflation got worse.

All over the country, people felt that the government had robbed them of their last resources in a perilous time. Bitterness mounted. Talk of government corruption increased. Those who had lost their money believed it.

Communist Wartime Build-up

During the war with Japan from 1937 to 1945 the communists built up strength in the northwest and penetrated much of the north. When the war ended they controlled 300,000 square miles and 95 million people, and had 900,000 men under arms.

The Nationalists had taken the brunt of the fighting, and the crack army that Chiang had built up over the years was largely used up.

The Communists were ready to take over.

Psychological Offensive

Mao had exploited their favorable position in the united front with the publication of his New Democracy in 1940. This served to soften up the intellectuals, and led them to believe that the united front was part of the communist policy, and that all parties would participate in a coalition.

The bright promises of the Communists were in alluring contrast to the drab and hopeless reality and the necessarily slow and difficult program of the Nationalists, which did not seem to be getting anywhere anyway.

Much of this seemed to be borne out by the discipline and politeness of the Communist troops.

"Let them come" was the mood in many parts of the country. "Things could not be worse."

American Policy

There was probably only one thing that could have prevented the Communists from getting control, and that was the possibility of American intervention.

But this situation was not realized. The fiction of their being agrarian reformers still persisted. A united front seemed the best solution. American policy was predicated on this and General Marshall was sent to mediate. The Communists stalled. The Nationalists saw more clearly and were reluctant. The negotiations broke down.

So in 1946 America cut off military aid to the Nationalist Government. In 1947 open civil war began. By 1949 the Communists had taken over the country and proclaimed the people's Republic of China.

Another United Front

In 1948 the Communists put forth a May Day slogan advocating that

> All democratic parties and groups . . . speedily convene a political consultative conference, discuss and carry out convoking of a people's representative assembly to establish a democratic coalition government.

An official editorial emphasized this.

> The revolutionary camp must be enlarged . . . It must embrace all persons willing to join in the present revolutionary cause.

Accordingly a number of so-called democratic parties held sessions to determine their new orientation.

Most intellectuals believed this and read into it their own hopes. They were over-sanguine as to the amount of freedom their organizations would have in the new united front.

PART V

THE PEOPLE'S REPUBLIC OF CHINA

The People's Republic was promulgated October 1, 1949. The Communists were now in control.

Land redistribution was extended to South China, which they had not previously controlled, during the period 1949–51 at a cost of a million and a half human lives.

But the new landowners were soon disillusioned. Mao's speech in July, 1955, marked the end of private property in agricultural land, and its complete collectivization in Agricultural Production Cooperatives.

New Democracy and Agrarian Reform now stood revealed as expedients for the seizure of power.

This power was now to be implemented by a new type of fanatical Communist devotee, produced by a process of psychological conditioning, who was given a vested interest in the Communist regime.

Agricultural Production Cooperatives emerged as the key to the whole Communist scheme of things. No food supply, no industrialization. No heavy industry, no armament. No strong nation.

The ultimate objective began to show up as world conquest.

Widespread resistance has begun to appear, and the Nationalist Government in Formosa remains as a symbol of freedom.

1

The Communists Take Over

The People's Republic of China was promulgated October 1, 1949.

The Communists have been portrayed in the preceding chapters as a group of professional revolutionists in pursuit of supreme power. Now they had it.

They had followed a "winding road," to use Mao's term. No stratagem had been too devious, no method too ruthless. Now they had arrived.

But the inner essence of what had happened was not apparent at that time to the people of China or to the world, so skillful had they been in hitching their wagon to the star of hope for a strong, united government that could repel imperialists, re-establish China as a great nation, and inaugurate an era of freedom and good times for all.

The Communists had a word for it—"liberation." So they took over. Enthusiasm ran high, although not a few of the elders shook their heads—but only in secret. For a time liberation was a reality, the revolution was a success, and China was a great nation once more.

There were scenes like the following in Shanghai.

The workers were really happy when the Reds took the city. We're the boss now, they said.

A comfort-the-soldiers drive was held . . . People thronged the park . . . The best actors and actresses sold donated objects, the best movie stars . . . I just drank beer and watched, thrilled . . . Darn it, I thought, under Communism actors come right out and mix with the people to help the soldiers. That's democracy, all right . . . There was . . . warmth in the air. I was deeply affected. . . . My inferiority complex was gone . . . I felt very happy. I felt free.

There were propaganda plays that were very popular.

When the curtain went down clapping reached a prolonged crescendo. People . . . climbed onto the stage and shook hands with the players . . . everyone on the stage burst into some fiery revolutionary song in which the audience joined. This happened at each performance . . . and was one of the reasons why people went.

Riding the Wave

This exhilaration went to the heads of the men at the top.

First, they would liberate Formosa, and late in 1949 eighteen armies were mobilized along the coast. But this did not come off.

A little over two months after the establishment of the new People's Republic, Mao was in Moscow, where meetings between him and Stalin went on from December 1949 to February 1950 resulting in a Sino-Soviet Treaty of Alliance. Rostow considers that "the only sensible assumption is that the top Soviet and Chinese leaders agreed on an offensive in Asia."

The treaty was signed in February. The North Koreans attacked in June. China gave backing to the Communists in Indo-China. On November 26, China entered the Korean War. In May, 1951, China took over Tibet.

The wave reached its crest when the Chinese armies were advancing against the retreating Americans in Korea. China had taken its place as one of the most powerful nations in the world.

This urge to expansion and conquest was natural to both Russia and China and was fostered by the situation. The Russian objective of World Communism had behind it the drive and history of Russian imperialism. Mao had established the equivalent of a new dynasty; and the First Emperor and the founders of the Han and T'ang dynasties had achieved far-flung conquests. Both the Russian and the Chinese Communists had made tremendous advances in the last few years. It looked easy to keep going. But in Korea they ran into the United States.

As far back as 1929 the Communists had considered America as the key imperialist enemy. This was increased by American backing of the Nationalist Government. So they went directly from civil war into a period of acute tension with the United States which arose largely from the inflated hopes of Moscow and Peking for Communist expansion.

Russia had taken over from Japan in Manchuria, the main area for Chinese heavy industry. The United States had demobilized at once at the end of World War II, so it was no use looking to America for help in that regard, even if the Chinese Communists had been inclined to do so. The only way to recover Manchuria was through a deal with Russia. If the North Koreans had retreated into Manchuria, it would have involved more Russian control there, perhaps Russian garrisons which might have stayed a long time, as has happened elsewhere. So China had to enter the Korean war. Also, Russia had already furnished economic assistance and technical help, and could give more, and further, it was part of the "Asian Communist dogma that the example of Soviet industrialization was more relevant to Asia than that of the United States."

They could count on Russia's long-term policy to weaken the West in Asia, as well as Japan.

So, in 1949, both Russian and Chinese Communists felt the time was ripe for a major extension of Communist influence in Asia. This called for joint action, for China was not able to exploit this without the backing of a great power. There was "a single wave" from the launching of open civil war in 1946, the Korean venture, to the exploitation of the Communist position in Indo-China and its diplomatic consolidation at Geneva in July, 1954.

These foreign adventures diverted the potential of the Communists away from domestic needs, but also served to divert the attention of the people from the difficulties they were facing.

From Revolution to Government

On arriving at full control in 1949, the Chinese Communist Party had nearly thirty years' growth, the hardening of a long war, and considerable administrative experience. But they had inherited the problems which the Nationalists had found insoluble. Propaganda, ideology, and the use of force had put them in control. But more than that was needed to restore and modernize the jaded economy of a vast nation.

Disillusion soon set in. Opposition developed, particularly in South China when forces were diverted to the northeast. The Communists began to resort to terror and to liquidate enemies of their regime. In February, 1951, a decree prescribed death or life imprisonment for a long list of "counter-revolutionary offenses." The illusion of a united front was fading.

This situation necessitated a change in policy, from the tactics of revolution to the methods of government.

Their domestic policy as of 1949 followed three main lines. First, the united front as set forth in Mao's "New Democracy" in 1940 was continued. Second, "land reform" was used as the method of gaining political control, especially in the south. Third, the communist-type organization of government and society was set up and consolidated. This involved expanding the Communist party, which dominated the government.

The publication of Mao's "New Democracy" had given noncommunist groups a hope of participating in the new regime, and this was now put into practice for the time being. The new government found it necessary to use existing government officials with experience, especially at the lower levels, and prominent noncommunists were put into ostensibly important posts, which temporarily gave the impression of a coalition government.

No effort was made to replace the bulk of the civil service. Private business was permitted. University curricula were little altered except for the addition of courses in Marxism.

This left them free to gain control through the process of land reform.

A program of land redistribution had enabled Mao to mobilize the rural riffraff into a Communist army and seize power. As "agrarian reform" it had served as a talking point to enlist the sympathies of liberal intellectuals and all who were looking for a new and better order. It misled America and other friends of China.

This had bound the surviving peasants to them on two counts. First, they had been brought into participation in people's courts that had liquidated landlords and wealthy peasants and had shared the guilt in what had amounted to semi-legalized lynchings. Second, large numbers had acquired a vested interest in the Communist regime which had given them land, buildings, and equipment belonging to the defunct bourgeois elements that they had helped to liquidate.

Under cover of guerrilla war against Japan, the Communists had consolidated their hold on the north and northwest. But they now controlled vast areas in the south in which they had as yet little or no peasant support. It was necessary to sell their program to them also. What could be better than the type of "agrarian reform" that had worked so well thus far?

So a nation-wide program of land distribution was set in motion.

Stages of Land Reform

This program was now more thoroughly organized, so as to serve not merely as a revolutionary expedient, but as basis for government organization. They had to begin at the bottom, for the masses in non-Communist China, prior to liberation, did not understand the objectives of Communist agrarian reform.

In new territory, this program was organized in five stages, which progressed hand-in-hand with the strengthening of the party and the other aspects of the Communist program.

First came the establishment of "revolutionary order," eliminating remnants of Nationalist troops, bandits, and anti-Communist forces. Cadres were sent in to instruct and direct. Local self-defense corps were set up. Second came the beginnings of administrative reform, the organization of peasant associations and regular militia, and various conferences. The third stage covered the final preparations for the process of land redistribution itself. Agrarian reform committees were set up at all levels. Peasant associations were expanded. Land was surveyed. The status of landlords was determined. The good work was begun in selected areas on an experimental basis.

The fourth stage brought action. Peasant conferences mobilized the peasants to "struggle" against the landlords. Land, houses, tools of the upper classes were confiscated. "Criminal" gentry were rounded up by the militia and tried by the people's tribunals. Peasant associations redistributed the confiscated land, and the People's Government issued title deeds.

The fifth stage consolidated all this, through election of village officials, grooming of peasant cadres for party membership, and establishment of peasant schools. It is estimated that half the land under cultivation was confiscated, along with some 7,000,000 buildings, 29,000,000 oxen, and a vast amount of food and implements. It was publicized that this was turned over to the poor farmers but experts consider it probable that most of the food, animals, and movable forms of wealth were taken over by the government, with an estimated value of eight billion American dollars. The new government had pillaged the people.

These five stages took two years or more.

People's Tribunals

The key agency in this process was the People's Tribunals which were established specifically for the period of agrarian reform and were to cease functioning when reorganization of the peasantry and economy was completed. They are to be distinguished from the permanent People's Courts, which have jurisdiction over ordinary civil and criminal cases.

The regulations governing these were promulgated July 20, 1950. Their duty was to deal with "criminals who violate the laws and orders pertaining to agrarian reform." They may pass the death sentence. The following description is from a Communist source (New China News Agency, Shanghai, March 20, 1951):

> On the basis of the data obtained from investigations and the accusations of the farmers, the people's tribunals, with the help of the militia, rounded up all of the despotic landlords . . . While trials were given by the people's tribunals, the masses were also mobilized to accuse them in public meetings.
>
> For despotic landlords deeply hated by the farmers, open trials attended by more than 10,000 persons were staged. In this manner the peasant's fervor was greatly increased.

The coming of formal political power led to a more regularized process of liquidation. Persons who were generally disliked were selected as examples for mass trial and condemnation, and this filled the rest with fear. Who might be the next target of some malicious accusation?

The total number executed during the process of land reform is conservatively estimated at a million and a half. (This covers only one period. The over-all figure is estimated by some as high as twenty million.)

How could such slaughter be justified?

During the earlier years of fighting, people were being killed all the time anyway, and it was just a part of the struggle that was going on. But now the Communists were the government, and peace and order had been established.

Slaughter Justified by Marxism

The official theory and explanation of land reform was presented by Liu Shao-ch'i in his formal commentary on the Agrarian Reform Law, promulgated June 30, 1950:

> The essential content of agrarian reform is the confiscation of the land of the landlord class for distribution to the landless and poor peasants.
>
> Thus the landlords as a class in society are abolished and the land ownership system of feudal exploitation is transformed into a system of peasant land ownership. This is indeed the greatest and most thorough reform in thousands of years of Chinese history.

But feudalism had been abolished with the establishment of the empire in 221 B.C., and land had been freely bought and sold ever since. Yet Mao, in his "New Democracy," had maintained that Chinese society was feudal until 1842. After which it became a semi-colonial, semi-feudal society.

Why this insistence on feudalism?

In the Marxist theory of the evolution of society, "ancient society" was followed by the feudal stage. It was therefore necessary to define Chinese society as feudal in order to justify a class war against the feudal landlords. This was deliberately and openly brutal, to make clear that a class war was going on.

But when Liu Shao-ch'i spoke of a "system of peasant land ownership" as quoted above, he did not explain to the peasants that this was merely a step in the process, and that in the not distant future their land was to be collectivized, and their private ownership disappear.

Land reform was primarily a means of seizing complete control, clear down to the village level. This would wreck the clan government and in its place install the Communist monolithic apparatus of power. This organization went hand-in-hand with land reform, and filled the vacuum created as the older system was destroyed. Also the loot from land reform, estimated at $8,000,000,000, along with a number of other exactions, enabled them to balance the budget and control inflation.

2

Communist Organization

The traditional government of China, as has been indicated above, was a makeshift conglomeration.

It had the emperor, his army and the government bureaucracy at the top, clan control at the bottom, and secret societies, local hoodlums, and bandits in the governmental gap in between.

The Communists set about organizing a monolithic apparatus of control from top to bottom.

Apparatus of Control

They did not confine themselves to a single, simple system of government, but set up multiple chains of command as follows: 1) party, 2) government, 3) military, 4) economic, trade unions in cities, cooperatives in country, 5) mass organizations for women, youth, children, labor, peasants, and many others. To these must be added two other areas of the utmost importance in the Communist regime, the agencies of agitation and propaganda, and the secret police.

Of course, all these could not be installed at once, particularly in regions where they had only recently assumed control.

Dominance of the Party

The party dominated and controlled the entire apparatus of government, largely by interlocking memberships, which put the party on the inside of every other agency at all levels.

The three main chains of command, party, government and military, all headed up in a small group dominated by Mao. Government and party employees numbered ten million military and militia and five million civilian officials.

It is unnecessary here to give details of the government struc ture as such. The distinctively Communist aspect was its control by the party and the other Communist agencies.

Mass organizations mobilized three former low-status groups: industrial workers, women, youth, as well as writers, students, and many others. No segment of life was left unorganized. All were controlled by the directives of the party.

There was an all-pervasive system of control in addition to the secret police. This included detailed reporting on individuals and families, permits for travel, party-managed local organizations, national mass organizations, and expanded education for indoctrination.

Consolidation of Control

The first internal task of the Communist leaders was to tighten their control. This was continued at first along the usual lines of agitation and propaganda. But the real object was not so much indoctrination as complete obedience.

This control had various aspects: leadership, party expansion, proletarian education, higher education, force.

The Communist ruling group in China consists of some fifty persons. Their characteristics derive from Chinese tradition, Soviet practice, and their own unique experience. They are revolutionists who now have to bear constructive responsibilities in the government they have taken over. The careers of forty-four as of 1945 were as follows: Communist party organizers and administrators, 20 (46%), military 17 (39%), labor 5 (11%), education and journalism, 2 (4%).

They are held together under Mao's leadership by a spirit of comradeship. They largely come from the three central provinces of Hunan, Szechwan, and Hupei, so that personal relations are reinforced by regional relationships and loyalties.

Theory vs. Reality of Power

This group has not been seriously concerned with Marxist theory. Nevertheless, it is "one of the well-established compulsions of Communism to rationalize courses of action in theoretical terms," and Mao is an intellectual, and perhaps the foremost living Communist theorist—certainly so in Chinese eyes.

But they are more concerned with the "reality of power." Witness Mao's unorthodox but successful basing of his revolution on peasants instead of urban proletariat. Rostow thinks that "if there is any authentic bias in Chinese Communism it is somewhat anti-theoretical." This fits in with the practical nature of the Chinese people.

Beginning with Lenin, Communist ideology has not been so much a theory of society as devotion to the party, particularly its methods of gaining power. Mao and his group may take the theory less seriously, but they have a profound devotion to the party and are "thoroughly professional Communists."

Yet there was at this time a distinct factor of ideological faith that matched their apocalyptic belief in the inevitability of a communist society as the certain result of the movement of history.

There is some indication that they tried to build what they thought were popular foundations for their rule. Perhaps this was chiefly on the part of the idealists and intellectuals who had been taken in by Mao's "New Democracy." Moscow had long since given up such persuasion and now emphasized material advance, power, and nationalism.

Party Expansion

Before liberation, the Communists had been in control in northwest China, most of North China, and in Manchuria. The Nationalists had held the Yangtze valley and the south. Their efforts to take over control in South China slowed them up.

To control the whole country a large increase in party membership would be necessary. Its growth was as follows:

1937	40,000
1945	1,210,000
1951	5,000,000
1954	6,000,000

But the rate of increase considerably slowed down over the three years, 1951 to 1954, and the party was too small to administer the greatly increased territory which they now had to govern. Their multiple chains of command and their intricate apparatus for the control of all aspects of life called for a huge bureaucracy.

To meet this situation, the Central Committee of the Chinese

Communist Party took action in 1952 and formally issued instructions for a campaign to recruit party members. This did not succeed very well.

Since its establishment in 1921 expansion of the party had been carried on secretly. This was the first time it was done openly with newspaper publicity. The reason was that the routine recruitment of new members had not resulted in sufficient strength. The *Yangtze Daily,* Wuhan (8/7/52) stated:

The party in the government offices in our Central and South Areas is not strong enough. Party members in some of the units only constitute 10.9% of their personnel.

In some business units, it is impossible to set up strong Party-branches owing to the scarcity of Party members in them. Some . . . are openly usurped in certain cases by unlawful bourgeois elements. . . .

We have to have the direct leadership of the Party in every unit of production. But at present, many of the productive units in the Southwest Area are without party-branches.

There are over 20,000 hsiang in the Southwest Area, of which 93% still have no Party-branches. . . .

The hsiang is the basic unit of rural administration, including one or several villages.

Party Control

The party was thus "unable to function as it should," and had to increase in size in order to do so. As a vice-premier put it (*People's Daily,* Peking, 1/31/53):

All the laws and directives promulgated by the Central People's Government are initiated by our Party. . . . Government is just an instrument of the Party, and all government organs are virtually Communist-Party-branches.

Therefore, everything depended on a sufficient supply of Party activists (cadres).

But the campaign did not always get results. Two years later it was reported:

In 24 counties in Kiangsi Province not a single new Party member has been recruited from May to October. About 50 per cent of the Party-branches in the government organs in Central and South Area are still marking time.

Kiangsi is the province where Mao had organized the first Soviet Republic in 1931.

Reason for Poor Results of Campaign

The Communists thought that, the Party being in absolute power, the people would scramble to join it. But five months passed with little development. An explanation appeared in three papers to the effect that "many party members did not want to take the . . . responsibility of acting as sponsors of activists (cadres)." This was true even among labor and students.

Among 150 workers in Amoy only one activist was selected. Less than 10 were selected from among the 600 members of the New Democratic Youth League in Amoy University.

Altogether about a million persons were trained, and about 400,000 recruited into the Party. This included a great number of new Party members with "unawakened consciousness."

This partial failure, however, is not very important in itself, as, even without recruiting a single new member, the Communist Party could still remain in absolute power. Its significance is that it has manifested the real attitude of the Chinese people towards the Communist regime.

Quality of Party Members

The quality of party members left much to be desired. Thus it was reported (*South Daily,* Canton, 9/19/52):

Many comrades, though knowing vaguely that life under Communism will be good, have only very faint ideas about what a Communist society is like, about how to bring about Communism in China, and about what they themselves have to do to achieve Communism.

A cross-section of one training class is given in the following report (*South Daily,* Canton, 10/21/52):

Total Trainees	590 (Men 457, Women 133)
Hired Farm Hands	107
Poor Peasants	463
Middle Peasants	16

This has a familiar look, and indicates that Mao and his group are continuing to use the ones at the bottom of the social scale. Their educational qualifications are not impressive, even for rural China. They are reported as follows (Junior primary is four years):

Illiterates	175
Having attended junior primary schools	372
Having attended senior primary schools	40
Having attended junior middle schools	3

These are the people who are to govern China at the grass roots.

Control Through Psychological Conditioning

The process of land reform was carried through under the direction of party activists. They sought out the landlords. They staged the public trials. They worked up the mass condemnations. They saw to it that the executions—a million and a half—were duly carried out.

What manner of men were they, and how could they be brought to deal in this inhuman fashion with their own people?

This leads to the most sinister aspect of Communism, the process of psychological conditioning, often called brain washing. It should be noted in passing that this was used not only in the training of activists, but variations of it were used to extort confessions, condition university professors, and the like.

The object was to secure party activists who would be wholly dedicated and utterly obedient, and the key to the inside working of Communist control in China is to be found in the nature and work of these dedicated and fanatical men and women.

The Activist

The Chinese technical term that is frequently translated "activist" means the one who activates whatever program or project he is ordered to put through. But it is more than that. The term "cadre" is still more frequently used. This word means framework. In military parlance it is the skeleton organization of trained men who whip the new recruits into shape and provide a framework of experience and discipline. But it is more than that. The best translation is probably "executive."

The activist may be visible and known but often operates secretly. He is an invisible executive.

These are men who have, in a very definite and actual fashion, stepped out of this real world into the artificial and fantastic fourth dimension of the Communist wonderland, where the end justifies the lie, and any crime is a virtue if it serves Communist ends, where the decencies that make up our humanity no longer apply, and the love between parents and children and between husband and wife, along with pity, loyalty, and truth, become merely bourgeois sentimentality to be sneered at.

This state is reached by a psychological convulsion analogous to conversion. It is akin to religious experience in that it is, in its own way, a new life, wherein the devotee does what he does voluntarily.

It is a break with the past, an entering into a different life. Here are to be found the roots of that strange emphasis on the principle of voluntariness, which has been noted above.

It has a theoretical foundation, in which philosophy, psychology, and physiology combine. The process of psychological conditioning carries the philosophical-psychological theory into effect.

Theoretical Basis

It is necessary, therefore, to understand the theoretical basis which the process of psychological conditioning translates into action.

This goes back to and is based upon the Marxist theory of knowledge, which was expounded by Mao in his essay "On Practice" in 1937. Excerpts follow:

> The epistemology of dialectical materialism raised practice to a position of primary importance. It regards human knowledge as being at no point separable from practice.
>
> Class struggle . . . especially exerts a profound influence on the development of man's knowledge. In a class society everyone lives with a certain class status, and all his thoughts are stamped with the seal of his class.
>
> Man's social practice alone is the criterion of truth in his cognition of the external world.

All of this being so, the Communist party must act accordingly in line with the following:

> At the present stage of the development of society the responsibility of correctly understanding the world and changing it has already fallen

with the whole weight of history upon the shoulders of the proletariat and its political party.

The struggle of the proletariat and revolutionary people in changing the world consists of carrying out the following tasks: to reconstruct the external world; to reconstruct their own subjective world, that is to remould their faculty of knowing; and to change the relations between the subjective and external worlds.

The external world which is to be changed includes the persons who are opposed to that change. To be remoulded they will have to go through a stage of compulsion before they enter into a stage of remoulding on their own accord.

Mao's last sentence above calls for special emphasis as combining compulsion leading to voluntary action.

The Training Process

Cadre training was a process which included:

(1) Organized indoctrination.
(2) Psychological conditioning.
(3) Self-criticism and confession, to cut them off from their past.
(4) "Steeling" the cadre to all sorts of violence.

By this process the carefully selected human raw material is turned into the ideal new Soviet executive.

Indoctrination

Indoctrination consists of the following: reading immense quantities of Communist writings, Marx, Lenin, Stalin, Mao; taking profuse notes on lectures that run from two to seven hours without a break; almost continuous discussion in small groups of reading and lectures in which all must participate constructively, and individuals are reprimanded if they fail to do so.

Psychological conditioning is based on the experiments and theories of the Russian physiologist, Pavlov, who held that "man integrates impressions from his environment into his reflexes" and was in line with the Communist dogma of "economic environmental determination." This was introduced by Liu who was the party's discipline specialist, and added a Chinese twist to the Russian techniques, on a mass basis. His technique was implemented by six factors in the Communist training institutes, such as the New China People's Revolutionary University with 8,500 students:

(1) Training takes place within a controlled area, which they are not allowed to leave.

(2) The merciless schedule involves constant physical and mental fatigue. During the first few months they are worn down by heavy physical labor. There is no opportunity to relax or reflect.

(3) There is constant tension. It is almost impossible for most to keep up with the work assigned. But they must be always alert or take the consequences.

(4) There is constant uncertainty. Each group of about 23 includes a secret cadre. They do not know who he is, only that they are being constantly spied on. They are never sure whether they are behaving correctly or not. Some disappear. A rumor is started that they have been sent to a forced labor camp. The rest increase their efforts.

(5) They must use a special language—the old ways are rotten, the new glorious.

(6) All is deadly—this is the appropriate adjective—serious. Humor is bourgeois and decadent.

Such is the atmosphere in which the process of psychological conditioning is carried out. The resistance of the trainee is worn down.

Breaking with the Past

Self-criticism begins with a diary and ends with public confession with criticism by the rest of the group. The diary reviews the past in the light of Communist theory. Most of the trainee's past has to be condemned. If he does not do a thorough job of it, he is criticized, and has to do it over, again and again. He may not believe a lot of this when he starts, but after days and weeks of merciless pressure in this hectic atmosphere he becomes conditioned by this environment. He comes to believe in spite of himself. At last comes confession. His past, his parents, have been all wrong. He confesses it publicly. The confession must be complete. Perhaps he cannot sleep. A neighbor—they sleep on the floor, 24 to a room—remarks on this to the effect that he must still have something on his mind, and better confess it. Thus he cuts himself off from his past. It is a time of terrific strain. Many weep. Not a few lose their minds.

Self-Criticism

The backbone of the Revolutionary University course was investigation into the views and attitudes of every student. This went back three generations, and covered home, school, personal relationships. They must point out the contradictions between their present thoughts and the bad capitalist society in which they had been reared. They must confess their dark past.

"If you don't reveal your wrong thoughts," they were warned, "they will become heavier until . . . you will no longer be able to bear their great weight."

"The ordeal when everyone had to read his thought conclusion aloud in class was horrible . . . Voices trembled . . . boys and girls cried openly in class. Some cracked up under the strain."

Steeling

"Steeling" comes next. The devil has been cast out. The mind is swept and garnished. "The Communists approach humans with a manipulative attitude." Their object is to make them into units in the party structure "which will function."

An actual piece of field work at the North China People's University is recorded by Hunter. A class of 200 students was taken to a village where a landowner's wife was on trial before a "peoples court" of some 250 farmers, presided over by a party member. Accusations were called for. Several said she was all right. Others accused her of oppression and cruelty. The party man then said she was obviously guilty and there was no need to hear from others. He asked what punishment they decreed. She was first ordered to strip. At this point some of the girl students began to weep. The fury of the crowd increased; the better element left until less than a hundred remained. Taunts and stones were followed by kicks and blows and the woman was beaten to death.

Next day in group discussion this was discussed "with the casualness of a lab experiment" and girl students were reprimanded for breaking into tears and "not knowing your friends from your enemies." This was sentimentality which must be cured by self-criticism.

"Self-cultivation" is the name given to this process by Liu Shao-ch'i.

Breaking the Family

For the first two months boy and girl students were segregated. Then they were considered politically mature enough to mingle and were free to go as far as they pleased. One former student reported that so far as he knew 17 girls were pregnant at graduation. They asked permission to marry and the boys wanted to marry them. The authorities refused. They would not be assigned to the same locality and marriage would only handicap their Party activities.

The girls asked, "Who will be the father of my child? It is shameful to have a baby without a father."

The university answered that this was a feudal idea. They were informed, "Your child will be the people's boy and will be raised by the government."

Many students were already married. They were advised to get a divorce.

"If you resume living together," they were told, "either she will influence you or you will influence her . . . Experience has shown that for the most part it is always the person who does not participate in idea training who influences the other."

The students asked why old thoughts should decisively influence new thoughts and overwhelm them. The answer was:

"After spending 20 or more years in the old society . . . remnants of it will still persist in your memories, and this is what makes it possible for you to suffer a relapse."

A number of the married students were persuaded to divorce wives or husbands. The ex-student reported that they were a pathetic looking lot.

"Don't weep," the Party member would tell them. "Be a man."

There were no marks and no formal exams. Revolutionary reliability was all that mattered.

A New Dimension of Power

Such is the training of the Communist activists who are the executives of Communism in China to-day.

If the picture seems overdrawn, it should be remembered that these are the ones who presided over the lynchings—invested with a Communist style pseudo-legality—of a million and a half of their fellow Chinese. Let their record validate the picture.

The chief development of cadre training came about 1942, after the Communists had taken control of a large area in northwest China under cover of the united front.

The leading Revolutionary University had trained 10,000 such activists by March, 1949. Previous to that a Moscow training school for Chinese had been graduating 500 a year since 1931, a total of 10,000 by 1950. But these were only a part.

Walker sums up the significance of this, and rightly comments as follows:

> This system of conversion, and changing of thought patterns in many ways constitutes a new dimension of power in the world to-day.
>
> The development of psychological control techniques has contributed far more to the thoroughness and success of the Communist regime in unifying China than has been apparent in accounts published in the West.

Let the free world beware.

4

Education and Intellectuals

There is no country in the world where education has been more highly honored than in China, or where it has brought greater rewards in official position, prestige and privilege. Nowhere has genuine scholarship been more highly esteemed. But today education in China is merely a means employed by the Communists to strengthen and consolidate their control.

A program was set up for the training of the masses. Its object was defined by the Minister of Education as follows:

> The political significance of proletarian education lies in the fact that it is indispensable in the consolidation and development of the people's democratic dictatorship, as well as in the building-up of a strong national defense army and a gigantic economic power.

This was further elaborated by the vice-minister, as follows:

> In a capitalist country . . . the objective of workers' education is to increase the workers' knowledge and technique so that they may be promoted . . . with better wages, positions and livelihood.
>
> Our education . . . is entirely different. Our objective is to educate the working class to contribute their efforts positively and efficiently towards the consolidation and development of the victory they have already achieved.

A system of spare-time education was developed which by 1953 enrolled some 3,000,000 workers and 42,000,000 peasants. Teachers were largely part-time, some being primary and secondary teachers who were already overloaded. Most were obtained from the masses by mobilizing literate workers, staff members, peasants, in accordance with Mao's dictum, "Make the people educate themselves." Such teachers received no pay. Teaching materials were defined by a high official as "Overstuffed with political indoctrination, and full of dry stereotyped political slogans."

Among workers, school conflicts with production, and many workers' schools closed down because of time shortage. In the country an official directive in 1953 stated:

> In this year's winter schools, political indoctrination should be the main work.
>
> To educate the peasants so that they can organize themselves, increase their grain production, and sell their surplus grain enthusiastically to the government.

The New Higher Education

In November 1946 there were 182 institutions of higher education, with 18,094 teachers and officers, and 80,646 students. By February 1953 there were 208 institutions, about 30,000 teachers, and by September 1953, 220,000 students.

Institutions were drastically reorganized. There had been 65 universities in 1950. This was reduced to seven universities for general studies. Technical schools were increased. Private institutions were eliminated.

At a conference in December 1945, the Minister of Education defined the new education:

> The Education of New China reflects the politics and economy of New China, and serves as an instrument of struggle for the consolidation and development of the People's Democratic Dictatorship. The key of educational work in the newly liberated areas is to win the intellectuals over and to strive for their unity and reformation. The present schools must be maintained and gradually reformed.
>
> After the rehabilitation of the schools in the newly liberated areas, the main task is to carry on political and ideological education.

Curriculum Reform

First came curriculum reform. The reaction of the teachers was largely passive. Most professors would not express their opinions at meetings; the majority of the younger lecturers and assistant-teachers were, however, very enthusiastic, being eager to display their progressiveness and hopeful to get more important positions in the new teaching plans.

When pressed to say something about the new curriculum, a department head in Peking said: "I don't think there is any necessity to ask for our opinions. The People's Government is always right."

The students were more enthusiastic. Changes were always welcome; and some were glad to get rid of some of the difficult courses. Most held a passive attitude. A student of Peking University remarked: "We are here to be trained. We are fed by the People. Naturally we must be given whatever courses our trainer considers proper."

The ideological remoulding movement (official translation) started in September 1951 and raged for a year. Tens of thousands of intellectuals were brought to their knees, accusing themselves relentlessly.

The Minister of Education of the Central and South Area stated:

> Ideological reform is different from the old political education. It is a severe political duty, an order which must be carried out. . . .
>
> Of course, ideological reform should be carried on a basis of voluntariness, by criticism and self-criticism, not by compulsory orders; but with the swift development of the revolution, whoever still lacks this "voluntariness" shall lag behind, unable to catch up with the march of times. . . .

There was scarcely any resistance. But this success, in the opinion of six refugee teachers who had experienced the ordeal, was one of intimidation, not indoctrination. Refugee teachers agree that in most it inspired, not faith in the Communist dogmas, but a sense of being hunted, of loneliness, depression, fear, and hate. They admit, however, that quite a lot of younger intellectuals have actually been indoctrinated by this process.

Reform of Teaching

Teaching was reformed by three innovations: the Specialty, the Group of Design and Direction of Teaching, and the Teaching Group.

A vice-minister defined the Specialty as follows:

Teaching is based on the specialty, the department becoming merely an administrative unit. The government plans the installation of specialties . . . according to the needs of national construction. Each has a teaching plan in which every course is compulsory, no course is optional.

The Group of Design and Direction of Teaching is the basic teaching organization, composed of all the teachers of one course, or of several related courses. The following is a sample report of the GDDT in action:

The teachers of Tsinghua University, since 1952, have all been organized into the GDDTs . . . The 40 GDDTs in the school have adopted such new methods as: collective preparation of lectures, discussion of teaching programs and materials . . . demonstration trial-lecturing by old professors, practising trial-lecturing by new assistant-teachers . . . study of the teaching methods of Russian experts.

These included 186 meetings for the study of teaching methods . . . 129 teaching programs for the next semester will be revised . . . all teachers will attend political studies six hours a week, and most will attend Russian language classes at least six hours a week.

Student representatives are to be present at trial-lectures and teachers attend each other's classes.

The teachers do not lecture freely [sic] or make arbitrary discourses as they did before. Now, the outlines and lectures of the courses must be approved by the GDDT . . . Democracy is also fully manifested in teaching, since the student representatives participate in the meetings of the GDDT and reflect the opinions of the students.

Each teacher is one of a teaching group. The class is not taught by the teacher himself. He is merely the representative of the GDDT.

The Russian Model

Russian scholarship is being followed to great lengths. A Chinese professor wrote an article entitled "Superiority of Soviet Russian Teaching Materials of the English Language" and praised the superiority of the Russian textbook "Advanced Reading of the English Language" which was adopted by his University in 1953.

The teaching of Chinese literature must also follow Russian materials.

The Department of Chinese Literature should study the part in Malenkov's report concerning literary problems, Stalin's treatise on philology.

China has translated and published nearly 3,000 scientific and technical books by Soviet authors . . . the combined print is more than 20 million copies . . . according to the Publication Administration Bureau of the Ministry of Culture (Peking NCNA 11/7/55).

The Educational Factory System

Teachers and students are overburdened with work. If there are five teachers in a GDDT, then, for each hour of classroom-lecture, each teacher has to spend at least one hour in the GDDT to deliver his own trial-lecture, four hours to listen to the trial-lectures of his colleagues, and four hours for reading and discussing each other's lectures, besides the time spent for preparing his own lecture. The Vice-Minister of Education defined the new system:

Institutions of higher learning, which are factories producing cadres for construction, must rely upon strict planning of teaching to ensure that the quality and quantity of products will be up to the standard.

The fundamental approach to this problem is to adopt the advanced experience of the Soviet Union as our blueprint, and then associate it with the practical conditions in China, besides critically adopting some achievements of the capitalistic countries in natural sciences.

There was a program of rapid expansion of higher education, with annual quotas. Thus, in 1952, it was planned to admit 50,000 to college, although there were only 30,000 high-school graduates. The quota for 1953 was 70,000. The Minister stated in 1953:

Educational work in the past three years has shown a tendency of blind development. The tendency to pay attention to quantity and not to quality has been very serious.

The most serious problem is the inadequate number and incompetence of teachers. In East China, where the deficit is less serious, the ratio of teachers and students in the advanced industrial schools is 1:80. In some GDDTs, young assistant-teachers have become the basic staff on account of the lack of professors.

The Finished Product

In the new higher education, a student is recruited into an institution of higher learning, assigned to a specialty which he may never have dreamed of, taught by representatives of GDDTs, and, equipped with a limited technical knowledge, sent to a job allocated to him of which he may know nothing. The whole process is governed by centralized planning and enforced by political control. The student cannot refuse to go to the school or take the specialty to which he is allocated; he has no optional courses; he cannot ask for transference to another school or department or specialty; he cannot give up attendance at school; and at graduation he has no choice but to accept the job given by the government. He is a piece of raw material going through a factory. An official article puts it as follows:

> Many students are still considering the problem from their personal point of view, placing personal interests above national interests, without seeing the glory and happiness of being a youth in Mao Tse-tung's Age . . . The proper attitude is to join the unified examination, and obey the unified allocation of the State. Any personal short-sighted plan, in the face of the great call of the State, is negligible.

The Intellectuals

In 1949 China had some five million college and middle school graduates and about 40 million with primary education. They had had a part in one attempt after another to modernize China. All they had to show for it was a little progress and a country devastated by war.

Over against this drab background were the glittering promises of the Communists. Their success in organizing their territory contrasted with the unsuccessful efforts of the Nationalist Government to deal with insoluble problems. Their genuine fervor and messianic double-talk masked their harsh measures.

The intellectuals had watched this process. In comparison the standard methods of education and national reorganization seemed too slow. They were in favor of a short-cut, something more drastic. To Christianity they said, "The Communists are doing things you only talk about."

Three aspects of the traditional scholar-official point of view fitted in with the Communist ideology and made them susceptible to Mao's "New Democracy": (1) government by an elite class—themselves, (2) the fact that the common man had counted for little, and the gentry ran things and spoke for him, (3) an anti-middle-class attitude which had always ranked businessmen low in the social scale.

A large part of the initial Communist success was due to the enthusiasm of youth, especially high-school students. Chinese students took themselves most seriously as a result of the traditional tie-up between scholarship and official position. They were "expectant" officials. They had a deep sense of their own dignity, and those of us who administered schools in China in those days learned that they could not be treated merely as school boys. They were different from students in America.

They had taken the lead in rousing the country against Japanese aggression in 1919. They had played a part in all subsequent upheavals.

Now the Communists appealed not only to a fiery patriotism but to adolescent pride. They were given leadership and enticing and exciting possibilities of rapid advancement to positions of power. It went to their heads. It was a wonderful improvement over the old Confucian rules of seniority.

The Communist leaders were concerned with obedience rather than ability. They whipped up a fanatic enthusiasm among the youthful educated who rode the crest of the Communist wave and uncritically accepted all their bright promises of the future.

There has since been disillusion. But youths who have come early to power have at least that to compensate for any disillusion. They are likely to hold on to it, particularly when there is no practical alternative.

Then came brain-washing and confession. The intellectual was made terribly aware that his entire livelihood, even his continued existence, was involved.

In the past the gentry had returned to their own clans and villages under adverse circumstances. Thus they had survived. Now the gentry—the landlord-scholar-official class—had lost their land. They had no place to go.

The Cadre

The young Communist activist in China belongs in the class of twentieth-century totalitarian enthusiasts along with Mussolini's Blackshirts, Stalin's party activists and Hitler's Brownshirts.

His initial task was war and propaganda. But with Communist control after 1949, constructive work was necessary. Here were hard cold facts that had to be faced and dealt with successfully. It was not at all as easy as Communist promises had led him to believe or his own ideals and enthusiasm had pictured.

Reaction of Intellectuals

In due course the university faculties began to reassert themselves, as has happened repeatedly in Chinese history. In January, 1957, seventy professors from twelve technical institutes came together in a symposium convened by the Ministry of Higher Education for revising the pedagogic plans for technical institutes. With them met representatives of seven national government business departments.

Almost total emphasis had been placed on technical education, and only three per cent of university students were allowed to study the humanities. But it had not worked out. The defects of the university mass production began to show up.

The government planners at the head of the business departments greatly overestimated the number of technicians they would need. So graduates of narrowly specialized technical courses had to change to some other occupation, for which they were not trained.

Highly specialized training had aimed to put graduates immediately into engineering positions in factories, but many had made a poor showing. It was clearly necessary to elevate the quality of university work. The professors urged more emphasis on fundamental theory. The foreign language problem came up in this connection.

There was a reaction among universities in Peking in 1956–57. They found that students who could read only Russian were barred from many technical publications in English or German, and have put increased emphasis on the study of these languages. Tsinghua

University opened courses in English and German for faculty members.

This was getting down to reality. This was not merely a question of party orthodoxy to be solved by more indoctrination. It was beginning to be apparent that it was necessary to get something that would work.

However, the main strength of Communism is in the vast number holding positions, large or small, of power and privilege who thus have a vested interest in perpetuating the Communist regime, and who, apart from it, would be nonentities.

5

Agricultural Production Cooperatives

Land reform with its mass trials reached its high point in 1951. In addition to the million and a half executed under the guidance of the cadres, untold numbers committed suicide. Some thirty-five million were branded as exploiters or class enemies.

But the transfer to peasant ownership brought about by land reform was only preliminary. Complete socialization was the goal. This took the form of Agricultural Production Cooperatives.

State Grain Monopoly

One of the earlier moves in this direction was in November, 1953, when the purchase of grain from producers and its sale to consumers become a state monopoly.

This established the "three fixed" norms, whereby the state set the production quota for each household, determined the quota to be collected in taxes or purchased, and established the quantity which each rural grain-deficient household may purchase from the state.

The object was to expand agricultural production so that it could provide for "around 100,000,000 inhabitants in cities and industrial and mining districts . . . some 50,000,000 peasants in areas producing industrial crops only, 50,000,000 who were short of grain, and some tens of millions in flooded areas" (*Peking Jen Min Jih Pao,* 3/9/55).

This was to "consolidate the alliance between the workers and the people," which meant that the peasants must provide the food for the workers in the state program of industrialization, or the whole Communist plan would break down. Hence the supreme emphasis that came to be placed on making the agricultural production cooperatives a success.

End of Peasant Ownership

This envisaged the end of the peasant ownership of land which had been the object of the land reform movement. Here is evidence —if needed—that the land distribution program had been merely the method of seizing power.

There was a doctrinaire reason. A key editorial in the *Peking People's Daily* (11/25/53) was in almost the same words as those used by Stalin in the 1920's:

> Socialism cannot be established on two entirely different and contradictory foundations, one of which is a great, progressive socialist industry, the other being a backward economy of small peasants that frequently promotes capitalism.

But the Russian failure in this regard had only recently been revealed by Krushchev's speech of August, 1953, and it is improbable that this was either unknown, or overlooked by them. This makes it unlikely that this was the real reason.

It was also a means to the further consolidation of power, to secure complete control in a way the Chinese empire had never attempted to do, by destroying the ancient structure of rural life, and extending the control apparatus of the Communist state to the local level, thus replacing clan control.

One observer suggests that the Communists began to realize their increasing unpopularity, especially when some 75 per cent of the war prisoners in Korea refused to return to Communist China, and therefore decided to speed up the process of securing complete control.

Peasant Resistance

As in Russia and in the European satellites, so in China there was peasant resistance.

Peking admitted that this program was poorly administered at first, and the confusion was enhanced by the disastrous floods of 1954. Early in 1955 food was short in many parts of China. The State Council on March 3, 1955, imposed stricter controls.

The *Peking Jen Min Jih Pao* editorialized on peasant attitudes (3/9/55). It noted:

The misapprehension that the more they produce, the more the state would purchase, and that what they could get out of the increased production would not be much.

This was confirmed by reports in the Communist press from widely separated provinces—Kwangtung, Hupei, Anhwei:

Only 29 out of 300 households accepted their production quotas.

Peasants in many places were neglecting their crops, this was menacing seriously the autumn harvest, and the peasant masses were worried to death.

The pooling of animals had a bad effect. When they were turned into common property, no one looked after them. The middle peasants did not want to spend money on fodder for animals that no longer belonged to them, and the poor peasants could not afford it. A village is cited where the cooperative acquired twenty-two oxen. In a short period, fifteen became dangerously emaciated and four died. There was a shortage of fodder, due to extension of the foodstuff growing areas, and to the plan for cultivating hillsides. The press stated: "The number of draught animals killed, or dying from starvation or cold is very serious." In one county the number was reduced from 3,424 to 1,993 within a year or so. The press demanded that the killing of animals be more severely punished.

All this came to a climax when the province of Chekiang dissolved 15,000 out of 53,000 agricultural cooperatives without the approval of either the provincial Party Committee or of the Central Government. An editorial in the *Hangchow Jih Pao* (5/4/55) gave the reasons as follows:

Among these three kinds of cooperatives, only the first is able to proceed with production in a normal manner.

The others have, since the spring of this year, revealed more and more faults, which had a harmful effect on spring plowing. In some . . . because of mishandling of financial affairs, members were reluctant to invest their labor, and fertilizers, seeds, and farm implements have not been properly prepared.

In co-ops whose members have not joined voluntarily, the situation was much more serious; the members had no plans for spring planting; they had no zeal for production at all.

Mao Forces the Issue

Mao took sharp issue with this and made an important speech on July 31, 1955. This was implemented by vote of the Sixth Plenary Session of the Seventh Central Committee of the Chinese Communist Party on October 11, 1955.

The agricultural production cooperative now emerged as the crux of the Communist program, and a sine-qua-non of industrialization. Mao's speech was important as defining the issue. He began by affirming belief in the predetermined advance of Communism, the enthusiasm of the peasants, and the capability of the party.

> We must believe (1) the poor peasants, the lower strata among the new middle peasants, and the lower strata among the old middle peasants, because of the economic difficulties . . . possess the active enthusiasm for pursuing the road of socialism . . . and (2) the party is capable of leading the people of the whole country to the socialist society.

> An agricultural production cooperative must increase the output of its crops compared with the individual peasants or mutual aid teams . . . Of the 650,000 agricultural producer cooperatives, more than 80 per cent have increased the output of their crops.

He then stated his program to cover some five five-year plans.

> The production of marketed grain and industrial raw materials in our country today is very low, and the state's requirements of these resources are growing year by year, this being an acute contradiction.

> If we cannot in the space of about three five-year plans basically solve the problem of the cooperativization of agriculture, that is to say, turn the small scale operation with animal power implements into large-scale mechanized operation, including the state-organized large-scale settlement reclamation schemes using machinery (in the space of three five-year plans, it is proposed to reclaim from 400 to 500 million mow of wasteland), then we shall not solve the present contradiction . . . and we cannot accomplish our socialist industrialization.

> During the first and second five-year plans, reforms in the rural areas will still be mainly social reforms, and technical reforms will only occupy a subsidiary place. Large-sized agricultural machinery will be increased, but will still not be very numerous.

During the period of the third five-year plan, reforms in the rural areas will consist of both social reforms and technical reforms promoted simultaneously, the use of large-sized agricultural machinery will be greatly extended annually. . . .

Also the use of mechanized operations in all departments and areas where mechanized operations are possible. . . .

The time needed for technical reforms may be longer than that needed for social reforms . . . the basic completion on a nation-wide scope of technical reforms . . . will call for four to five five-year plans. . . .

Crisis

It was recognized that this was a crisis. But the agricultural production cooperatives that Mao demanded could not be set up merely by common peasants who are "not always thinking in terms of the benefit to the cooperative." A trained cadre had to be put inside each co-op to "guide" it. This led to an all-out effort. The *Study Monthly* (11/2/55) stated:

Various places in the whole country have detached large numbers of cadres from leading organs at various levels, and sent them deeply into the rural villages. . . .

These included a Vice-Director of the Posts and Tele-Communications Bureau, and a number of others of similar high rank.

Social Reform Measures

In this speech, Mao distinguished between social reforms and technical reforms.

Up to now the Chinese Communists have had their chief success in the area of social reforms, which they have ruthlessly put through regardless of the human cost, but now they faced the "acute contradiction" between the increasing needs of the state to feed its industrial workers and the low yield of grain.

The campaign was pushed vigorously everywhere by such special measures, and on November 21, 1955, the New China News Agency was able to report that up to November 10 of that year 1,200,000 agricultural production cooperatives had been established, 590,000 of them since July 31, when Mao had forced the issue. By January 1, 1956, it was 1,900,000. And on February 9, Radio Peking reported that the government had decided to grant an "unprecedented amount of agricultural loans for 1956, which altogether would total about a billion American dollars."

The agricultural production cooperative had emerged as the key issue in the whole Communist program.

Technical reforms were put off. Mao stated that during the first and second five-year plans, "technical reforms will only occupy a subsidiary place." During the third, social and technical reforms will be "promoted simultaneously." But the "basic completion on a nation-wide scope of technical reforms . . . will call for four to five five-year plans."

6

THE REAL COMMUNIST OBJECTIVES

Communism is imperialism in a new guise—or rather disguise. This appears in the ruthless conquests of the Russian satellites in Europe, and in the readiness of Russia to starve to death four millions of her own people so that by exporting their grain she could buy machinery for heavy industry as a basis for overwhelming military power. It appears again in the Stalin-Mao plan for taking over Korea and Indo-China, and in the Chinese seizure of Tibet.

In China this has been approached step by step: Mao's mobilization of rural gangsters, the stratagem of the united front, the communist seizure of power, and the nationalization of the food supply through agricultural cooperatives.

"For the people"—such is the slogan that has captured the imagination of idealists in all lands and raised up a prolific crop of devoted doctrinaires, fanatics, parlor-pinks, fellow travellers, and traitors in nearly all lands.

But who are the people? Not all the people in the usual sense of the word, but the chosen classes. Here is Mao's definition:

> Who are the "people"? At the present stage in China, they are the working class, the peasantry, the petty bourgeoisie and the national bourgeoisie.

But who decides who are the people and who are not? The Party.

One of the most astute observers in Hong Kong states that the communist leaders in China know perfectly well they can expect no considerable increase from the agricultural production cooperatives in a large part of the country, and are merely using these as a pretext for consolidating an iron control over rural China.

Outside observers tend to assume that it is necessary that they make a success of their agricultural program. But this is mere honest democratic thinking. It is necessary to inquire, success for whom? Not for everybody in the democratic fashion, but for the professional communists in power.

There is an ideological reason for this, as witness the dictum of Lenin quoted by Stalin, as referred to above.

As long as we live in a country where small-peasant farming predominates, there is a firmer base for capitalism in Russia than for Communism. Socialism must encompass agriculture as well as industry.

There is also a solid practical reason. The Chinese Communist dictators cannot feel secure as long as a socialized industry is superimposed on an agriculture based on private property and including eighty per cent of the population.

They cannot have failed to note that the Russian cooperatives have not been a success. They do not care. For example, in the disastrous floods of 1953, it was reported that peasant relief in only four provinces was costing Yuan 1,670,000,000. This was followed by drastic reductions. The official attitude was that the starving peasants would have to depend on "self-aid by production."

The question of slave labor bears on this. In October, 1952, the Ministry of Water Conservancy reported:

In the past two years, 10,370,000 conscripted workers participated in water conservancy work throughout China, under the supervision of 320,000 armed police.

The Nationalist delegation to the United Nations presented an estimate of 24,000,000 slave laborers in China, based on statements and documents from Communist sources.

This is in cynical contrast to the pronouncement in the magazine *Political Study* (June 1955)

Marxism-Leninism is the revolutionary doctrine that leads the laboring people of the world to a happy life.

Racing with the Capitalist Countries

Much closer to the real objectives is an article written for the National Day, entitled "Racing with the Capitalist Countries." (*Peking Kwang Ming Jih Pao* 10/1/55)

It is a very serious task for China to catch up and surpass capitalist countries.

During the first five-year plan of our country, steel output will be stepped up from 1,350,000 tons to 4,120,000 tons. It took the United States 17 years to do it, Germany and the United Kingdom 23 years, France 48 years and Japan 11 years . . . Our five years will equal 11 to 48 years in capitalist countries.

In the course of this peaceful race, the annual iron and steel output in our country has exceeded 1,000,000 tons. We should understand the meaning of a country producing 1,000,000 tons of iron and steel . . With that amount of iron, England was able to mechanize . . . her textile industry, build large numbers of merchant vessels and warships and control her seas. It was also this huge mass of iron that enabled England to break open China's doors during the Opium War.

In 1931 Japan produced 1,600,000 tons of steel and established the puppet Manchukuo and seized our territory and assumed leadership of East Asia. Now we are able to say that this will not happen again . . . In 1936 Japan produced 4,590,000 tons of steel. Japan was then the strongest nation in Asia and one of the capitalist powers of the world. The Chinese people were fighting those 4,000,000 tons of steel.

In the course of the peaceful race, China envisages an output of 10,000,000 tons by the final year of the second five-year plan . . . By 1914 Germany produced 8,200,000 tons of pig iron and 1,390,000 tons of steel. This represented the important capital of Kaiser Wilhelm II in his attempt to subjugate all Europe. By 1937 German output reached 17,490,000 tons while British output stayed at 13,900,000 tons.

Between the last two wars, first-class imperialist powers dominating Europe were essentially nations capable of producing over 10,000,000 tons of iron and steel. Japan produced only 6,850,000 tons during 1940. This figure had already boosted the ambition of Japanese militarists to the extent of subjugating Southeast Asia.

It is obvious to see where we will be going in the race with imperialist nations. Our iron and steel output has now surpassed that of England at the time of the Opium War and has overtaken that of Japan during the September 18 incident (1931). We are now heading for the target matching the scope of Japanese iron and steel industry during the earlier phase of China's war of resistance against Japan. Looking toward the future, our country may be able to catch up with and surpass Japan . . . by the time our second five-year plan is put through.

We should be able to catch up with industrially advanced imperialist nations in Europe during the period before and after World War II by the time we carry out the third five-year plan.

We will catch up with them and surpass them step by step.

The All-Asia War

The present situation in China is international.

This is particularly true of the Communist psychology and world strategy. In this connection Hunter quotes the evidence of the diaries of guerrillas in Malaya, and sums up as follows:

We were thinking in patches . . . Americans were talking about the "Korean war." Englishmen were speaking about the "Malayan war." Frenchmen were referring to the "Indo-China war."

But neither the Chinese Communists nor any other Communists in Asia used that terminology. They spoke of the "All-Asia War," of the "Korea-China-Indo-China-Philippines front," of the "Anti-Imperialist War."

While non-Communist authorities . . . were thinking and acting locally, the Communists were operating globally. Asia was one front to them.

Communism is imperialism in a new disguise. The Chinese Communist leaders seek power. First for themselves in China. Then throughout Asia.

7

Communist Contradictions

The agricultural production cooperatives have involved the Chinese Communists in a fundamental contradiction. The poor peasants are the ones on whom their control depends, but the middle peasants have the agricultural know-how.

The magazine *Political Study* dealt with this contradiction in several articles from May to August, 1955.

> The poor peasants, including the new middle peasants who originally were poor peasants, are the political sinews of the party . . . in rural villages. We have to rely on them.

> But the middle peasants are the essential factor in actual production.

> The individual middle peasants have more land, labor, draught animals, farm tools, and rich experience in agricultural production and management. . . .

> When unified purchases of grain and cotton are effected by the state, those who have surplus grain and cotton to sell are mostly such middle peasants . . . their production potential is greater.

> Since at the moment it is still impossible for the state to produce huge quantities of modern farm machinery and fertilizer . . . it will have to depend not only on mutual aid teams and cooperatives, but on the production ardor of the peasants. If the peasants cease to be zealous, there is nothing you can do about it.

The magazine suggests that a third of the leadership cadres in the industrial production cooperatives should be middle peasants instead of practically none as at that time. But it acknowledges the great difficulties:

When a cooperative is led by middle peasants who care more for individual interest, there will grow in it a tendency to capitalism.

So the poor peasants must be kept in the lead.

The poor peasants are the political pillars of the party in rural villages. To . . . hit them . . . cripples the strength on which the party depends for rural work.

Class Struggle vs. Unity and Cooperation

The Communists have been promoting a class war that has brought death to millions, and broken up clans and families. This has a psychological repercussion. The middle peasants have been through the terror of land redistribution at the hands of the poor peasants. Doubtless many of them narrowly missed being liquidated. They cannot easily work up a warm feeling of cozy comradeship for the poor peasants who are now in power over them.

Financial Contradiction

But where will the billion dollars come from that Red China proposes to lend its agricultural production operatives?

There is only one place where they can get it, and that is to take it from those who have, to lend it to those who have not. In rural terms, it means taking it from the middle peasants to lend to the poor peasants—taking it from the producers, to lend to those who fail to produce enough—taking it from those with ability, industry, thrift, to lend to those who in greater or less degree lack those qualities.

This may be good doctrinaire communism, but it is not good economics.

The middle peasants are sure to realize this, and it will not help to promote that "unity and cooperation" that is held up as desirable.

What can the Chinese Communists get for their proposed billion-dollar loan to the agricultural production cooperatives?

The bulk of the population, who live in rice-producing areas, one family per acre, have for centuries cultivated every square foot with loving patience. Here the law of diminishing returns applies. How much more can be gotten out of the land? Will it be enough to justify the additional expense?

Bureaucracy

Another aspect of the contradiction between party organization and control and economics is bureaucracy.

The machinery of rural collectivization and planned quotas of production and purchasing calls for an immense amount of paper work. The vast bureaucracy necessary to impose all these drastic changes on a quarter of the human race superimposes an almost impossible burden on the already overstrained economy of China, and it will be remembered that it was this overstrain that had been causing peasant revolts since 1774—nearly two hundred years. An economist who visited China in December 1955 estimates the communist bureaucratic burden at twenty-five per cent.

An immense number of cadres infest every line of activity—farm, factory, business—directing, keeping accounts, setting quotas, checking all sorts of details. A recent announcement indicates the extent of this new overhead. (*NCNA Peking*, Oct. 31, '55)

> A plan to train cooperative functionaries . . . calls for the training of two million book-keepers, three million skilled experts in farming technique, and half a million stock breeders from among young peasants by the spring of 1958.

When all Shanghai business firms were brought into joint government ownership in January, 1956, it was announced that 20,000 cadres were taking charge.

It seems likely that most of the proposed billion-dollar loan will have to go into supporting this vast, non-productive bureaucracy.

It has been pointed out that these bureaucrats have a vested interest in the Communist regime. They have tasted power. It went to their heads. There were complaints from the militia that even in small country villages the local cadre would demand their services to do sentry go outside his office, or to act as an escort of honor when he went abroad.

Inefficient Bureaucracy

The indications are that this immense bureaucracy will be far from efficient. This was the case in a check on private business, which lends itself to accounting methods better than does Chinese agriculture. The data obtained were reported by the *Peking Jen Min Jih Pao* (10/16/55) as incomplete and very inaccurate.

Many government-owned business enterprises have been grossly inefficient. Overstocking and unsalability of goods were first noticed in 1950. In 1952 a communist report stated:

The amount of capital funds invested in the commodities and goods of second grade and in goods now remaining unsalable in various state-owned trading departments came up to 20 to 31 per cent of the total operating funds of these departments.

Reports from widely separated cities gave details: overstock of cotton cloth, 1,390,000 rolls; 60,000 cartons of cigarettes became mouldy; 60,000 dozens of toothpaste containers had undergone chemical change; 150,000 dozen of stockings and 100,000 dozen towels "just could not be disposed of." And much more of the same.

In 1953 it was worse.

Such was the result of bureaucratic planning in place of following the law of supply and demand.

Another reason was that speed-ups and emulation drives had produced goods of inferior quality that could find no market. Still another cause was that in order to control private handicraft industries the government had committed itself to "total purchase and total sales."

This had a far-reaching effect on the communist economy, for they had publicized that "in 1953 revenue from state-owned enterprises had constituted 59.79 per cent of the total budgeted receipts."

The communists have seized and organized their power on this basis. They have to go through with it, or lose their power and all that goes with it.

Social Versus Technical Reforms

Mao's distinction between social reforms and technical reforms is important for an understanding of the present status of the Communist program in China. They are in conflict.

In the West, social reforms have followed and grown out of technical changes. Thus the industrial revolution completely changed the structure of Western society, and the process is still going on. Under Communism the social changes come first in accordance with Communist doctrinaire theory, which plans to implement them later with technical reforms.

In the West the social changes have followed the natural course of events in accord with economic laws. Communism has used bloodshed to impose its social reforms upon an economy with an insufficient foundation.

Technical Reforms

At the end of his speech ordering a drive for agricultural production cooperatives, Mao made two admissions. One was when he spoke of "mechanized operations in all departments and areas where mechanized operations are possible," thus implying that there were areas where mechanization would not work—such as the vast rice areas of the south two-thirds of China. The second was when he said that "the basic completion on a nation-wide scope of technical reforms . . . will call for four to five five-year plans."

Nevertheless, he stuck to his faith in the program of mechanization to which the whole Communist ideology was committed.

This ideology was not on a solid basis. It was in contradiction with the real state of things. It was based upon a doctrinaire feudalism which had little real existence, and a theory of exploitation that was only partially true.

It ignored basic problems like over-population. The government planners used as a base line a population of 400,000,000 or 450,000,000. Then their census revealed a total of 600,000,000. But large areas in China had long had a population too large for the food supply. Here was an increase of a third in the number of mouths to be fed. This would absorb a large part of the grain increase which the planners had envisaged as a basis for state industrialization.

Yet the magazine *Political Study* (8/13/55) stated:

> We will have to go back to fundamental causes. The reason why the peasants became poor is because they have for long suffered ruthless exploitation at the hands of landlords and rich peasants.

That was the social reform aspect. On the technical side the reason was given in the same article:

> At the moment we cannot yet make tractors, and the poor peasants' means of production are very limited.

To this was to be added complete socialization as the panacea for poverty.

Agricultural cooperativization is aimed gradually to eliminate private ownership in rural villages and uproot the cause of poverty for the poor people.

It has been indicated above that in a considerable part of the rice-producing areas, a family of five live on one acre of cultivated land. To that must now be added the population increase, the new bureaucracy, and on top of that the quota of increased production.

Opposition

The people of China responded in characteristic fashion. Peasant revolts were difficult under the present iron control. But the Minister of Justice reported that the courts had handled 364,000 counter-revolutionary and sabotage cases during the year ending May 1, 1955. This was thirty per cent of all types of cases handled by the courts. Further details appear in a later chapter.

Interim Expedients

Meantime, the program had to go forward, often by forced labor on a massive scale.

The following is the proud report of a District Military Commander, on the Peoples Liberation Army in Production and Construction in Sinkiang. (Peking, *Jen Min Jih Pao* 9/27/55)

The PLA units of the Sinkiang garrison had, on the one hand, to firmly carry out the task of suppressing bandits and guarding the borders, and on the other, to join in the grand production movement.

Material conditions at this time were extremely difficult. Those units engaged in agricultural production and water conservancy projects opened up wasteland, dug irrigation ditches, and plowed fields in parts of the Gobi plains where no people inhabited. There was no shelter for most of the troops who were exposed to extreme cold and heat and had to work with primitive digging tools and man-pulled plows in the open fields.

The material conditions for those engaged in engineering projects (including capital industrial production), transportation, and subsidiary processing industry were equally hard.

Though conditions were so difficult, the entire officers and men . . . under the firm and strong leadership of the party . . . strove selflessly to fulfil the task of production and construction. They lived frugally and thus saved money with which large quantities of agricultural implements as well as industrial equipment were procured.

The New Northwest

The turning to the northwest is in part a tacit acknowledgement that communist theories—particularly rural mechanization—will not work well in the southern rice areas.

Across Central Asia, from Manchuria to the Caspian, lies a wide belt of steppe which has been the habitat of nomad tribes since the dawn of history. At the west end of this belt Russia has plowed up almost 75 million acres of virgin land since 1952 in a grandiose effort to boost grain production. The Food and Agriculture Organization of the United Nations reported on this in June 1956.

Events so far have lessened early optimism. In part of the newly opened regions there were frequent droughts in 1955 and the quality of some soils had forced abandonment of grain production in favor of stock raising.

At their end of this steppe belt, north of China proper, the Chinese have been following the Russian example, as indicated above, in spite of the fact that the attempts of Chinese settlers during several decades to push north into this area—as some 20 million had gone into Manchuria—had met with little success.

The Alternative—Mass Starvation

It seems clear that if the increased production quota of the state planners cannot be met, the state will extract its quota just the same, leaving the peasant to stand the loss, and that this was what the peasant feared and what robbed him of initiative.

This is borne out by the cynical standards for grain-short households as follows (*Tientsin Ta Kung* Sept. 4, 1955):

The grain consumption standard . . . in the case of grain-short households . . . should be slightly lower than the standard for local grain-surplus households. This is based on the actual living conditions . . . grain-short households may be divided into three types:

(1) Grain-short households that have little land, many persons, and do not produce enough for consumption. Such grain-short households always maintain the excellent tradition of economy in the consumption of grain. Because of this and limited purchasing power their consumption level is generally lower than that of the local middle peasants. To fix their grain-consumption level lower than that for local grain-surplus households is completely in conformity with their economic conditions and actual requirements.

(2) Grain-short households . . . because they are not industrious. It is only proper and rational for the state to fix their grain consumption standard slightly lower than that for other local grain-short households. If they feel that it cannot meet their normal requirements, the only thing they should do is to do a better job and strive to be self-sufficient in grain.

(3) Standards in famine areas should be lower than the standard for local grain-short peasants in normal years. This is because peasants hit by natural calamities will encounter financial difficulties . . . and will certainly pay attention to economy in consuming grain.

The Two Viewpoints

To understand this crisis in Communist China it is necessary to look at it from two points of view, that of the democracies, and that of the Communists. It is a mistake to attempt to judge the situation merely from our own angle.

As we see it, it is necessary for the Communist program to achieve economic success in the form of reasonably good living conditions for all. Otherwise it is a failure, and will inevitably have to be discarded. From the Communist point of view, this is a secondary consideration as long as they can maintain their people's dictatorship.

8

Communism vs. Chinese History

A recent writer thinks specialists on communism will soon be better qualified to analyze events in China than sinologists. This has a large element of truth, but in view of the four thousand years of China's history as compared with the eight years of Communist control, it seems a bit premature.

The following summary attempts to relate the basic aspects of the present situation to the structure of Chinese society, the movement of Chinese history, and the development of Chinese thought. It follows Mao's own distinction between social and technical factors.

It is in the field of the social factors that the Chinese Communists have had their successes thus far. The technical factors present more stubborn obstacles.

The main factors growing out of China's history and social structure which made China vulnerable to the Communist attack were the historical trend, the governmental gap, the clan structure of society, and the unique place of the intellectuals.

The Historical Situation

The key to understanding the confusion in China is that the impact of the modern world came just at the end of the dynastic cycle.

The three syntheses under the empire had been achieved by the founders of dynasties—Chin and Han, Sui and T'ang, Sung. The fifth synthesis was overdue, but the Manchus had been under two handicaps in this regard: a synthesis could scarcely be brought about by an alien dynasty, and the modern influences which posed the necessity for a far wider synthesis came to a climax when the dynasty was in decline.

A strong China might have withstood the shock. But it was a

China in process of breaking up that faced the forces of the modern world—and later those of Communism.

A comparison with Japan will make this more clear. Japan had been more tightly closed against foreign influences than China. Its opening came later, and as the result of diplomacy, not of force of arms as was the case with China's "unequal treaties." The restoration of 1868 gave the emperor the backing of the nation. China was torn by a succession of revolts. Japan had the able leadership of the Meiji Emperor. The best China could do was the Empress Dowager. The Japanese emperor had the immense prestige of divinity. China had had the Confucian idea of the mandate of heaven, and Sun Yatsen had used the slogan that this mandate was not eternal. China's relations with the West were haphazard. Japanese relations were largely of their own choice, and predominantly German.

Communism is really less a synthesis than a destruction of Chinese traditional values. It does not build on Chinese history, but twists it to suit its theory of feudal society as a pretext for class war.

Any synthesis to be stable must have a sufficient Chinese basis. In the present situation, where the doctrinaire Russian type of theory fails to work, its more impractical aspects are likely to be replaced by Chinese ways of doing things. This has already taken place to a decisive extent in Mao's use of peasants instead of proletariat as a basis of power. The tendency will be for China to revert to type.

But that may take a long time. The previous syntheses of Chinese history have always taken a long time. And many most unpleasant things may happen in the interim.

Small Experience in Choice of Other Cultures

In working out a synthesis it was necessary to make a choice among the Western political and social systems which varied widely among themselves.

Previously, foreign influences had entered China and established themselves, becoming partly Chinese in the process, and were then merged into Chinese culture. But the Western ingredients were too various, too indigestible. The changes necessary in China itself were far greater than had ever been the case before. The process was bound to be much more complicated.

This was the more difficult because the West too was in crisis.

It was the day of Mussolini, Hitler, and Stalin. It was the day of a transitional psychology, when peoples, new to the responsibilities of democracy, lost their revolutionary self-confidence and sought the guidance, exaltation, and security of totalitarian regimes. Communism was one manifestation of this.

China had to choose among the cultures of the West, but nothing in China's history prepared her to do so.

China had a single culture that had shown a power of penetration and a persistence unmatched by any other. It had been unaccustomed to alteration. Outside influences and peoples had been absorbed. The result had still been Chinese.

The fact that Chinese culture had been unaccustomed to change had made it resistant to change.

China had commonly spoken of itself as "T'ien Hsia," all under heaven, in other words, the world. It was the "Kingdom of the Midst," at the center. This world was now rudely shattered. China was no longer the center, but a fragment of an uncertain international situation in bewildering change under the impact of two world wars.

Japan had had experience in adopting other cultures—Korean, Chinese, and, to some extent, Indian. Japan was able to choose, and acted promptly and practically, while China engaged in academic and political window-shopping.

Absorbing Conquerors

One aspect of previous syntheses was the absorption of conquerors—of peoples as well as their cultures.

The earlier invaders who established dynasties were compact tribes of barbarian fighters, often semi-nomads, who broke into China during a time of confusion or dynastic weakness, took over as much of China as they could manage and settled down to enjoy the spoils.

But while conquest was fairly simple, the bureaucratic machinery necessary for water control, the collection of taxes in grain, and its transport was usually too much for them. The Chinese gentry, who had had a monopoly of this, usually refused to cooperate, and retired to their ancestral villages. No others had the requisite education and experience.

This situation brought most such dynasties to an early end. They could not make the bureaucratic machine work, or by the time they had learned, they too became Chinese.

Even the Mongols, who had set up an empire reaching from the Black Sea to the Yellow Sea, lasted only 88 years as the rulers of China, and largely for the same reason. The Manchus rapidly took over Chinese culture, and able emperors secured the cooperation of the gentry scholars and bureaucracy, and lasted 268 years.

To what extent will this pattern apply to the present communist regime in China?

The previous invaders were on a lower culture level, and were influenced and usually overcome by the advantages, refinements, and prestige of Chinese culture. Except for the Mongol minority who withdrew, these invaders have been assimilated and today can scarcely be distinguished from other Chinese.

The communist inroad is something different. It comes from a technically higher culture level. It has the prestige of the West. It is backed by massive brute force and wickedly clever propaganda.

Communist Seizure of Power Affected by Political Structure

Several aspects of the political and social structure have rendered China vulnerable to the Communist attack. The political weak spot was the governmental gap.

China had a makeshift, conglomerate government. Above was the nation-wide structure of the empire. At the bottom were the disunited clans of China, a million of them, product of the new stone age, local, biological, unicellular units, that governed themselves on a traditional basis of ancient family custom. In between was a governmental gap, a sort of no-man's land.

The government was not articulated with the people. It had no democratic base. It was cut off from the people by this gap, and democracy could not develop. The feudal system had been destroyed, and there were no barons to wring a Magna Carta from the ruler, as happened in England. Their Chinese counterpart was the landlord-scholar-official class, who were firmly tied to the imperial structure as its bureaucracy.

It was in the area of the governmental gap that Sun Yat-sen and Mao operated. Sun used the secret societies. These were strongest in cities, which he tried over and over to capture. But the government forces also were strongest in cities. Mao mobilized the rural gangsters, and had among his early forces two bandit gangs. There were few government forces in the rural areas, and his movement was able to grow and flourish.

Sun and his revolutionists overlooked the key item of the army at the capital and garrisons at strategic centers which had the real power of the ruling dynasty. It was not till 1922 that Sun realized that the government must have an army and set one up under Chiang Kai-shek. Mao early developed his peasants into an army.

Factors of the Structure of Society

The long history of China is due to the stability of Chinese society. This is often characterized as conservatism. It is far more than merely psychological and is rooted in the biological and anthropological structure of Chinese society.

From the sociological point of view China is a loose aggregation of clans. The clan is a biological entity. Can the communists abolish biology? The father is still father. The son is still son. He may repudiate his father—many have—but the biological relationship cannot be abolished.

The communists are trying to destroy the Chinese family. Will blood prove thicker than ideology? Particularly if the ideology does not work, and people begin to find it out. In China biology and ethics are closely linked, for Confucianism is the rationalization of the Chinese social order, the putting into words of the clan and family relationships. Can Marx overcome Confucius?

That is one side of it. On the other hand, a refugee intellectual in Hong Kong told me how his own powerful and wealthy clan had been broken up.

When the communists came the head of the clan went into hiding. They tortured his son until he revealed his father's hiding place, then tortured and killed both of them. This crippled the clan organization, for no one else dared to step in as head of the clan.

They then redistributed the land. In a large clan some were rich and some poor. But a two-class society had been taken for granted for centuries, mitigated by clan solidarity and mutual responsibility, so that the poor were looked after. However, some were the landlords, and some were tenant farmers paying rent to others of the clan. The communists exploited this to break up clan solidarity. A nephew might be the tenant of his uncle. He now attacked him in order to possess the land for himself. Son was turned against father. Bitterness and strife took the place of mutual cooperation. The clan's concentration of wealth and power was dissipated, and with it went much of the clan's influence.

It did not stop there. Children were taught that their first loyalty was to the communist state, and were trained to spy on their parents. They had previously depended on parents for getting an education. Now the state decided who should go to school, and provided the money. Children ceased to look to their parents for anything.

Furthermore, men were brought into men's organizations, women into women's organizations, and the same with children. All were kept busy with tasks and meetings. Thus separate interests were developed and the family unity destroyed for lack of common interests. They might live together. The old shell was there, but the content was changed. Love was replaced by suspicion and hatred.

There is evidence of reaction against this. In agricultural cooperatives the division of product according to labor performed left out parents and children, too old or too young to work. Previously each family owned land handed down from father to son, which gave parents a right to share its proceeds. Communism cancelled this, for the land now belonged to the cooperative. This led to heartless treatment of parents and children, and the number of lawsuits involving their support greatly increased. Papers editorialized on certain more flagrant cases: "this has aroused public opinion." Another wrote, "the traditional morality of our people and the real love of children for parents will never perish." The communists made new regulations so that by March 1957 six provinces reported 700,000 old people being cared for by the cooperatives.

Moreover, there is the beginning of an aftermath. Even the communist authorities are getting worried over juvenile delinquency, and are calling on parents to control their children. But parents no longer feel the responsibility for doing so. Even if they do, they do not have the heart to try and they are by no means certain that they could do anything about it even if they did.

Psychological Factor

The communists deny man's basic humanity. But this is strong in China.

It was related above in connection with psychological conditioning that the authorities of the Revolutionary University urged married students to get a divorce. They gave this reason:

> Experience has shown that it is always the person who does not participate in idea training who influences the other.

Why?

> After spending twenty or more years in the old society remnants of it will still persist in your memories, and this is what makes it possible for you to suffer a relapse.

There is considerable evidence that this sort of thing is going on, as will appear in the following chapter on people's resistance.

9

People's Resistance

South China had never been under communist control, and their attempt to institute "land reform" and similar measures met with immediate and widespread resistance. This soon developed in the north also, and has continued up to the present and even increased.

These resisters were described up to 1950 as bandits, which justified drastic action to the Chinese people who were ostensibly being protected, and signified to the outside world that this opposition was not political. But in 1951 the "Law for the Punishment of Counter-Revolutionaries" virtually admitted that the resistance was political.

The people's resistance is analyzed by Shih Ch'en-chih for the years 1950–1955 from reports in communist periodicals. He finds evidence that within a month after China entered the Korean War, October 25, 1950, anti-communist forces became active.

Peasant Uprisings

A number of uprisings took place in five provinces in the northwest in 1952, one of which spread to five counties. Reports of the Central-South Military Region indicated that resistance had spread to sixteen counties. The Southwest Military report killing 120,000 "bandits." There were a large number of such local uprisings in various parts of the country.

By August 1953 the situation was serious enough to call forth a statement by Chu Teh, Commander-in-Chief of the Red Army, which indicated that it was necessary for the public security force to aid the militia and local factory guards. In one case troops had fought the peasants for eleven days.

In June 1954 communists reported that they had cracked up three "serious counter-revolutionary cases" in the Peking-Tientsin-

Paoting triangle. One was described as "during the last four years . . . plundering villages and slaughtering people in as many as 17 counties." This was an area of 500 square miles, a region which the communists had long controlled, close to their capital. It must have been well organized to last four years.

In the province of Shansi there were 170 cases of attempted assassination of cadres in six months, resulting in 93 deaths (Peking *Jen Min Jih Pao* 11/11/55).

In the province of Fukien there were 30 cases of burning forests in the first two months of 1955 which destroyed a larger area than had been reforested since liberation.

Workers' Resistance

There were reports in 1955 of "laxity in labor discipline." There were slow-down strikes. Several engineers were found to have altered blueprints, causing accidents or faulty products. The Minister of Justice summed it up in his report:

> From the beginning of 1953 to the end of May 1955, the people's courts at various levels have dealt with 364,604 counter-revolutionary cases concerning economic construction.
>
> In Shantung Province the number of counter-revolutionary cases handled during the first quarter of 1955 was two times more than in the corresponding quarter of 1953.

By June 1955 it was reported that in Shantung and Szechwan "over 90% of the agricultural production cooperatives have organized guard teams . . . to strengthen the supervision of counter-revolutionaries and criminals, to guard against their further sabotage."

Secret Societies

The organization of these movements generally took the form of a secret society. These were religious in character, chiefly Taoist, sometimes eclectic.

In a peasant revolt in 1952, secret societies were uncovered in a third of the local administrative units of the county affected, and usually from 50 to 66 per cent of the peasant households were members. A new crop was uncovered each year. A selective list of those uncovered in 1955 includes some 31 organizations in 13 provinces.

One of the most widespread was a Taoist secret society, the "I Kuan Tao." One of its chiefs was reported to have 12,000 Taoist chiefs under his command in the northwest. Another such society had 51 leaders and was active in 60 cities in the Yangtze valley and along the Lunghai Railway.

Youth

The magazine Literary Studies in March 1957 published a short story by a 22 year old writer in which the leading character, in a high government office in the capital, fights bureaucracy as exemplified by a former enthusiastic revolutionary now become cynical and his colleague, superficially able but indifferent to the problems of the people. This set off a nation-wide controversy and the magazine received 1300 contributions on the subject. Many branded it, piously, as mere exaggeration, quite impossible in the capital. The majority, especially youth, agreed with the author.

There was widespread student disillusionment. In China education had always led to a career. Now hundreds of thousands of primary and junior high graduates were returned to work in their home villages. Many became "dejected and pessimistic." Many families who had economized, hoping to see their sons go up in the world, were chagrined. Many left school. In the province of Kwangsi the primary enrolment in 1955 was 240,000 less than in 1953.

Unreliable Cadres

The analysis by Mr. Chen indicates that the spread and continuance of resistance in many cases could not have taken place without some degree of sympathy on the part of the local communist leadership. This increased. It was reported in 1954 that in a single county 171 party members, Youth League members and cadres had been "bought over by reactionary elements," and that in coal mines in two provinces "directors, foremen, security officers and cadres . . . joined ranks with the workers in staging go-slow strikes."

This was augmented by resistance in the Youth League whose Central Committee in July 1955 urged members to guard against sabotage by counter-revolutionary elements inside the league. It admitted that "there are a certain number of counter-revolutionaries in our League . . . but compared with the over 90% of good comrades, the percentage of bad elements is very small." There was also increasing resistance among students.

This indicates a certain amount of deterioration of the inner structure of the communist apparatus itself.

Resistance Trends

Resistance appears to be on the increase. But it is to be noted that it has been crushed wherever found. How much more there may be under the surface is unknown. However, Mr. Chen analyzes certain trends.

The 1952 suppression campaign was conducted with fanfare and counter-revolutionaries were tried in public meetings and often shot immediately. In 1955 there were few public trials, largely because the campaign was directed to a considerable extent at cadres inside the party. Also, the people had become more sober after years of experience of the communist regime and were not so easily aroused. The term used had been changed from "suppress counter-revolutionaries" to "purge counter-revolutionaries."

This continued resistance resulted in some softening of the communist position. First came retrenchment, cutting the bureaucracy at all levels. Then a certain amount of decentralization at the small business and handicraft level in the provinces—approval was given to small mines and blast furnaces using native methods. Wage reform came in 1956. A renewed united front wooed non-communist parties. An effort was made to reclaim, rather than liquidate, counter-revolutionaries, and a propaganda drive featured reports of their being won over by the leniency of the government. Even with Formosa, threats gave way to an appeal to come and be united as they had been in the two previous united fronts.

In a secret speech in February 1957 Mao admitted: "The question of whether socialism or capitalism will win (in China) is still not really settled."

What Possibilities?

Thus far no over-all pattern of resistance is apparent. Movements are sporadic and unrelated. Each group goes its own way. Peasants retaliate by setting fires, assassinations, uprisings. Workers sabotage plants and production. Industrialists evade taxes and hoard materials.

China has little experience of government arising from the people —only the million or more disunited clans. The secret societies provide only a partial substitute. At present the one most widespread is a Taoist society. One such band was thus described in an official report: "Part used swords and spears; others were bare-handed, chanting liturgy and drawing spells and incantations." This develops a do-or-die morale, but is no substitute for organization.

At this point the leadership of the intellectuals is a necessity. China has always depended on the landlord-scholar-official class. However, they have changed their base from the ancestral village, and modern educated sons of the old gentry families have infiltrated business, and the professions, including education. They are still there, but without the old cultural unity and singleness of aim.

What can come out of such a situation?

Shih distinguishes two kinds of factors—intentional and accidental. It was pointed out above that Sun Yat-sen engineered ten uprisings in various cities which got nowhere, until a fortuitous correlation of local and national objectives touched off the revolution in 1911.

The Chinese communists count on a doctrinaire interpretation of history that makes the conquest of communism inevitable, and on a doctrinaire economic program that has not worked elsewhere. They appear to be firmly in control. Such is the report of various ones who have visited China recently. Doubtless they would have made similar pronouncements two years ago concerning Poland and Hungary.

Factors in the Present Situation

There are three factors in the present China situation: the Communist strength on the mainland, the Nationalist government in Formosa, and the international situation.

Those who assess this situation in terms of the ability or inability of the Formosa government to invade the mainland miss the main point.

The overwhelming factor is the degree of Communist strength among the six hundred million. This in turn depends on how it interacts with the movement of Chinese history and the basic character of the Chinese people.

If this strength deteriorates, due to doctrinaire error, inefficiency, lack of human decency, increased people's resistance, or whatever cause, some fortuitous combination of circumstances—as in the revolution of 1911—may trigger an explosion.

Formosa remains of great value as a symbol of freedom, as was Chungking during the war with Japan. It was a haven of freedom to the eighty per cent of the Chinese prisoners of war in Korea who chose to go to Formosa rather than be repatriated to communist China. It is a symbol of freedom today hidden in the hearts of millions like them who have learned to hate the communist regime.

What Formosa might be able to do in some crisis might be just enough to tip the scales.

Bibliography

Part I Structure of Chinese Society

Andersson, J. Gunnar. *Children of the Yellow Earth: Studies in Prehistoric China.* London, 1934
Turner, Ralph, *The Great Cultural Traditions.* New York, 1941
Granet, Marcel, *Chinese Civilization.* London, 1950
Cressey, George B. *Land of the Five Hundred Million: A Geography of China.* New York, 1955
Jones, Clarence F.. *Economic Geography.* New York, 1935
Buck, John Lossing. *Land Utilization in China.* Chicago, 1937
Lattimore, Owen. *Inner Asian Frontiers of China.* New York, 1940
Yang, Martin C. *A Chinese Village.* New York, 1945
Chiao, C. M., Thompson, Warren S., and Chen, D. T. *An Experiment in the Registration of Vital Statistics in China.* Scripps Foundation, Oxford, Ohio, 1938
Feng, Han-yi. *The Chinese Kinship System.* Cambridge, 1948
Cressy, Earl Herbert, co-author with Wong Su-ling. *Daughter of Confucius.* New York, 1952
Kirby, E. Stuart. *Introduction to the Economic History of China.* London, 1954
Chi, Ch'ao-ting. *Key Economic Areas in Chinese History.* London, 1936
DuBois, Cora. *Social Forces in Southeast Asia.* Minneapolis, 1949

Part II History

Creel, Herrlee Glessner. *The Birth of China.* New York, 1937
Dubs, Homer. *History of the Former Han Dynasty.* Baltimore, 1938
Goodrich, L. Carrington. *A Short History of the Chinese People.* New York, 1943
Latourette, Kenneth Scott. *The Chinese, Their History and Culture.* New York rev. ed., 1946
Fitzgerald, C. P. *China. A Short Cultural History.* London rev. ed., 1950
Eberhard, Wolfram. *A History of China.* Berkeley, 1950
Wittfogel, Karl A. and Feng, Chia-sheng. *History of Chinese Society, Liao.* New York, 1949
Legge, James. *The Chinese Classics, Vol. V, The Ch'un Ts'ew with The Tso Chuen.* London
Waley, Arthur. *The Book of Songs.* London, 1937
Waley, Arthur. *The Analects of Confucius.* London, 1938

Waley, Arthur. *The Way and Its Power.* London, 1934
Waley, Arthur. *Three Ways of Thought in Ancient China.* London, 1939
Mei, Yi Pao. *The Ethical and Political Works of Motse.* London, 1929
Dubs, Homer. *The Works of Hsun Tse.* London, 1928
Duyvendak, J. J. L. *The Book of the Lord Shang.* London, 1928
Goodrich and Fenn. *A Syllabus of the History of Chinese Civilization and Culture.* New York

Part III Development of Chinese Thought

Fung, Yu-lan. *A History of Chinese Philosophy.* Vol. I Peiping 1937. Vol. II Princeton, 1953
Fung, Yu-lan. *A Short History of Chinese Philosophy.* New York, 1948
Fung, Yu-lan. *The Spirit of Chinese Philosophy.* London, 1947
Hughes, E. R. *Chinese Philosophy in Classical Times.* London, 1942
Waley, Arthur. *Three Ways of Thought in Ancient China.* London, 1939
Wieger, Leo. *History of the Religious Beliefs and Philosophical Opinions in China.* Hsien-hsien, China, 1927
Waley, Arthur. *The Way and Its Power.* London, 1934
Fung, Yu-lan. *Chuang Tzu.* Shanghai, 1933
Liebenthal, W. *The Book of Chao.* Peking, 1948
Hu Shih. *The Development of Zen Buddhism in China.* In "Chinese Social and Political Science Review." 1931
Huang Siu-chi. *Lu Hsiang-shan.* New Haven, 1944
Bruce, Joseph Perry. *Chu Hsi and His Masters.* London, 1923
Wei, Francis C. M. *The Spirit of Chinese Culture.* New York, 1947
Yang, Y. C. *China's Religious Heritage.* New York, 1943
Chan, Wing-tsit. *Religious Trends in Modern China.* New York, 1953
Carter, Thomas Francis. *Invention of Printing in China and Its Spread Westward.* rev. ed. New York, 1956
Brewitt-Taylor, Charles Henry. *San Kuo or Romance of the Three Kingdoms.* Shanghai, 1925
Buck, Pearl S. *All Men Are Brothers.* New York, 1933

Part IV Break-up and Attempts at a Modern Synthesis

Rostow, W. W. *The Prospects for Communist China.* Boston, 1954
The Annals of the American Academy of Political and Social Science, *Report on China,* Philadelphia, Sept., 1951. Including articles by
Taylor, George E. *The Hegemony of the Chinese Communists 1945–50*
Pritchard, Earl H. *Political Ferment in China 1911–1951*
Cole, Allan B. *The United Front in the New China*
Steiner, H. Arthur. *The Role of the Chinese Communist Party*
Skinner, G. William. *Peasant Organization in Rural China*
Glick, Carl, and Hong Sheng-hwa. *Swords of Silence: Chinese Secret Societies Past and Present.* New York, 1947
Brandt, C., Schwartz, B. I., and Fairbank, J. K. *A Documentary History of Chinese Communism.* Cambridge, 1952

Mao Tse-tung. *Report on the Peasant Movement in Hunan.* 1927
Mao Tse-tung. *Concerning Practice.* Univ. of Washington, 1951
Mao Tse-tung. *Collected Works.* New York
Mao Tse-tung. *China's New Democracy.* New York, 1945
Schwartz, Benjamin I. *Chinese Communism and the Rise of Mao.* Cambridge, 1951
Hauser, E. D. *Shanghai, City for Sale.* New York, 1940
Kirby, E. Stuart. *Introduction to the Economic History of China.* London, 1954
Cressy, Earl Herbert. *Yellow Rivers: Adventures in a Chinese Parish.* New York, 1932
Ting Li. *Militia of Communist China.* Union Research Institute, Hong Kong, 1954
Shih Kuo-heng. *The Rise of the Modern Chinese Business Class.* Part II. New York, 1949

Part V The Peoples Republic of China

Rostow, W. W. *The Prospects for Communist China.* Boston, 1954
Walker, Richard I. *China Under Communism.* New Haven, 1955
Hunter, Edward. *Brainwashing in Red China.* New York, 1951
Department of State, External Research Staff. Mimeographed translations from Chinese Communist Sources. Washington 1951–57
Current Background
Survey of the China Mainland Press
Extracts from China Mainland Magazines
Review of Hong Kong Chinese Press
Union Research Institute, Communist China Problem Research Series.
Fang Shu. *Campaign of Party Expansion.* Hong Kong, 1953
Chung Shih. *Higher Education in Communist China.* Hong Kong, 1953
Hsiao Chi-jung. *Revenue and Disbursement of Communist China.* Hong Kong, 1955
Shin Ch'eng-chih. *People's Resistance in Mainland China.* Hong Kong, 1956
News Release of Union News Agency. (weekly)

Index